© 2003 by Jenny Blum

About the Author

Howard Blum, an award-winning former reporter for the *New York Times* and a contributing editor of *Vanity Fair,* is the author of several bestselling nonfiction books, including *The Brigade, The Gold of Exodus, Gangland*, and *Wanted! The Brigade* is being made into a major motion picture by Miramax Films.

THE EVE OF DESTRUCTION

ALSO BY HOWARD BLUM

NONFICTION

Wanted! The Search for Nazis in America

I Pledge Allegiance . . . The Story of the Walker Spy Family

Out There

Gangland

The Gold of Exodus

The Brigade

FICTION

Wishful Thinking

THE EVE OF DESTRUCTION

The Untold Story of the Yom Kippur War

HOWARD BLUM

Perennial
An Imprint of HarperCollins*Publishers*

A hardcover edition of this book was published in 2003 by HarperCollins Publishers.

HarperCollins books may be purchased for educational, business, or sales promotional use. For information please write: Special Markets Department, HarperCollins Publishers Inc., 10 East 53rd Street, New York, NY 10022.

FIRST PERENNIAL EDITION PUBLISHED 2004.

Designed by Joseph Rutt

Maps by Paul J. Pugliese

The Library of Congress has catalogued the hardcover edition as follows:
Blum, Howard.
The eve of destruction : the untold story of the Yom Kippur War / by Howard Blum.—1st. ed.
p. cm.
Includes index.
ISBN 0-06-001399-0
1. Israel-Arab War, 1973. I. Title.
DS128.1.B59 2003
956.04'8—dc21

ISBN 0-06-001400-8 (pbk.)

2003056563

04 05 06 07 08 ❖/RRD 10 9 8 7 6 5 4 3 2 1

For my children,
Tony, Anna, and Dani.
With boundless love.

And my sister, Marcy,
always ready to ride to the rescue.
With love and gratitude.

CONTENTS

On Rosh Hashana their decree is inscribed,
and on Yom Kippur it is sealed.
How many shall pass away, and how many shall be created;
Who shall live, and who shall die;
Who shall come to his timely end, and who to an untimely end;
Who shall perish by fire, and who by water;
Who by the sword, and who by beast;
Who by hunger, and who by thirst;
Who by earthquake, and who by the plague;
Who by strangling, and who by stoning;
Who shall be at rest, and who shall wander about;
Who shall have serenity, and who shall be confused;
Who shall be tranquil, and who shall be tormented;
Who shall become poor, and who shall become wealthy;
Who shall be brought to a low state, and who shall be uplifted . . .

—Traditional prayer recited on the
High Holidays of Rosh Hashana
and Yom Kippur, attributed to
Rabbi Ammon of Mayence.

A NOTE TO THE READER

Nations make wars, but men fight them. This is the true story of the men, Arabs and Jews, who fought in the conflict that became known in America as the Yom Kippur War.

It is an account of battles, and of soldiers. Of governments, and of armies. Of honor, and of betrayals. And it is, no less, a love story, a tale of a young bride and groom tossed about in this swirl of history.

To write such a story with accuracy and drama, I relied on a variety of sources, including previously classified Israeli government documents and reports, captured Egyptian and Syrian documents and letters, books on the war in English, Hebrew, and Arabic, and unpublished research papers written by veteran Arab officers studying at the U.S. Air Force Air University at Maxwell Air Force Base, in Montgomery, Alabama.

Another essential resource was the many interviews I conducted with soldiers, Jews and Arabs, who fought in the war, as well as past and present members of the Israeli intelligence community. A complete chapter-by-chapter attribution of my sources follows at the end of the narrative.

I would be derelict, however, if I did not publicly acknowledge at the outset the role of Nati and Yossi Ben Hanan in helping and encouraging my pursuit of this story. It was while I sat on Nati's terrace in Haifa, looking at her wedding pictures in the fading evening light, that this book first began to take shape in my mind.

—H.B.

CAST OF CHARACTERS

ISRAELIS

Soldiers

Lt. Col. Yosef "Yossi" Ben Hanan, Battalion Commander
Lt. Einat "Nati" Friedman, wife of Yossi
Col. Avigdor "Yanosh" Ben Gal, Brigade Commander
Maj. Shmuel "Shmuli" Askarov, Deputy Battalion Commander
Lt. Col. Avigdor Kahalani, Battalion Commander
Col. Amnon Reshef, Brigade Commander
Col. Yitzhak Ben Shoham, Brigade Commander
Capt. Yonathan "Yoni" Netanyahu, Commander of Commando Reconnaisance Force

Generals

Lt. Gen. David "Dado" Elazar, Chief of Staff
Maj. Gen. Yitzhak "Haka" Hofi, Commander, Northern Command
Maj. Gen. Shmuel "Gordish" Gonen, Commander, Southern Command

Maj. Gen. Avraham "Bren" Adan, Commander of a division on the southern front

Maj. Gen. Ariel "Arik" Sharon, Commander of a division on the southern front

Intelligence

Zvi Zamir, head of the Mossad

Gen. Eli Zeira, head of Aman, Military Intelligence

Lt. Col. Shabtai Brill, Operation Director, unit 8200, Aman

Col. Yoel Ben Porat, Commander, unit 8200 Aman

The In-Law, code name of Mossad agent serving in the Egyptian government

Cabinet

Golda Meir, Prime Minister

Moshe Dayan, Minister of Defense

Chaim Bar-Lev, Minister of Trade

EGYPTIANS

Generals

Lt. Gen. Saad el Shazly, Chief of Staff

Maj. Gen. Ahmed Ismail, Commander-in-Chief and Minister of War

Lt. Gen. Mohammed el-Gamasy, Director of Operations

Maj. Gen. Ali Mohammed, Commander, Engineering Corps

Intelligence

Maj. Gen. Fuad Nasser, head of Defense Intelligence

Cabinet

Anwar el-Sadat, President

Ashraf Marwan, Ambassador-at-Large, Presidential Adviser

Bahieddin Nofal, Secretary, Syrian-Egyptian Armed Forces Supreme Council

SYRIANS

Generals

Maj. Gen. Yusuf Shakoor, Chief of Staff

Maj. Gen. Abdelrazzak el Dardary, Director of Operations

Maj. Gen. Nagy Gamil, Commander, Air Force and Defense

Intelligence

Maj. Gen. Hikmat el Shihaby, head of Defense Intelligence

Cabinet

Hafez al-Assad, President

Gen. Mustafa Talas, Minister of Defense

JORDAN

King Hussein

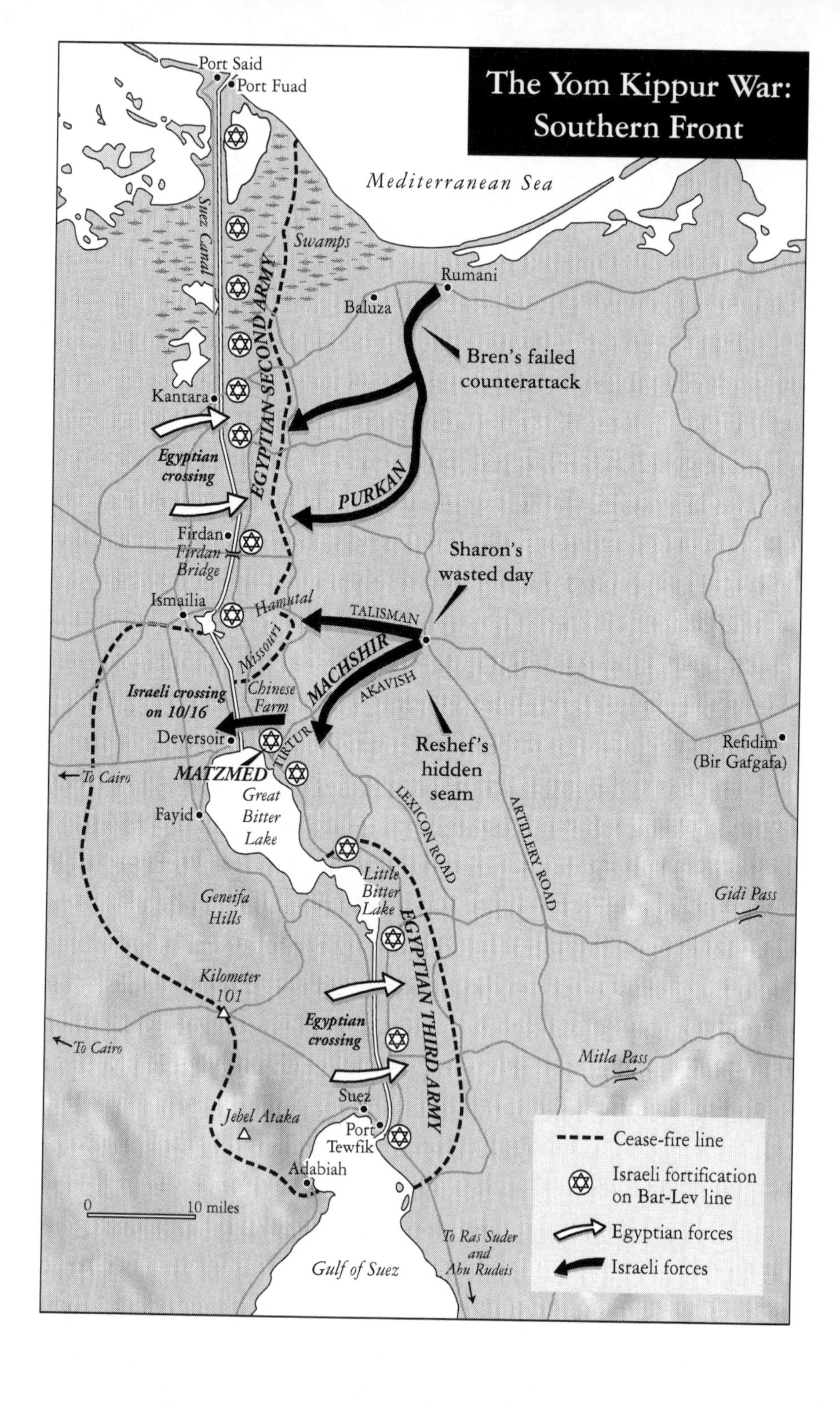
The Yom Kippur War: Southern Front
Port Said
Port Fuad
Mediterranean Sea
Suez Canal
Swamps
EGYPTIAN SECOND ARMY
Rumani
Baluza
Bren's failed counterattack
Kantara
Egyptian crossing
PURKAN
Firdan
Firdan Bridge
Sharon's wasted day
Ismailia
Hamutal
TALISMAN
Missouri
MACHSHIR
Israeli crossing on 10/16
Chinese Farm
AKAVISH
Deversoir
TIRTUR
Reshef's hidden seam
Refidim (Bir Gafgafa)
To Cairo
MATZMED
Great Bitter Lake
Fayid
LEXICON ROAD
ARTILLERY ROAD
Little Bitter Lake
Geneifa Hills
EGYPTIAN THIRD ARMY
Gidi Pass
Kilometer 101
Egyptian crossing
To Cairo
Mitla Pass
Suez
Jebel Ataka
Port Tewfik
Adabiah
0
10 miles
To Ras Suder and Abu Rudeis
Gulf of Suez
Cease-fire line
Israeli fortification on Bar-Lev line
Egyptian forces
Israeli forces

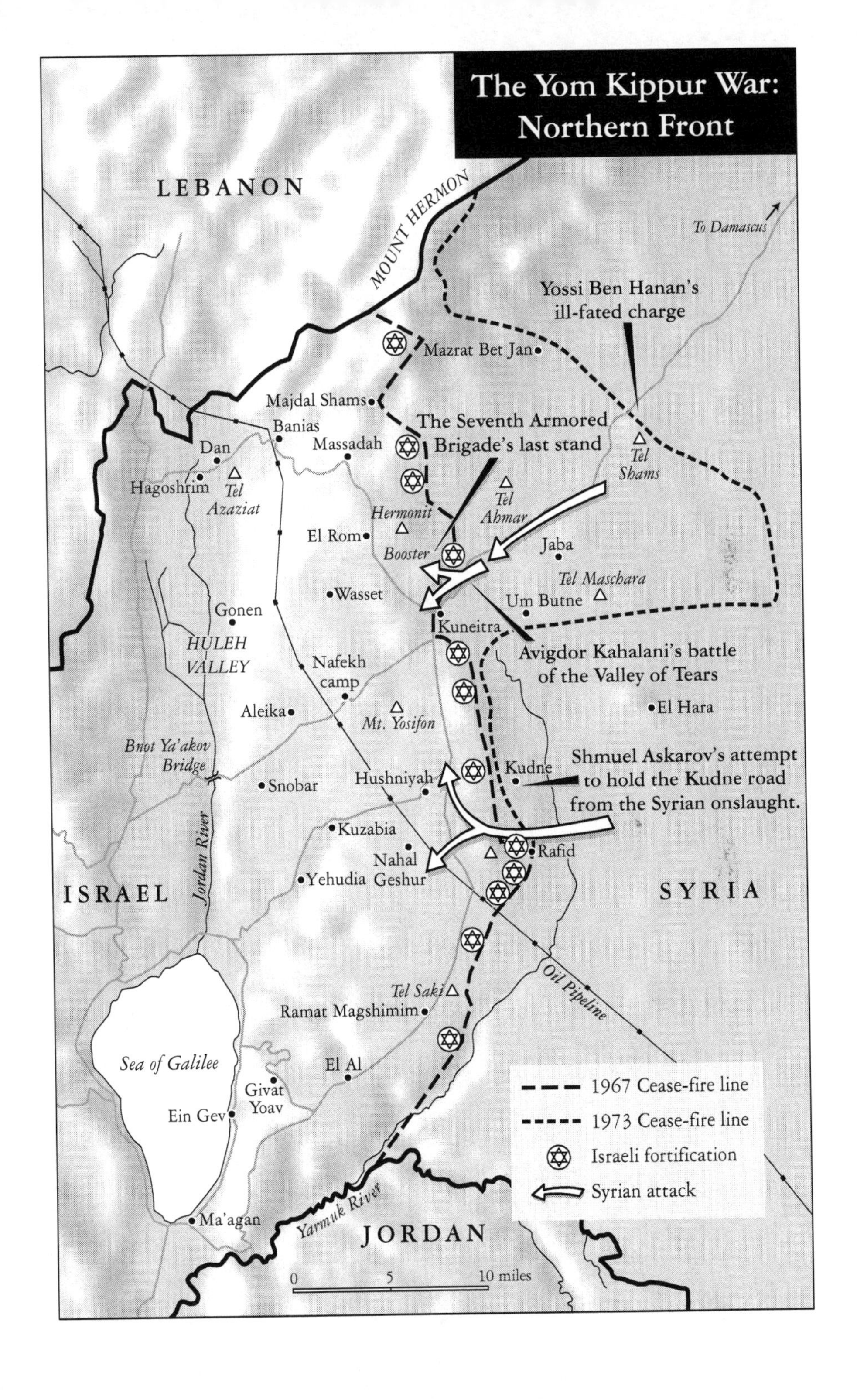
The Yom Kippur War:
Northern Front
LEBANON
MOUNT HERMON
To Damascus
Yossi Ben Hanan's
ill-fated charge
Mazrat Bet Jan
Majdal Shams
Banias
Massadah
The Seventh Armored
Brigade's last stand
Dan
Hagoshrim
Tel Azaziat
Tel Shams
Tel Ahmar
Hermonit
El Rom
Booster
Jaba
Tel Maschara
Wasset
Um Butne
Gonen
Kuneitra
HULEH VALLEY
Avigdor Kahalani's battle
of the Valley of Tears
Nafekh camp
Aleika
Mt. Yosifon
El Hara
Bnot Ya'akov Bridge
Shmuel Askarov's attempt
to hold the Kudne road
from the Syrian onslaught.
Kudne
Snobar
Hushniyah
Kuzabia
Nahal Geshur
Rafid
Yehudia
Jordan River
ISRAEL
SYRIA
Oil Pipeline
Tel Saki
Ramat Magshimim
Sea of Galilee
El Al
Givat Yoav
Ein Gev
1967 Cease-fire line
1973 Cease-fire line
Israeli fortification
Syrian attack
Ma'agan
Yarmuk River
JORDAN
0
5
10 miles

PROLOGUE

THE WATCHMEN

Jerusalem / Cairo
Summer 2002

Who shall live . . .

The custodian sat at his desk, lunch hour spent as usual leafing through his scrapbook, when the bomb exploded. The blast took him by surprise. He rose from his chair as if yanked to attention. The red-covered photo album tumbled to the floor. Yet as he looked down at the scattered photographs, at the letters neatly typed on ministry stationery, at the precisely underlined newspaper articles, at all the years of carefully collected and cataloged evidence that now lay in a wide puddle on the cement floor, he also realized he was safe.

A suicide bomber had struck again. The explosion had rattled the two windows facing Hakhayal Street, but nothing broke. The intifada, fierce and primitive, raged on. But his building, his tenants, and—though in truth it was of little consequence to him—his own life had been spared.

He stood by his desk without moving for a while. His stance, after all the years of training, was by instinct a soldier's: parade rest. He did not dwell on his escape, his luck. His mind filled with another knowledge.

During the long, difficult months as he watched his beloved Jerusalem become an anxious city of flaming targets, an understanding had been slowly building. It began as a premonition and evolved, incident by grim incident, into a theory. But now it coursed through him full blown, all-powerful. The connections were indelibly forged. This bombing was his irrefutable message. Now he knew. He alone.

It was all happening again, he realized. Nearly thirty years had passed since October 1973, since the Yom Kippur War, since he stood guard for the nation. But now there was a new call to duty.

He saw the choices that lie ahead, and a weary resignation overwhelmed him. His mind went dull. For the moment, he focused instead on gathering up the papers and photographs that had escaped from the album. He stacked them in a tall pile on the floor.

Deliberately, he did not allow his eyes to linger on any of his mementos. Each would only be a further provocation, a goading reminder of what he had to decide. Of whom he had once been, and what his future might be like in the aftermath of another call to serve the nation.

His life had spiraled down to this low station. But even in his ignominy—a custodian! an office above a parking garage!—he had no doubt there were worse fates. Or that propelled by another act of defiance, another challenge to the men of power, there were lower depths to which he might descend.

When the custodian was done, after the album along with the stack of loose "exhibits" (as he insisted on calling them) was returned to his desk and the drawer once again locked, he went to the window. He looked out at the boulevard lined with its familiar shops: the bookstore, the strictly kosher bakery, the bank, the grocery. The sky above was a dome of Jerusalem blue, a masterpiece of color and illumination that was his daily proof, despite the constant threat of new horrors, of a continued Divine Presence in this holiest of cities. And farther down the avenue, in the distance, rose a cone of dense gray smoke.

Sirens yelped. Ambulances and police cars, lights pulsing, weaved expertly through the mass of stalled traffic. Two men wearing yellow reflector vests, skullcaps on their heads, raced toward the smoke. A team from Zaka, he decided. The Disaster Victims Identification Squad. They would blot up blood from the walls, and scrape stray bits of flesh from the floor. They would make sure all the human detritus was accounted for, placed in plastic bags, and buried along with the dead. A person's soul, the Law says, resides in his blood.

And what about my soul? he wondered. Is there any hope for me if I don't act?

The years had led him to this new, small life. "My exile," he called it, full of self-pity. Yet once again he alone had worked it all out, had deciphered all the clues.

He knew where the bombers would strike next.

Once again, he was their Watchman.

He could shout the warning.

But he hesitated.

Would they listen this time? Had they learned anything in the past thirty years? Or would there be a new "Concept"? A new rationale for ignoring his evidence? And in the aftermath, would they once again make him pay for their mistakes? Their ignorance? Their arrogance?

He stayed at the window for a long time, staring out at his wounded, grieving city. The custodian had to decide, and he did not dare.

As coincidence would have it, that tense summer, nearly 300 miles to the west in the sprawling city of Cairo, another man who had lived with his own secrets for the past thirty years was also coming to realize that the past was never past.

But while his counterpart in Jerusalem had paid a steep price for his role in the shadows, he had only prospered. His work had made him rich, as wealthy as a sheik. And when he retired from the government, it was with honor and respect.

Nevertheless, he was a cautious man. He made it a point to keep up his connections in the ministry, and to talk with his former business associates abroad. And now suddenly, after all the years, there was trouble.

He learned that the authorities in Tel Aviv, as they tried to grapple with a new, perplexing war, had begun to talk more freely about secrets from an old one. A distraction strategy, a shrewd way of diverting a besieged nation's attention, he presumed. But from his perspective, it also was a growing danger.

Israeli Military Intelligence, he was told, had commissioned a secret history of the Yom Kippur War. A professor of political science from Haifa University had been given the task. The professor marched through the corridors of official power, and each of his interviews, his sorting through the pages of classified documents, culminated in his posing one still perplexing question: How could Israel, with all its resources, all its might and manpower, have been taken by such complete surprise on that October afternoon nearly three decades ago? As this professor asked his questions, old men, eager to find justifications for their mistakes before the record was sealed on their lives, finally talked. They made accusations. The name of the man from Cairo had not yet been revealed. But his long-hidden role, his contribution, was suddenly being challenged. And reevaluated.

While he was at home in Egypt, there were for the first time disconcerting moments, too. For years he had thought his secret was safe. When President Sadat was assassinated, he truly believed that part of his own past was now dead and buried. But lately he felt people were avoiding him. No one telephoned anymore, he told his daughter. No one in the government sought his once-valued advice. He also confided to a former associate (who was quick to spread this morsel of gossip) that he had been ignored the last time he had been at the Sporting Club, his club since he had been a young functionary serving Nasser. The other members, usually eager to talk business or politics, left him alone with his newspaper and coffee. In his mind, it felt deliberate. He was certain people were afraid to be seen with him, reluctant to be identified as his friends.

Now he preferred to stay at home. He lived in a large white concrete house with a broad, sheltered terrace that faced the Nile. Day after day he sat on this terrace. He would take to his chair early in the morning as a thin breeze rose up from the river and floated toward the stifling city. In the evening, as the muezzin's call to prayer came across the water, he would still be there.

That summer as Israel was once again under attack he did not travel. He did not, as he had in previous years, go off to relax in the cool and calm of Alexandria. Or to the blue waters and invigorating sun of Majorca, another favorite escape. Instead, he followed the intifada—Sharon's war again! he marveled—quite closely. He listened attentively and, another occupational habit that lingered into his retirement, tried to decipher the true warnings hidden in the threats from Al Qaeda and Hezbollah broadcasts on Al-Jazeera. And he waited.

He waited for someone to come to kill him. He feared the Jews. And the Arabs. And, worse, he knew they both had reason.

PART I

"RETURN TO ZION"

Haifa/Alexandria Summer 1973

. . . and who shall die

ONE

Haifa/27 June 1967

Nati fell in love with Yossi before she ever met him. She was sixteen, still in high school, and all it took was just one look. But at that moment in Israel's history, the entire nation, or so she would grow to complain, was in love with Yossi—the tousled-haired soldier with the coal dark eyes and the gleaming smile in the famous photograph.

The photograph first appeared on the June 27, 1967, cover of *Life* magazine. Newspapers and magazines across Israel, full of xenophobic pride for the local boy who had made good in the larger world, were quick to purchase reprint rights. Soon it was everywhere. It even had a second life as a poster; sales, especially to teenage girls, were impressively strong.

The image was clever in its directness. Twenty-two-year-old Yossi Ben Hanan, wearing tanker's overalls, a battle-scraped AK-47 assault rifle clutched in his hand, stared straight up into the camera. The soot-covered face, the strained brow beneath the fringe of haphazard curls, spoke of hard combat. Yet the grin bursting through all the weariness left no doubt: This soldier had fought and won.

But the picture's true power, and the source of its enduring fame, lie in the complex story it succinctly told. For as Yossi crooked his head up into the lens, he was cooling off from the heat of battle in the Suez Canal—water that until that day had been as Egyptian as the Nile.

This soldier's spontaneous celebration, the editors of *Life* realized, captured in a single snapshot the totality of Israel's victory over the Arabs in the Six Day War. It effectively condensed all the "astounding"—this was the unrestrained yet not inaccurate adjective on the magazine's cover—battle reports from every front.

In the air, within two hours and fifty minutes after launching preemptive strikes on June 6, 1967, Israel had destroyed 300 Egyptian planes. The Egyptian air force, for all tactical purposes, simply ceased to exist. The Israeli bombers quickly moved on to maul airfields in Syria, Jordan, and Iraq. By noon on the first day of the war, 452 Arab planes were lost and Israel controlled the sky above the Middle East.

On the Syrian front, the fighting was brief, too. Protected by concrete bunkers and rocky mountainous terrain, the Syrian troops at first grappled with the Israelis in bloody hand-to-hand combat. But as the sun rose on a second day of battle, the Syrian officers began to flee. Israeli troops pushed rapidly up the Golan Heights, taking strategic towns and peaks. A rout followed. After only twenty-seven hours of fighting, the road to Damascus was wide open, the Syrian capital ready to be seized if the Israelis decided to advance.

Jordan, despite Israel's diplomatic attempts to convince King Hussein not to get involved in the conflict, also entered the war. Its artillery opened up on the Jewish section of Jerusalem and shelled Tel Aviv. In response, eight Israeli brigades poured into the West Bank. On the morning of the third day of the war, Israeli soldiers reached the Western Wall in the old city of Jerusalem, rejoicing as they reclaimed the sacred religious site that had been lost a quarter of a century ago in the War of Independence.

And in the battle against Egypt, Israeli armor swiftly penetrated on three axes through the heart of the Sinai Peninsula, only stopping when they reached the east bank of the Suez Canal. The Egyptian force, 100,000 strong and outfitted with modern weapons and tanks provided by the Russians, was left in shambles. They fled in disorganized droves, leaving more than 15,000 of their dead and almost all of their equipment behind in the sand. More than 12,000 soldiers—including nine humiliated generals—were taken prisoner. Israel had 275 casualties in the desert campaign.

In less than a week's fighting, Israel's soldiers had decisively changed the political—and, no less significant, the strategic—geography of the Middle East. On the seventh day the nation, even if it were too jubilant to rest, could for the first time since it came into existence breathe easily.

The old territorial boundaries, a relic of the 1949 armistice, were history. Now the Sinai, the West Bank, a united Jerusalem, and the Golan Heights belonged to Israel. And with this new land, Israel's leaders were convinced, came safety. Egyptian forces would now need to cross the Suez Canal and, as if that alone were not enough of an obstacle, then march across a 150-mile-wide desert before being able to threaten a major Israeli city. The unification of Jerusalem placed the holy city for the first time in more than two decades out of the range of Jordanian artillery. Similarly, the villages in the northern Galilee were no longer easy targets for Syrian shelling.

In fact, the potential for a devastating first strike was now reversed. From their outposts in the newly seized land, the Israeli forces loomed ominously closer to the Arab capitals: Cairo was sixty miles away, Damascus only thirty-five.

An impressed community of nations, both friends and foes, uniformly acknowledged the strength of the Israel Defense Forces (IDF). "The Israelis are very patriotic, brave and skillful soldiers, brilliantly led," announced one widely reprinted, and quoted, editorial essay that seemed to sum up the international reaction to the incredibly one-sided war. And the editorial did not stop there. It bluntly went on to ask "an impolite but unavoidable question: What *is* the matter with the Arab armies? Was there ever a people so bellicose in politics, so reckless and raucous in hostility—and then so unpugnacious in pitched combat—as Nasser's Egyptians?"

But even this reaction was restrained when measured against the swaggering confidence many Israelis expressed. "Israel is now a military superpower," Gen. Ariel Sharon, a commander in the Sinai campaign, boasted. "Every national force in Europe is weaker than we are. We can conquer in one week the area from Khartoum to Baghdad and Algeria." The Arab armies, Sharon and many other Israeli generals believed, were no longer a threat—just an annoyance. It would only be a matter of time before they became an irrelevancy.

And thanks to the editors of *Life* and the powerful shorthand of journalism, one handsome face became the symbol for Israel's bursting pride. The chosen image of a chosen people. Yossi Ben Hanan, a novice platoon commander, became the link in the minds of the young nation for all the suffering that had come before, and the glittering future that lie ahead. The Holocaust launched to annihilate the Jewish people, the two decades of war intent on destroying the Jewish state—all these deep fears could finally be laid to rest. For now there was a new generation of Jews and a new generation of Jewish soldiers. Men who were brave, robust, and perhaps even invincible. Men like Yossi Ben Hanan.

And so the nation applauded Yossi, as with equal enthusiasm, they applauded themselves. He became a celebrity, unable, he would say with a twinge of embarrassment, to walk down a street in Tel Aviv or turn a corner in Jerusalem without someone calling out, "Shalom, Yossi." He was quickly promoted to captain, and the government sent him off to show the resolute face of the new Jews—a warrior people—to adoring crowds in Japan, Europe, and, of course, the United States. With his easy charm, his natural friendliness, his self-deprecating candor, and his smile, his nearly incandescent grin, his success seemed assured. Chief of staff would someday be his for the asking. Or, perhaps politics was his destiny. Would minister of defense or even prime minister be out of the question?

Yet as his comrades in the armored brigades speculated at what was in store for their beloved Yossi—"our Greek god, our golden boy," his close friend and commander Col. Avigdor "Yanosh" Ben Gal described him without irony—Nati quietly and confidently made her own plans. By the time she went off to do her compulsory military service two years after she had first seen the photograph on the cover of the magazine, Nati still had never met the object of all her fantasizing. But the passing of time and the blur of adolescent dalliances had diminished neither her ardor nor her conviction. Nati knew that someday she would meet Yossi and when she did, he would want her, too. No other outcome was possible. In her mind, their love had the force of a biblical prophecy. It was inevitable.

TWO

Golan Heights/June 1971

Four years to the month after the photograph had appeared on the magazine cover, they finally met. Capt. Yossi Ben Hanan, a battalion commander in the Seventh Armored Brigade, hurried into Col. Shmuel Gonen's briefing, apologized for being late, and then growled at a lieutenant, "What are you doing sitting in my seat? Get up."

Lt. Nati Friedman was not intimidated. She fixed the superior officer with her honey-colored eyes. A moment passed. Then she rose, and standing ramrod straight as if at attention, executed a smart salute. In the Israel Defense Forces, a populist army where even commanding officers are addressed by their first names, her gesture was clear parody, an implicit reprimand for the sharp tone. But in case the famous captain missed the point, there was more to her performance. Nati walked from the conference table with a deliberate, unmilitary slowness. A tall, slim woman, her dark hair piled into a neat bun, she wore tight green fatigues. Her back was to Yossi, so she could not see his eyes following her every step. But she felt them, she would say. She knew he was watching, appraising.

And all the time, undaunted by the discordant circumstances, she was thinking, I knew someday we would meet.

When the briefing ended, Yossi went off to confer further with Gordish, as Colonel Gonen was known to his troops. Yossi had served under the colonel in the Sinai, and knew too well whom he was up against. Gordish was a slight, prim tanker, frosty as a monk, and as devout as a rabbi. He would not respond well to a frontal assault. So Yossi dutifully asked question after question about the upcoming maneuvers in the north. The colonel, who enjoyed talking about the complicated mechanics involved in getting a column of tanks to the battle line, responded to each successive inquiry with eager detail. Yossi listened respectfully. He desperately wanted a cigarette, but he knew Gordish considered smoking a vice, and, therefore, unsuitable behavior for an officer. It was only hours later as the two men were leaving the briefing room that Yossi, with an impressive casualness, eased into his primary mission. "Your aide who was sitting in my chair," he asked. "What was her name?"

They went for a walk that night. The moon, as if Nati's coconspirator, illuminated the water as they strolled along the rocky shore of the Sea of Galilee. It was an auspicious beginning, a childhood prophecy made real.

And it was an illusion. The relationship quickly became complicated, even hurtful. For the next two years, Yossi and Nati suffered through a tumultuous on-again, off-again courtship. Nati's commitment did not waiver. But Yossi, with a hero's prerogative, grabbed his opportunities as quickly as he found them. He would return to Nati, but his excursions, always guiltless, always predictable, took their toll.

Nati finally had enough. She grew tired of sharing Yossi with, as she put it, "the rest of them." The sense of his absences became too wearying. She announced that she did not want to see him again. Determined to prove her sincerity as much to herself as to Yossi, she made plans. She would leave the army and, trading one uniform for another, become a stewardess for El Al. It would be a new life full of new possibilities.

Yossi accepted her decision. But, with his charm as manipulative as ever, he cajoled Nati "for old times' sake" to spend one last weekend with him. Reluctantly, she agreed. But she was surprised when they rode in Yossi's jeep up north, back to the Sea of Galilee.

The moon was not as full, not as theatrically bright as on their first night. But nevertheless it shined down with drama on the ancient water where Peter had fished, and remained her ally. They were walking hand in hand, tenderly, old friends, when Yossi said, "Why don't we just go ahead and do it?"

Months ago she had given up hope, dismissed all her previous fantasizing as a young girl's silliness. Now Nati understood she had been right all along. Her love was justified. A single word leaped up in her mind: destiny. But still this would not do. She refused to accept so passive an acquiescence.

"Do what?" she asked, full of innocent wonder.

Yossi fell to one knee. He took her hand, cradling it in his. And fulfilling her prophecy, he asked, "Will you marry me?"

She kissed his lips, and he held her. A long moment of complete stillness filled the night. The silence deepened, and stretched taut between them. When she finally spoke, it was a single word, as solemn and serious as a vow. "Yes," she said.

Later that night, they sorted through the practicalities. Yossi was now a lieutenant colonel, a battalion commander of an armored brigade. The ceremony would take place as soon as possible, as long as it did not interfere with his command responsibilities. Of course it would be in Haifa, at her parents' house. The back lawn, they both agreed, would be perfect. "But I don't want a big wedding," Nati said.

"Neither do I," he agreed. "Just my friends."

THREE

Haifa/Summer 1973

By the time they added the last name, they had invited 830 people to the wedding. Yossi had a lot of friends.

But more was inflating the quickly growing guest list than the many fellowships of arms of a professional soldier. Nor could the stack after stack of invitations that Nati mailed simply be attributed to Yossi's diligent ambition. As soon as the engagement announcement appeared in the newspapers, "shofars," Nati imagined with only a hint of facetiousness, "blew throughout the land." Each day the phone rang and there was someone new—an obscure relation, a long-forgotten friend of a friend—wishing Nati a genuinely heartfelt mazel tov. Each day another apparent stranger offered congratulations as Nati bought groceries or boarded a bus. Each day things seemed to get more and more out of hand. Yet as the weeks passed, as the buildup to the carefully planned day drummed on, she began to understand.

Her marriage was not simply another summer wedding between two young people who had fallen in love. She had chosen August 13, 1973, for the festivities because it was the fifteenth of the month of Av on the Hebrew calendar, the biblical Valentine's Day. Now she recognized the timing brought with it more powerful symbolism.

Everyone was eager to come, to be invited. She sensed that it wasn't just Yossi and Nati they wanted to celebrate. It was something more. Larger. *It was becoming a national celebration.*

Nati's mother was sixth-generation Israeli. Her family's roots were deep into the land since the days of Ottoman rule. They were farmers when the arid, sunbaked earth was strewn with formidable boulders, and a Jewish state, a land of plowed fields, of milk, honey, and commerce, existed only in biblical stories.

Her father's family had arrived in Palestine one generation earlier, and had also lived through the early struggles. In the War of Independence, Ephraim Friedman's parents had to abandon their home on the banks of the Jordan River. Along with their neighbors, they ran in panic from the Arab advance, leaving behind all they owned, all they had built in the Galilee wilderness. Yet he was a son who made a heartfelt promise to his parents and fulfilled it: An army commander, Ephraim led troops in fierce hand-to-hand combat to reclaim the home where he was raised. In his second life, he labored to design and build the highways that linked the northern towns and cities to the urban heart of the nation. The much traveled road stretching from the hills of Haifa to the shoreline of Tel Aviv was his accomplishment; and as the nation prospered, he did, too.

Yossi's family had been part of Jerusalem forever, or so it seemed in this young, immigrant state. When not caught up in the chaos of war, Michael Ben Hanan taught math and physics to generations of students. But it was not his accomplishments as a soldier or a teacher that had made him, almost as much as his son, renowned throughout the country. Since 1945, at 6:10 every morning, Michael Ben Hanan's hearty, no-nonsense voice boomed from the radio, leading a conscientious nation in its daily exercises.

On both sides, Nati and Yossi were children of pioneers, offspring of the men and women who had built the state, the generation that fought the Turks, the British, and the Arabs. They served in the illegal underground armies, the Haganah and the Palmach—adventures that today are recounted to Israel's children as if they were the tales of knights at the Round Table. They volunteered for the nascent defense force and won hopeless battles against overwhelming odds. They raised families and built homes, while all the time living under the threat of annihilation, of Arabs vowing to push them into the sea. They killed out of necessity, and for revenge. They endured the pain of wounds and maimings, and, no less scarring, saw beloved friends and relatives die in combat or terror attacks. They served alongside the generals and statesmen who became legends, and still knew them as intimates, as Moshe or Golda. Their biographies are volumes that span the entire history of the country, from its hard-won creation in 1948 to the triumph of the present.

In a country as small and tightly knit as Israel, the parents of the bride and groom had deep, even mythic connections. They were, by blood and deed, the Founders. And this storybook marriage, an occasion of such complete happiness, proved that all the sacrifices of an entire generation were worthwhile, that all their resilience was justified, and that the hope-fostered imaginations of the forefathers who had left the shtetls to come to an inhospitable desert land were visionary.

"Look at Nati, at Yossi, these strong, beautiful children," a nation of beaming mothers and fathers was exclaiming. "Our new Davids, our new Sarahs. And look at the world, prosperous and fecund, we, with our own hands, our own labors, created for them."

And no less than a family wedding, the celebration promised to be a military event. In a country that reveres its soldiers, Yossi was a warrior prince, a lieutenant colonel in the elite Seventh Armored Brigade. Ever since the magazine cover, his face symbolized the entire corps of professionals, bold and determined, who protect the state on land, sea, and in the air. How could the staff officers, the well-known generals who had molded this force of patriotic fighters, their new Maccabees, not share this occasion? How could they not raise a glass to Yossi and his bride, as at the same time they silently toasted all he had come to represent?

The junior officers, colleagues who had stood in the turrets of the massive Centurion tanks with Yossi during the years of training and who had charged with him under enemy fire across the Sinai, were no less eager to attend. They waited for the off-white card to come in the mail, and then they waited for the day itself. Just to be in Yossi's proximity, they had come to understand from past experience, brought with it the promise of something extraordinary, be it a large victory or a memorable "afters," as the tankers' nights out were known.

"You could always count on Yossi to make things happen," Maj. Shmuel "Shmuli" Askarov, his second-in-command recalled, a swift smile bursting from his face. "All summer we were waiting, looking forward to our Yossi's wedding."

But the connection that brought all these strands together, the unifying force that turned the event into a national celebration, lie in the exhilarating moment it shared in history. "We are on the threshold of the crowning era of the Return to Zion," Moshe Dayan, the military hero of a previous generation who was the minister of defense, predicted that May to a convention of cheering paratroopers. His confidence exuded not only from the victory in the Six Day War, but also from all that had happened in the six years that followed: the cease-fire along the Suez Canal, the apparent collapse of many terrorist groups, and the tension lingering between Egypt and Russia since the expulsion earlier that year of 14,000 Soviet military advisers.

It was a time "the likes of which our people has probably never witnessed in the past, and certainly not since the modern Return to

Zion," Dayan proclaimed in another confident speech that spring. "The superiority of our forces over our enemies" and "the jurisdiction of the Israeli government from the Jordan to Suez" assured, he predicted, peace and prosperity for decades to come.

And so the reasons to celebrate fused in merry anticipation. It was an occasion to rejoice over a nation's good fortune, as well as a young couple's. Many were invited, and they all were only too happy to come.

FOUR

Haifa/13 August 1973/1700

The white, squat flat-roofed villa stood by design at the crest of one of Haifa's many hills. The bands of windows were also carefully placed, facing west toward the sparkling blue waters of the Mediterranean. Today, festive baskets of wildflowers—Nati had picked them herself—lined the wrought-iron balcony. From there, the view opened past tall Carmel Mountain pines straight to the sea. It was, people would invariably say, like standing on the deck of a ship.

This afternoon the guests were not encouraged to linger. Instead, they were directed to a white-pebbled path scented with the fragrance of flourishing jasmine bushes. A canopy of pines shaded this narrow walkway, but after only a short stroll one emerged from the shadows into a bright green lawn sloping toward the sea. And here, in the late afternoon August sun, more than 800 guests began to gather as they waited for the wedding ceremony to begin.

At its center, the expanse of grass was as flat and wide as a soccer field. The bulk of the guests, without thinking too much about it, quickly separated on this level plain into two distinct groups. A crowd of generals and cabinet ministers huddled near the house. The younger officers drifted down to the far end, keeping their distance. By five, with the first hints of an evening breeze rustling the tall pines, the lawn had filled.

Deep in the scrum of festive tankers, Lt. Col. Avigdor Kahalani stood close to his wife, Dalia. His eyes darted across the lawn. "Only Yossi," he kept whispering to Dalia as, awed, he pointed out one distinguished face after another.

There was short, broad-shouldered "Haka," as Maj. Gen. Yitzhak Hofi was affectionately called in the press. For a little more than a year, he had been the general officer in charge of the Northern Command. He was flanked by his subordinate from the Syrian front, Brig. Gen. Rafael "Raful" Eytan, the taciturn former paratrooper who commanded all the forces along the Golan. And standing nearby was the man who had been Hofi's predecessor in the Syrian border command, Maj. Gen. Mordechai Gur. Gur was the defense attaché in Washington, but he had made it a point to schedule his week of cabinet briefings so that he would be in Israel for the wedding.

Chaim Bar-Lev was spotted, too. After serving as chief of staff and designing the string of defensive fortifications along the Suez Canal, he had moved on to politics. Now the minister of trade and finance, Bar-Lev huddled in a remote corner, seemingly trading secrets with the stern, imperious former paratrooper who ran Military Intelligence and was rumored to be the next chief of staff, Maj. Gen. Eli Zeira. Meir Amit, the former head of the Mossad, Israel's intelligence agency, stood in another circle, just an elbow away.

The Southern Command, the nation's first line of defense against Egypt, was well represented, too. Gonen, Nati's old boss and now a major general, had been appointed to head the Suez front in May and he held court with his divisional commanders: Maj. Gen. Avraham "Albert" Mandler, who in seven weeks was scheduled to retire from his post as head of the forces holding the Suez Canal line and the Sinai; and Maj. Gen. Avraham "Bren" Adan, who, poised at Gordish's side, seemed more like a thoughtful, lanky graduate student listening to his professor than the commander of an armored division. Even the air force had turned out. Gen. Benjamin Peled, the first Israeli air force commander trained entirely in the country, had known both the bride's and groom's families since childhood.

Kahalani stared at all the famous guests, watched as squads of waiters hurried from the grand house to offer up trays loaded with glasses of wine and bowls of olives and hummus, and found himself remembering his own wedding seven years earlier. The son of Yemenite immigrants, he grew up outside Tel Aviv in a house built by his father. There was no indoor plumbing, but his father made sure the walls were thick concrete, reinforced to withstand the sporadic gunfire from the adjacent Arab neighborhood. It was a hardscrabble childhood, and the future seemed to offer no promise of larger opportunities. Then he joined the army. By 1966, without brooding too much about how much more was demanded of him because of his dark North African skin, he had risen to battalion Operations officer in the Seventh Armored Brigade. But he still could not afford a wedding hall or a reception.

When Yossi heard this complaint, he announced that something had to be done. A soldier, a brother Israeli officer, deserved better. And as resourceful as a magician, Yossi came up with a solution. The men, part jest, part testimony to Yossi's ingenuity, dubbed it Operation Bride.

Four gleaming Patton tanks formed a circle, their long cannons pointing to the center. Wrapped around each nozzle was a heavy iron chain. Each chain, in turn, was attached by a lock and bolt to a metal cage. And standing inside the cage were Avigdor and Dalia, as well as a very skeptical rabbi. On command, the four cannons rose in unison, hoisting the cage high into the air. As the cage swung unsteadily, the iron chains creaking ominously, Kahalani put the ring on Dalia's finger and the petrified rabbi chanted the marriage prayers.

"Only Yossi could make this happen," Kahalani had told Dalia at the time. Today, even more astounded, he echoed the sentiment. "Only Yossi," he said repeatedly as he stared across the lawn with bewildered admiration.

Col. Amnon Reshef also was impressed, but there was a twinge of envy in his appraisal, too. He was a proudly self-made man. Ejected from school at fourteen, the year after his mother's death, he said a blunt good-bye to his tailor father and went off on his own. There were farming jobs in the morning, then backbreaking labor on construction sites, the work days starting at five in the morning and stretching until ten at night. He went straight into the army without attending high school. To his surprise, he was selected for the officers course. This was an opportunity to reinvent himself and he grabbed it with full determination. A decade later he commanded an armor brigade on the Suez front. Tall, ramrod straight, an air of perpetual menace embellished by a thick handlebar mustache, Amnon kept strict reign on his troops. Success, his hard life had taught him, was achieved through perseverance. He demanded much from his men, but no less than he extorted from himself. As he sneaked glances at the assembly of generals and the ministers across the manicured lawn, he could only wonder what his life would have been like if he had the gift, the offhanded presence, to be at ease in such worldly company. He instinctively measured Yossi's natural advantages, the exuberance of charm and the network of connections, against his own dogged talents. All he could do, Amnon realized with typical resignation, was resist the urge to be bitter. He had come this far on his own. The Yossis of the country would one day see his military career was not nearly done. With luck, he would have his opportunities. And with tenacity, he would make the most of them.

For Maj. Shmuli Askarov, however, it was an occasion celebrated with only generous, unjudgmental joy. In his uncomplicated world, it was blessing enough to serve alongside Yossi, to be his friend. Three years ago, his rash decision to quit the army at twenty-three had led him to despair. Returning to his kibbutz, the elders put him at the wheel of a battered truck, and ordered him to make deliveries. Driving an old Dodge through the crowded streets of Tel Aviv was not at all, Shmuli quickly learned, like racing a Centurion across the Sinai sand dunes. For six months his kibbutz life rambled on, leaving him numbed and indifferent.

Then one afternoon he returned from another day of deliveries and found Yossi, his old comrade from the Six Day War, waiting for him. "I've just been appointed to head a tank battalion," Yossi announced. "How'd you like to be my deputy?" They left together that evening, and Shmuli had never regretted it. Every day in the field with Yossi brought invigorating responsibilities and challenges. And the nights carousing alongside Yossi as his always eager sidekick brought their own adventures, too.

Shmuli looked around, at all the "high society" as he called it and silently thanked Yossi Ben Hanan for making him, "with my two feet on the ground," part of this shimmering world even if only for a few hours. And full of hope, he wondered if Yossi would remember to keep his promise and find a moment to introduce him to one of Nati's glamorous friends.

Only Yanosh Ben Gal, standing tall in a horseshoe of tankers, his rowdy, uninhibited laughter distinctive above the stream of merry chatter, seemed uninterested in the bigwigs across the way. His mind, even as he spun one ribald story after another, was busy with another matter. It filled with suspicion. And the later it got, the more the ceremony appeared to be unexpectedly delayed, the stronger his conviction grew.

Yossi, he decided with an immense satisfaction, wasn't going to go through with it! He was going to call the wedding off. Walk away with a shrug and a helpless grin, and Yossi, being Yossi, would get away with it.

Yanosh had reason for his suspicions. It wasn't that long ago that the two of them, full of wine and mischief, had spent the night on the beach at Caesarea entwined with two El Al stewardesses, the cool waves lapping them like another set of tongues. And there was the evening in the Sinai, not that long ago either if his memory wasn't playing tricks, when, with the turret of their tanks wide open to the desert stars, they made the best they could of the confined space below with two energetic young female lieutenants. There was little chance, Yanosh told himself, that Yossi would give up their extravagant life, a soldier's rightful spoils, for the shackles of marriage. Even one as brilliant as this one.

When Yanosh heard a commotion, an excited building rumble of voices coming from the path by the house, he knew with sly certainty that he had guessed right. In his mind he could already see Nati's father, the old Palmachnik full of weary resignation as he went off to one last hopeless battle, heading to the veranda to make an embarrassed announcement to the guests.

But Yanosh was wrong. When he turned toward the buzz of noise, in its midst was not Friedman, but another old soldier. It was a face so immediately identifiable that it could serve as an icon for the state. Moshe Dayan, the celebrity minister of defense, his bald dome of a head held high, the massive forehead sliced on the diagonal by the chord of his pirate's black eye patch, walked stiffly through the adoring crowd. To everyone who hurried over to shake his outstretched hand, he announced, "Golda wanted to come, too. She insisted I give her regrets."

Now that Dayan had arrived, the wedding could begin. Yossi, in his open-necked dress uniform, and Nati, in a long, slim white toga, a garland of wildflowers in her dark hair, stood side by side under the marriage canopy. Yanosh held one of the poles raising this symbolic tent above the couple. Shmuli grasped another. And Dayan, a new groom himself, marrying his second wife just days before his fifty-eighth birthday three months earlier, stood nearby.

"Blessed art thou, O Lord our God, King of the Universe, who hast created joy and gladness, bridegroom and bride, mirth and exultation, pleasure and delight, love, brotherhood, peace and fellowship," the rabbi chanted as he began the last of the seven blessings. "Soon may there be heard in the cities of Judah and in the streets of Jerusalem the voice of joy and gladness. . . ."

When the rabbi concluded, Yossi, as centuries of tradition dictate, brought his heel down sharply on a shard of glass. The smashing of the glass commemorated the destruction of Jerusalem and the holy Temples, first by the Babylonians in 586 B.C., and then by the Romans in A.D. 70.

As the jubilant guests shouted out mazel tovs to the new bride and groom, how were they to know that within weeks the cities of Judah and Jerusalem would wail with tears, not "joy and gladness." Or that the Third Temple, their hard-won state, would be in danger of destruction. And that many of them, the sword of the nation, would be fighting for their lives, if not already dead.

FIVE

London/14 August 1973

One invited guest never made it to the wedding. In all the tumult, with all the crowd of well-wishers, his absence went unnoticed.

Still, his ties to both families were old, and affecting. He had stolen guns from British army camps scattered across the Mandate territory with Nati's father in the Palmach days. Then he had fought alongside Yossi's father, quite possibly with those very Bren guns, in the battle for Jerusalem during the War of Independence. When peace came, his wife was one of Michael Ben Hanan's algebra students.

Yet two days before the wedding, a cable arrived at an office in Herzliyya, north of Tel Aviv. The patient, it read in part, would be in for a checkup. The next morning he boarded the El Al flight to London. His travel documents identified him with an alias—he used work names on a one-time basis whenever he left the country—and listed his occupation vaguely as "commerce." But the slight, rumpled, balding grandfather sitting in the business class seat was a major general. His name was Zvi Zamir. He was head of

Israel's Institute for Intelligence and Special Operations. Or, as it is more commonly called, the Mossad. And the "patient" he hurried to see was the most valuable spy he ran.

Foreign agents, the Mossad teaches its talent spotters, are usually recruited to spy against their own countries by any of three inducements. The three Ks, they are called in the Midrasha, the agency's hillside training academy: *kesef*, or money; *kavod*, respect; and *kussit*, which, in its crude, slang way, comes down to sex. The tempting prizes are dangled, the greedy turncoat bites, and a mutually beneficial relationship begins.

But what sets off alarm bells in the Mossad, or any intelligence agency for that matter, is the "walk-in"—the volunteer who comes unsummoned to your door bearing gifts. Even more suspicious is the walk-in who insists he's betraying his country for none of the usual base, and therefore easily understandable, reasons. If he's not a "double"—that is, an enemy agent assigned to spread disinformation—then he is much too unpredictable, an embarrassment waiting to happen. Inevitably he'll get burned, and so will the operation.

Yet the In-Law, as the Mossad's prize agent became known to the prime minister and the half dozen other top government officials who regularly received copies of the debriefings, began his operational life as a walk-in. And despite the efforts of several of the agency's psychological profilers, the In-Law's true motivation was never definitively identified. He was the exception to all the cautious rules. In the end all that mattered was the material he offered. No spy in the history of Israel ever delivered such intelligence. The yield, raved the head of Aman, Israel's Military Intelligence agency, was "raw documents, one miraculous one after another"—straight from Egypt's secret files.

The In-Law made his initial contact in the spring of 1969, as the sporadic skirmishes between the Israeli and Egyptian forces along the Suez Canal settled into a War of Attrition. Like a genie, he simply appeared offering the Mossad a seemingly unlimited number of wishes. He was, a hastily convened council of Mossad wise men debated, either too good to be true, or truly a whole lot better than good: manna from Heaven. But even the skeptics had to admire the planning that went into his approach to Israel.

He was sick, and he was scared. A sharp pain throbbed in his stomach. He could not sleep, he complained nightly to his wife. And to the people he worked with—ministers, cabinet members, even Gamal Abdel Nasser during their regular conferences at the president's home in Giza—he tentatively shared his large, building fear. Cancer, he worried out loud. The word, once spoken, lay there ominously. It brought an anxious, sympathetic pause to every conversation. No one, no matter how much power he wielded, was immune.

He visited the best doctors in Cairo, but their diagnoses were inconclusive. Yet all the while the pain continued unabated; and, he confided gravely to anyone who would listen, his fears grew, too. After nearly eight months of sharing his anxiety, he applied to the National Intelligence Service (NIS) for a visa to visit London. He explained to the NIS, which routinely reviews the foreign travel requests of all high government officials, that he needed to consult with a medical specialist. The NIS granted the visa without delay.

The next stage of his operation moved forward with a similar astuteness. As soon as he arrived in London, he kept his appointment with a Harley Street gastrointestinal specialist. The doctor's medical credentials were well established. However, he also held another affiliation that was only known to a much smaller circle.

The doctor was a *sayan,* a Jewish volunteer who, when asked, assisted Israeli agents working in his country. He, in fact, had played an important role in the start of confidential Middle East diplomatic negotiations. King Hussein of Jordan, another of his foreign patients, conducted his first meeting to discuss a permanent peace with an Israeli representative, Yaacov Herzog, general director of the prime minister's office, in this Harley Street office. The talk was a closely held secret; Hussein feared that if his discussing even the possibility of stabilized relations with the enemy became known, he would be assassinated just like his grandfather. Yet the meeting, or at least a rumor of it, had not escaped the attention of one high government official in Cairo. And he had come to London to act on this knowledge.

He moved quickly. In the opening moments of the consultation, as he sat opposite the doctor, he interrupted himself to announce that he had brought a sheaf of X rays taken by a battery of Cairo physicians. Would the doctor be interested? Of course, the doctor answered.

Reaching into his briefcase, he took out a folder and passed it across the desk. As he continued talking, the doctor did a cursory appraisal of the various X rays. Suddenly—as the moment is described by members of Israeli intelligence services who had knowledge of the case files—the doctor broke in.

"I think, sir, there has been some mistake. Some papers have been included in error."

The patient assured him that there was no mistake. He wanted the doctor to deliver these documents to the Israeli embassy.

The physician protested vehemently. He most certainly knew no one in the embassy. Perhaps, he said with authority, the gentleman would be kind enough to leave his office. But when the patient mentioned the meeting between King Hussein and Herzog, the physician lapsed into silence.

"And your examination?" he asked finally.

"I think we should proceed as you normally would," said the patient. "If you don't, it would look most irregular. Besides, my stomach *is* a bit off."

Three days later, as he wandered through a crowded floor of Harrods searching for a present for his wife back home in Cairo, a shopper bumped into him as if by accident—except the quick apology very casually included his name. And a whispered suggestion: Perhaps he would like to leave. Take the tube to the British Museum, and then proceed to the Main Reading Room. Before he could respond, the stranger disappeared into the crowd of shoppers.

He never arrived at the British Museum. He was met as he walked from the Holborn tube station. A man he had never seen before grabbed his arm and, without a word of greeting or instruction, hurried him into a waiting car.

His identity, of course, had already been investigated by a team of overexcited Mossad vetters. But that afternoon he proudly confirmed all the Mossad's findings. His wife was a daughter of Egypt's President Nasser. His title was Ambassador at Large, but his specific governmental responsibility was to serve as the liaison between the president and the Egyptian intelligence services. He was not yet thirty, but he sat at conference tables with the small circle of men who planned Egypt's future.

By the end of the interview, his operational life as a spy for the Mossad had begun.

Four years later, as Zvi Zamir traveled to his face-to-face on the weekend of Yossi and Nati's wedding, the running of the spy referred to in the upper circles of government as the In-Law had grown into a small industry within the Mossad. A safe house only a meandering walk from the tony neighborhood of the Dorchester Hotel, the agent's ostensible refuge during his medical consultations in London, had been purchased at outrageous expense, then furnished with similar, uncharacteristic extravagance. While this new home was being outfitted, a team of *shicklut* technicians, the agency's department in charge of listening devices, flew in from Tel Aviv. When they had finished, every conversation, every whispered aside, could be automatically recorded anywhere in the house.

Plus, an army of full-time staff served the operation. Israeli handlers maintained discreet contact with the spy when he was in Cairo or on state business elsewhere in the Middle East. Housekeepers arranged the details for each meeting in London down to a favorite brand of ouzo. Research teams analyzed the mountain of raw documents the In-Law delivered on each trip. And clerks with top security clearance transcribed the one-to-one conversations with both the case agent and, with increasing frequency over the years, the head of the Mossad. Within forty-eight hours of each face-to-face, the strategic and political insights from a member of Egypt's inner political circle were shared with the prime minister, the army chief of staff, the head of Military Intelligence, and the handful of other top officials cleared for the In-Law distribution list.

And there was one more expense. While the In-Law was wealthy, and insisted he had volunteered because he "believed in the ultimate triumph of the Zionists" and felt "ashamed of the disgraceful performance of the Arabs in the last war," Zamir persuaded him to accept a fee. It would, the head of the Mossad graciously insisted, help soften the burden of his trips to London. They agreed upon a payment of 100,000 British pounds sterling, delivered in cash at each face-to-face. And when the deal was done, the Mossad was even happier than the recipient; the profligate attitude in intelligence is the more you pay for something, the less you doubt it.

By the time all the expensive nuts and bolts were fastened together, the total cost of running the agent during the four years of his operational life had soared to a staggering $20 million. But it was money, the leaders of Israel agreed, that was well spent. In their strategic poker game with Egypt, where the stakes were nothing less than the survival of the state, they were able to see every card their opponent held.

Two incredible documents, both delivered by the In-Law, became the foundation for the nation's entire long-term threat assessment of the enemy. The first was a transcript of a conversation Egyptian President Nasser had in Moscow on January 22, 1970, with members of the Russian general staff.

Still unsettled by Egypt's devastating defeat in the Six Day War, Nasser explained he had come to realize that before he could launch a successful war to liberate the lost territory, two preconditions must be satisfied. First, Egypt would need Scud missiles to terrorize Israel's cities. And second, his air force required long-range fighter bombers capable of striking deep into enemy territory and destroying their fortified command centers. Moscow, the transcript revealed, was unwilling to provide these items. Furthermore, the Russians rudely suggested—and the Israelis read with gloating pleasure—the problem was not lack of equipment, but rather the quality of the Egyptian soldier.

The second purloined document was a confidential letter written by Anwar el-Sadat, who became president of Egypt upon Nasser's death. In this August 30, 1972, letter to Russian President Leonid Brezhnev, Sadat reiterated the necessity of having both missiles and bombers before Egypt could make war against Israel. He wrote:

"I mentioned in our frequent discussions that we needed a retaliatory weapon which would deter the enemy . . . because of his knowledge that we would then be able to retaliate in kind and attack his inland positions . . ."

But it was the sentence that followed that Israeli officials always underlined and quoted. "It was obvious, and still is," Sadat confided in apparent frustration, "that, deprived of such a retaliatory weapon, we would remain incapable of taking any military action."

In addition to these revelatory documents—although what intelligence could be more unimpeachable than the president of Egypt's private thoughts? the insiders who read these letters agreed—there were the many transcripts of conversations with their agent. He was an eyewitness as decisions were made at the highest level; and, as a perfect spy, he could reiterate with a mimic's gift the flow of conversations, the fever in any debate. His performance was pure theater.

In these sessions he also revealed another hidden cornerstone of Arab policy: no Arab state—especially Egypt—was willing to launch a war against Israel on its own. And Arab unity, despite all the resolute public pronouncements, was an illusion. The In-Law described with amused disdain the constant feuding between the Arab leaders. They were parochial heads of state more inclined to fight each other than the Jews.

For four heady years the spigot of incredible information had continued to flow and flow. And from all that the spy delivered, both his raw documents and his eyewitness reports, Israeli Military Intelligence developed *Ha'kontzeptia*—"the Concept."

The Concept became an article of faith throughout the nation's military and political establishment. It proclaimed with a biblical certainty that until (1) the Egyptians had missiles and long-range bombers, and (2) the Arab states were a unified coalition, war was impossible. And since these preconditions were unfulfilled wishes, the nation could go about its business without concern.

So trusted was this spy that when he worried, the leaders of Israel immediately worried, too. In April 1973, in startling contradiction to all his previous reports, he sent a flash message to his case agent using the word *radish*. This was the prearranged code for an imminent war. May 15, he told Zamir in a hastily arranged meeting in the London safe house, would be the date of an Egyptian–Syrian surprise attack. Five infantry divisions would cross the Suez Canal, while helicopters carried commandos to Sharm el-Sheikh. At the same time, Syrian infantry would march over the northern border.

Upon Zamir's return to Israel, a key group of the country's political and military leaders gathered at Prime Minister Golda Meir's home on April 18 to hear his report. The In-Law's pronouncement of imminent war was given even more credibility because of other disturbing news: A week earlier a squadron of sixteen Iraqi Hunter jets and their pilots had reached Egypt, and sixteen Mirages that France had sold to Libya had also been transferred to Sadat's command. Suddenly, it seemed plausible, and perhaps even likely, that Egypt was readying a strike force.

Eli Zeira, the head of Aman, in his customary curt, confident way, dismissed all the concerns. Despite the spy's warning, and "signs of concrete preparations," he insisted that war was unlikely. "Truth is," he told the group that included the prime minister and David "Dado" Elazar, the army chief of staff, "we are finding more signs that he [Sadat] is not going to start a war. . . ." And even if the Egyptians were to attempt to cross the Suez Canal into the Israeli-held Sinai, he said with convincing authority, "I am sure we will know ahead of time and be able to give not only a tactical but an operative warning as well. I mean a few days ahead of time."

Syria, he went on in the bombastic way that had earned him the nickname of "sergeant major," was not a realistic threat. "The Syrian president [Hafez al-Assad, a former head of the country's air force] knows that if our air force wants to, it can destroy the Syrian air force within two hours. Therefore, when the Syrians say to the Egyptians, 'Our army is at your command and we are ready for a coordinated plan in an event war will break out,' they don't mean it."

Dayan and Dado's assessment differed. It would be, the chief of staff argued, a "disaster" if only the relatively small standing army was in position in the event of an attack. To fight a war, Israel needed her reserve battalions mobilized and placed at the front lines. Of course, he reassured the prime minister, even in the unlikely event of an attack before the reserves were called up, the air force would still undoubtedly have at least forty-eight hours' notice, and would be able to neutralize the Egyptian air defenses.

"If war happens, let it happen," Dado told the group. But Israel needed to be prepared. "We have no interest in war, but if one breaks out in 1973, it's an historic opportunity to deal a crushing military and political blow that will last for a very long time to come," he said. Dayan agreed, and so did Golda Meir.

On May 7, they launched Condition Blue-White. This was the code name of the general staff's plan to deal with the possibility of an Arab surprise attack. Tens of thousands of reservists were called to duty, while troops and support equipment were deployed along the front lines in the Sinai and the north. It was a major mobilization, and it came at a major cost. A flash message from a spy had set in motion events that cost the Israeli treasury, already overburdened by defense outlays that hogged more than 40 percent of the country's total budget, an additional $35 million.

It was a false alarm.

Yet the alert cautiously dragged on for another three months. As coincidence would have it, the week Zamir flew to London, the week of Nati and Yossi's wedding, the army finally canceled Condition Blue-White. The reservists returned to their angry families, and the front lines were once again manned by thin, defensive forces. The nation gladly settled into a renewed complacency.

Nevertheless, as Zamir remembers it, he began his meeting with his agent that August evening in London as he began all the sessions.

"Is there anything out of the ordinary I need to know about?" was his customary opening question. "Anything that has changed?"

"No," said the In-Law before they moved on to other business. "Nothing at all."

SIX

Alexandria/22 August 1973/1400

Eight days later, halfway east across the globe from the comfortable town house in Mayfair, Saad el Shazly paced impatiently back and forth along a wooden dock. It was two o'clock on a broiling August afternoon in Alexandria, but he did not search for shade. Instead, he remained on the open dock. And each new glance at his watch reminded him that the boat carrying the six men was very late.

Wearing civilian clothes, an open-necked shirt and trousers, only added to his discomfort. He felt incomplete without his paratrooper's beret, jump boots, and the weight of his general's stars. There was something demeaning in the Egyptian chief of staff's skulking around in disguise. Furtive. Like a spy.

In sudden reaction to his own thought, he looked toward the crowd squeezed into the small holding area beyond Customs. Were all of them waiting for their friends and relatives to arrive? Or, was someone watching him? He flew in yesterday on the short commercial flight from Cairo. Was the enemy onboard, too? Did they know whom he was meeting? What they were planning?

As fiercely as if he were addressing a jumpy private, he ordered himself to find some calm. His fears were unwarranted. Everything was going well. Up to this moment, all the months of complex preparations had moved forward without creating a ripple of suspicion. There was no reason to believe anything had changed.

The Soviet liner, already a disturbing forty minutes overdue, was on its normal run from the Syrian port of Latakia. On board were several hundred vacationers making a late summer's trip to the beach. And hidden among them, using aliases, wearing disguises, were his six men. His long road to war, Shazly told himself, was finally nearing its end. But for now all he could do was wait, a solitary figure marching with nervous excitement under the violent sun. . . .

In the beginning, there was the will. On a moonlit night in June 1967, Shazly had hurried his division of paratroopers in humiliated retreat back across the Suez Canal, as Sharon's troops chased at their heels. The memory was a constantly twisting knife. When he reported to Command, he impudently lectured the staff officers: Reclaiming the territories lost in '67 must be Egypt's primary military mission. As soldiers, it was their duty. As men, honor required action.

But revenge was not the prevailing mood in Cairo. In reaction to his frank, bellicose talk, the generals sent him to an isolated post by the Red Sea. On his first day, an aide showed him to a general's villa. He rejected it. Instead, he slept in a 6-by-10-foot shack; it fitted his self-contained, independent mood.

In his exile, night after night reliving his painful battlefield memories in the solitude of the vast desert, Shazly began his search. On his own, he would conceive of a plan to fight the Jews—and this time win.

Yet he was, by nature and military training, a realist. As he brooded on what needed to be done, he quickly bogged down. The continuing superiority of the enemy forces, particularly its squadrons of fighter jets and bombers, had to be conceded. No matter how honorable the cause there was no honor in sending Egypt's youth out to certain slaughter.

Another inescapable reality sunk his thoughts deeper into the doldrums: A new defeat would bring unbearable consequences. If the cocky Zionists once again quickly repulsed an all-out Arab attack, the shame would be a permanent poison. Dishonor would be a curse seeping into the blood of unborn generations.

But even as he acknowledged the difficulties, his resolve did not falter. And in time, nurtured by the isolation of his Red Sea Command, goaded by his undiminished anger, and shaped by a mitigating sense of reasonableness, he found a strategy taking form. Admittedly, it was still broad; certainly he had no illusions that it supplied all the rigorous tactical solutions that were necessary. But at the same time he was convinced its core logic was overwhelming: Fight the war you can win and your enemy can't.

The idea—his Concept—translated into revolutionary shifts in Egypt's military thinking. And Shazly could only imagine how the stubborn, old-school professionals in Cairo who ran the army would scream when they heard it.

Far from headquarters, he played out in his mind the briefing he hoped to deliver.

First, Egypt had to stop believing its own propaganda. There was no realistic possibility, at least in the next round of fighting, of pushing Israel into the sea. Or, for that matter, even of liberating the entire Sinai and the Gaza Strip. Decades of wishful thinking had only brought three successive and stunning defeats.

Instead, using the weapons it already possessed, Egypt had to train to fight a limited war. Cross the canal, smash through the Bar-Lev Line forts, and, just as the troops were poised to charge ahead—*stop!*

If the invading Egyptian army established bridgeheads ten to fifteen kilometers from the Canal, if they dug in immediately after entering enemy territory, then they were in a fight they would win—a defensive war. As long as the Egyptian forces did not charge beyond the range of the thicket of surface-to-air missiles (SAMs) that, thanks to the Russians, had already been established on their own west bank of the Suez Canal, they were protected. Let the Israeli jets counterattack their positions. Heat-seeking missiles and antiaircraft fire, as they had proved in the War of Attrition, would shoot the enemy planes out of the sky. When mobile SAM units were brought across the Canal, Egyptian troops could advance farther into the Sinai, but even then only for a symbolic five to eight miles.

The key to victory lie in never moving forces beyond the missile shield. With the enemy bombers thwarted, prevented from pounding away with their past savagery, Shazly felt confident the Egyptian army, outfitted with Russian T-62 tanks brandishing powerful 115-mm cannons and handheld Sagger antitank missiles, could be trained to hold out against the Israelis.

While at the same time, this was precisely the sort of long, drawn-out campaign that Israel had neither the will nor the capabilities to fight. To wage war Israel needed to mobilize 600,000 soldiers, more than a fifth of its population. Initially, only the convenient rhythms of daily life would be disrupted. But if weeks of fighting dragged into months, the economy would sputter, then break down. Israeli politicians could not allow their generals to conduct a war without the promise of a quick end. They would insist on a rapid drive, a furious blitzkrieg of charging planes, armor, and infantry, to expel the invaders back across the Canal.

Which was just what Shazly desired. He wanted the Jews to assault his fortified positions. He was confident well-trained Egyptian troops, hunkered down in their bridgeheads, the skies above protected by SAMs, could stand up to any charge.

And as his guns and planes mauled the advancing enemy columns, as one costly, bloody day followed another, the Zionists would pull back. They would beg for a negotiated peace.

The Jews, he had come to realize after four wars, were a particularly sentimental people. Shazly still could not get over how the loss of a single soldier had them lamenting. As a Muslim, he had difficulty understanding their squeamishness; death in a holy war, the Koran promises, opens the door to Paradise. But as a soldier, he was willing to exploit it. Once troops started dying in the futile struggle to push the entrenched Egyptian force back across the Canal, Israel would be eager to trade land for peace. He did not expect, or, for that matter, require much. Even a sliver of the Sinai desert would be a restoration of honor. What a sweet victory, a reversal of fortunes and morale for the first time in twenty-five years, would be symbolized in those few miles of liberated sand.

With these broad strokes, Shazly, while still a relatively junior officer, had worked it all out. "A calculated risk, rather than a quixotic gamble" was how he described his strategy for winning the next war.

But he did not dare share it. His briefing remained locked in his mind. Who in the High Command would listen to, let alone support, a low-ranking paratroop officer's call for a limited, defensive war? He would be accused of cowardice, if not treason.

Then on the morning of May 15, 1971, an excited aide hurried into his small office. The president's secretary had called. Anwar el-Sadat wanted to see him tomorrow afternoon in Cairo. It was, the secretary said, urgent.

SEVEN

Cairo/16 May 1971/1100

Plots and purges rocked Cairo as Shazly arrived in the capital for his meeting with the president. Only eight months earlier, Anwar el-Sadat, then vice president, had assumed power on Nasser's death. The new president had boldly promised 1971 would be "the year of decision." But it still remained unclear to Shazly what the decision would be.

In February, Sadat had announced to a stunned Egyptian parliament, "if Israel withdrew her forces in Sinai to the Passes [Mitla and Gidi, strategic positions about forty-eight kilometers east of the Canal], I would be willing to reopen the Suez Canal . . . and sign a peace agreement with Israel. . . ."

Israel, however, was intransigent. After its heady victory in the Six Day War, Prime Minister Golda Meir saw neither the logic nor the advantage in returning land won in battle for what, in her judgment, was less than a guarantee of Israel's permanent right to exist. Until Egypt coupled its proposal with a condemnation of Palestinian and other Arab terrorist groups who remained determined to destroy the Jewish state, she felt Sadat was only posturing. She responded in a hard, uncompromising speech to the Knesset. "Golda extended him a finger—not a hand," was how one of her own dismayed foreign ministry officials described the rejection.

Having been rebuffed in his attempt to make peace, Shazly watched with greater interest as Sadat began, apparently, to reconsider war. An important first step, the president decided, was to merge the Arab states into a unified military bloc. In April 1971, Shazly attended a session of the Armed Forces Supreme Council to discuss the newly formed Union of Arab Republics between Egypt, Libya, and Syria. To his soldier's mind, Sadat's creation of a political alliance with the potential to mobilize for combat in unison against the Israelis, a union that envisioned employing the combined armed forces and wealth of the Arab world in a concerted attack, was a masterstroke. Yet Shazly sat at the conference table only to listen with frustration as Egypt's highest-ranking military leaders attacked the union, and by implication the new president who had sponsored it.

More unsettling, when he spoke out forcefully in favor of the plan, his superiors heckled him. Shazly drove back to his own headquarters convinced that a political storm was building, and that his outspoken dissent ensured that his thirty-year military career would be washed away when it broke.

Far from the capital, ostracized to the stifling heat of the Red Sea coast, Shazly still managed to hear rumors. Visitors came and whispered stray pieces of the budding conspiracy. Ali Sabry, the air force officer who was vice president, and War Minister Mohammed Fawzi, along with a group of army officers and with tacit backing from the Soviets, were poised to seize power.

But Sadat struck first. He dismissed Sabry on May 2, 1971, and placed him under house arrest. When Fawzi attempted to lead a squad of tanks to free the prisoner, presidential guards overwhelmed the force before they could fire a single round. Ninety-one people were arrested, and all faced death sentences. By May 15,

Anwar el-Sadat, for the first time since taking office, was Egypt's undisputed leader.

When Shazly entered the president's home the next day, his mind buzzed with all the capricious swings of power and policy in the past year. He could not even begin to guess why he had been summoned. The unexpected presence of Gen. Mohammed Ahmed Sadek, the newly appointed minister of war, and one of the ruder critics of his support for the Union of Arab Republics, however, was a despairing sign. Immediately Shazly saw his fate reduced to two possibilities. The best he could hope for was dismissal. But more likely within the hour there would be ninety-two prisoners condemned to death.

He stood at attention as the president entered the room. Shazly had been a soldier his entire adult life, since his graduation from the Egyptian Military Academy. A paratrooper and a commando, at fifty he still had the rock-hard physique that he demanded of all the men who served under him in the special forces. He had trained with the Americans at Fort Benning, and then, as the political winds shifted, with the Soviets. He had fought the Jews in 1948 as a commander of an infantry platoon, and he had rushed to the battlefield against them in every successive war. His career, he proudly believed, was an honorable one. As he saluted the president, he was determined to meet his fate with courage.

The president returned the salute. Then he announced that he had selected Shazly, over thirty more senior officers, to be chief of staff.

For the next two hours, the astonished Shazly, the war minister, and the president discussed what had to be done to restore the confidence and the morale of the Egyptian army. They discussed war with Israel in only vague, strategic terms. They still did not have the weapons to fight the battles that would drive the Jews out of the occupied territory. The Soviets still would not sell them the bombers and missiles that would allow them to target Tel Aviv. But as the conversation continued, despite all the candid talk about the daunting challenges ahead, Shazly began to grow excited. He began to understand what the president had finally come to decide in this "year of decision." He began to understand why he had been chosen to lead the Egyptian armed forces. He began to understand that the president shared his deep, consuming ambition. Sadat wanted to fight.

EIGHT

Cairo/Summer 1971

"No!" Gen. Mohammed Ahmed Sadek decided quickly. "The plan is without either political or military value."

It was July 1971, less than two months after Shazly's promotion to chief of staff, and when he finally shared his strategy for a war against Israel, the minister of war peremptorily dismissed it as if Shazly was still an adjunct exiled to the Red Sea command.

Politically, the minister explained with dismissive impatience, the operation accomplished nothing: The bulk of the Sinai would still remain under enemy occupation. Militarily, it placed Egyptian troops in greater danger: Once they crossed over to the far bank, the Suez Canal would no longer be a protective barrier between the two armies.

Give me a plan, the minister insisted, that will lead our troops through the Sinai and into the Gaza Strip. A plan the Russians will support. Our goal must be to liberate all the occupied territories.

"Impossible," Shazly said. "It's impossible because the resources are impossible."

From that first meeting, Shazly, emboldened by his new title, argued back. He had come too far, too much was at stake, for him to give in. And within months, after bringing his commando's tenacity and ingenuity into this new ministerial battleground, he engineered a compromise. Then, with even more cunning, he persuaded Sadek to accept another one. But this deal would be their secret.

Operation 41, as drawn up by Shazly, was an attack to seize the two key Sinai passes, Mitla in the southern Suez Gulf sector and Gidi farther north. It was not the unlimited war the minister envisioned. While to Shazly's dismay, it pulled Egyptian troops far beyond the SAM missile shield; the passes were forty miles east of the canal.

But its great strength, at least in the judgment of the politically cautious minister of war, was that the Soviets would not be able to accuse Egypt of a lack of ambition. They were urging boldness, and this was an invasion deep into enemy territory. Another plus, Moscow, an increasingly reluctant benefactor, would also have to concede that the shopping list of necessary weapons—mobile SAM-6s, new MiG-21 jets—was not too extravagant.

Sadek's instinct was astute. After a single briefing, the Soviets were ready to enter into discussions to provide missiles and the planes. But even as their military advisers in Egypt helped prepare this attack, there was, unknown to Moscow, another plan. These battle orders, one more compromise between the chief of staff and the minister of war, outlined the actual invasion.

High Minarets had the limited goal of only a five- or six-mile penetration into the Sinai. It was the plan Shazly had first conceived a year ago. And now as chief of staff he set out to find a way to implement it.

The new chief of staff raised his head above a wall of sandbags and peered through binoculars across the Suez Canal. Three hundred yards of dark, racing water separated him from the Israeli positions. He needed to lead an invading army to the other side.

He continued his reconnaissance for a while longer, then he put down the binoculars and took out the pad he always carried. In his precise, orderly way, he began to enumerate the problems.

One: Steep concrete walls rose up from the Canal bed and stretched past the waterline. Designed to shore up the eroding banks of sand, they also made any crossing a treacherous, perhaps hopeless attack. Amphibious assault vehicles would be stranded on these parapets, helplessly dangling ten feet above the ground, and exposed to scorching enemy fire.

Two: As if this were not sufficient, Israeli bulldozers had spent the past six years conscientiously piling dense mountains of sand behind the concrete bankings. At the most likely crossing points the hard, gray sand rose, he estimated, sixty feet high—as tall as a three-story building. And the sand was packed thick; a dozen solid brick walls might just as well have been placed back-to-back.

Three: Perched on top the formidable sand walls were the Bar-Lev Line forts. Named after the Israeli chief of staff who had championed them, they provided an early warning of attacks, and served as firing shelters to hold off, if not hold back, the initial enemy assaults. There were thirty-five of these structures spread in a line ten kilometers apart, although they were grouped closer together where the Canal below ran straight enough for bridging. Each was a stronghold: walls thick enough to withstand a 1,000-pound bomb; surrounded by minefields and barbed-wire fences; firing positions looking straight down at the canal. The entire line was manned by only a single infantry brigade—a lean force of less than 1,000 men. But backing them up, in camps deeper in the Sinai desert, were three armored brigades: 360 tanks. The moment lookouts spotted an invasion fleet crossing the 300-yard-wide canal, even as gunners swept the boats with machine guns and cannons, a call from the forts would summon the tanks. Within fifteen minutes, a half hour at most, the tanks would be in their assigned positions between the forts, joining in on the barrage of fire raining down on the invaders.

And four: A final deterrent. Every time Shazly considered it, he filled with fresh rage against an enemy who could conceive of such a weapon. Its viciousness was primitive and barbaric. Buried deep in the sand ramparts were reservoirs of flammable liquid. When the men in the forts turned the release valve, the oil-based substance would rush out into the canal. A thermite bomb would ignite the thin pool settling on the surface. And instantly the water would blaze with soaring flames, trapping the invaders in a fiery moat, burning them alive.

The chief of staff reviewed the discouraging list he had written and immediately had renewed appreciation for the enemy's confidence. Nearly every day he read an intelligence memo reporting that the arrogant Israelis were giving the grand tour of their impregnable canal fortifications to another undoubtedly impressed foreign military expert. And what had their General Gavish, the head of the Southern Command, boasted to the press? "The Suez Canal, minefields, fortifications, the armored division, and the air force—let's see them against *that!*"

Yet despite all he saw, Shazly vowed he would find a way.

NINE

Giza/24 October 1972/2100

Shazly threw himself into the long preparations for war. He trained his attack force. He worked with his engineers to develop a plan for the crossing. He discovered a secret weapon made in West Germany that would, he hoped, allow his invaders to storm through the sandbanks. But ultimately, war is a political decision. And in the midst of all his activity, he took an evening off to attend a dinner at the Saudi Arabian embassy in July 1972 and learned that President Sadat, with a single rash decision, had made all his work futile.

As the party in honor of Prince Sultan continued on merrily, Sadek guided Shazly to a quiet corner. "The president," he said without preamble, "has decided to expel the Russians."

Shazly was stunned. There were more than 14,000 Soviet advisers in Egypt, but what concerned him were the Russian field units who controlled vital, highly sophisticated military equipment. Russians directed the SAM-6 sites, flew MiG-25s, and independently operated electronic reconnaissance and jamming squadrons aimed at Israel. "You must realize how dangerous this decision is," he complained. "There is no question it will affect our capabilities."

"I tried to convince the president not to do it," said the minister. "But I couldn't."

That night, Shazly left the Saudi embassy believing war was no longer possible. And if revenge was not to be achieved, then, by default, his resignation held the only path to honor.

But he had misjudged the president. Sadat had not simply marched off in a huff from a difficult alliance. With brassy nerve, he was gambling that a disappointed Moscow would try to win him back. And in their eagerness, there would be unprecedented generosity.

Sadat won his high-stakes bet. Less than three months after Egypt severed the alliance, the Russians promised to provide two squadrons of jets, both MiG-23s as well as SU-20s, and an even greater treasure, ground-to-ground Scud missiles. These R-17Es, as the Russians called them, were too inaccurate to use tactically against a military target, but with a range of 150 miles they would spread terror deep into Israeli territory.

Encouraged by these developments, Sadat, just six days later, on October 24, 1972, called for a meeting of the Armed Forces Supreme Council. That evening Shazly arrived at the president's house in Giza full of anticipation.

Sadat began slowly, as if deliberately letting his anger build. He reviewed his attempts to make peace with Israel, his disappointment at the United States's halfhearted attempts to bring Israel to the negotiating table, and his realization that the Russians would never give Egypt all the weapons the army needed.

Then with his preamble delivered, his mood abruptly changed. It was as if a switch were thrown and an animating electricity coursed through him. "The Soviets are not sure we are going to fight," he said, nearly shouting. "That is why they are reluctant to give us weapons. At all my meetings with them, the leadership has indicated this in so many indirect, insinuating ways: 'When are you going to fight? When are you going to act like men and liberate your lands?' . . . If they were in our position, they said, they would fight to liberate their country even if they had nothing but rifles."

Sadat not only challenged his generals, he taunted them. And all the while, Shazly silently applauded. This was remarkable. He listened on with mounting anticipation.

"The issue facing us now," Sadat declared, "is 'to be or not to be.' We cannot simply load blame onto the Russians. They have armed and equipped two entire field armies—with arms and equipment of their own choosing, certainly, but equipped nevertheless.

"This is not a matter about which I'm taking your advice. The time has passed for that. Today the armed forces are faced with a test. . . . If we don't act . . . if we remain passive, our cause will disintegrate and die by the beginning of 1973."

The president bluntly concluded: "We will simply have to use our talents and our planning to compensate for our lack of some kinds of equipment. God bless you."

Shazly felt the thrill of vindication. This was the call to war—a limited war, a war that could be won—that he had championed for so long. And yet even as he rejoiced, other voices around the table began to protest.

The minister of war and several of the other generals questioned the decision to fight without the long-range weapons capable of destroying the cities of the Jewish state. Their arguments were careful, delivered with a diplomatic restraint. But Gen. Abdel Kader Hassan, the deputy minister of war, was bold: "We might embark upon a limited offensive . . . we might succeed in the initial phase of our attack, but then we would undoubtedly be forced on the defensive by the enemy. . . . And what of us? We have to consider that most of our interior has no proper defenses against air attacks. The enemy's air force could inflict heavy damage. . . . Syria's is even weaker. . . ."

Sadat exploded. "Abdel Kadar, you don't have to tell me what to do and what not to do. I am responsible for this country's independence and I know what my duties are."

Shazly listened uneasily, but with fascination. He thought Sadat was ready to jump from his chair and put his hands around the impudent general's neck.

"You must not interfere in something that is not your responsibility," the president warned. "I do not want to have to tell you again. Keep to your limits. You are a soldier, not a politician."

With that reprimand, any further challenges remained unspoken thoughts. Still, it was past midnight before the meeting ended.

And there were repercussions. The next afternoon Sadat summoned Shazly to Giza. He announced the dissenters, a group including four generals and the minister of war, had all been removed from their posts. From this moment Shazly had total control of the armed forces. He was to prepare a force to cross the Suez Canal. "The countdown to war," the president declared, "has begun."

Shazly finally had what he wanted. What he had carried in his heart, what he had crafted in his mind, was now real. Yet only a moment later, Sadat, always capricious, once again surprised him.

"Now," the president said, "let us consider who is to be the new minister of war. I am considering Ahmed Ismail."

Ismail! The general who had lost Egypt the Sinai in '67! Shazly was appalled.

The last time they had worked together was more than a decade ago in the Congo. When Ismail objected once too often to the way Shazly ran the United Nations's contingent, Shazly, tired of all the arguing, knocked him to the ground with a single punch. Shazly could not imagine leading the nation to war in tandem with such a brusque, indecisive commander. Any chance of success would be doomed.

"Mr. President," he argued, "it would be impossible for us to work together in harmony."

They talked for over an hour, but Sadat refused to reconsider. He offered only a small balm to Shazly's anger: Ismail would not revise the battle plan that Shazly, during his past eighteen months as chief of staff, had already begun to put in motion. Beyond that, Sadat was adamant; there would be no other concessions.

The choice was Shazly's. Either he fight with Ismail as his partner, or he resign—and not fight at all.

"You will guarantee that Ismail will not change the plan?"

"Yes," said the president.

"I will prepare the troops for the battle that will determine the destiny of our country," Shazly decided.

Six months later, in April 1973, Ismail informed Shazly that the battle plans would need to be revised.

"Impossible," Shazly yelled. "I have the president's guarantee."

"It is the president," the minister of war explained, "who is ordering the change."

What had happened was politics: Days earlier, in a former British Colonial army base hidden away in Egypt's western desert, Sadat held a secret meeting with Hafez al-Assad, president of Syria.

"I've decided on a battle this year," Sadat told Assad. "What do you say to this?"

Assad paused as if to shape his thoughts. Victory, Sadat knew, could rest in the answer. If the attack on Israel broke out simultaneously on two borders, in the north with a push toward the Galilee as well as in the south across the Suez Canal, the Zionists would be forced to divide their forces.

At last Assad replied. "I'll be with you. We're going to fight and are preparing for it."

But, as Ismail explained to Shazly, there was one condition for Syria's support. Egypt must engage Israel aggressively in the Sinai. Otherwise, the Syrian generals feared the enemy's tanks and planes would be quickly diverted north for a counterattack.

"If the Syrians realized our plan is limited to the capturing of a line less than ten miles east of the canal," Ismail lectured Shazly, "they would not go to war alongside us."

"I would prefer us to go it alone."

That was not an option, Ismail flatly announced. The president had decided an alliance with Syria was a political necessity.

An operation beyond the missile shield will be a military disaster, Shazly responded. The enemy jets will slice our troops apart.

Back and forth the two generals went. But this time their argument ended without a punch being thrown. The solution was Ismail's, and it filled Shazly with shame.

There would be two plans. One outlined a bold attack to the passes; an update of the old Operation 41. They shared this strategy with the Syrians. But it would never be implemented.

The other was much more limited: the crossing, and then the establishment of defensive positions. This one Shazly gave to his commanders. It was the war plan.

And so throughout that uncommonly warm spring of 1973 Shazly covertly prepared for war. It was still his resolute ambition, but he no longer treasured the prospect as he had in his lonely nights by the Red Sea. He moved forward with the final arrangements in partnership with a mercurial president, a minister he did not trust, and an ally, he acknowledged with considerable guilt, who should not have trusted him. He could only wonder what other unanticipated problems lay ahead. But he would do his best, and that was all Allah asked.

. . . The high-pitched roar of a boat's claxon pulled Shazly back from his uneasy thoughts and into the present. He hurried up the dock to the late-arriving liner. There remained one final issue to resolve, and he was eager to find the six men and get it done.

TEN

Alexandria/22 August 1973/1530

Shazly took one look at the men coming down the gangplank, and tensed. The Syrian High Command in their disguises—loose-fitting shirts, trousers, sandals—looked like six middle-aged tourists arriving for a summer's holiday at the beach.

He was accustomed to seeing these men striding through state offices, attended by doting aides, resplendent in their generals' uniforms. The image they now presented was not only informal, but also disconcertingly less substantial. How can I count on these old men? Shazly asked himself.

Then he remembered that he was out of uniform, too. No doubt he looked the same unconvincing way to their critical eyes.

Reassured, he shook hands and offered a quiet greeting to each man as he stepped off the gangplank and onto the dock. While their dress was casual, years of discipline prevailed and they disembarked in a rigidly hierarchical order. The minister of defense, the cold, strong-willed Gen. Mustafa Talas, led the way, trailed by his more genial chief of staff, Gen. Yusuf Shakoor. The heads of the air force, Operations, and Intelligence followed, while the naval commander took up the rear.

The ceremony was deliberately low-key. But this caution, the latest in a succession of tense, complicated arrangements, reinforced Shazly's awareness of what was at stake.

Moving quickly, Shazly led them to a small convoy of unmarked cars parked a distance away. Feeling a bit like a tour director, he shared the itinerary. They would be driven to the officers' club in the center of the city. Later, just before six, the cars would return to take them to the Ras el-Tin Palace. Their eight Egyptian counterparts would be waiting, and the secret session of the Syrian-Egyptian Armed Forces Supreme Council would convene.

In less momentous times, King Farouk had frolicked in the Ras el-Tin Palace. He hosted fabulous, fabled seaside parties, gleaming with extravagance, giddy with excess. Tonight few lights shined in the sprawling building. The grand, ornate chambers were empty. Silence stretched down the long, cool marble corridors. Night shadows fell over the unwalked garden paths leading to the stilled fountain. All seemed abandoned, and only a heavy, deep, thick quiet remained.

But the palace was not deserted. On its third floor, behind a pair of locked doors, in a room looking out over the inky waters of the Western Harbor, the council gathered. Hidden away, the fourteen men plotted.

The attack had been discussed, worked on, and revised so often over the past months that now only its formal ratification was required. This came quickly. Unanimously agreed: The two countries would hit the Jews simultaneously, Syrian armor charging over the border in the north, Egyptian invaders crossing the Suez Canal in the south.

Now there was no possibility of turning back. War was inevitable. With a show of hands, they had tilted the course of their lives into another orbit. Win or lose, history would be transformed.

Their mood was grave yet excited, as they now turned to the one question that remained: When to launch the attack?

Since last winter, Gen. Mohammed el-Gamasy, the Egyptian chief of operations and his staff had been gathering the facts needed to make this decision. Gamasy was a precise, pedantic man, full of a lawyer's caution. But, these ponderous qualities served him well as he directed the research. He consulted a wide, often inventive collection of sources: the old Suez Canal Company water current charts, astronomical tables, meteorological predictions, the election cycles in Israel and the United States, and, a last-minute idea, lists of national holidays. His intent was to identify the days that promised Syria and Egypt optimal attack conditions; and, the other edge of his sword, those that were worst for Israel.

He wrote the final report by hand—it was too secret to trust to a typist—and personally delivered it to the minister of war. The president was impressed. "El-Gamasy's notebook," he called it, full of enthusiastic approval.

Now, from his seat at the head of the conference table, Ismail summarized its findings. He acted, Shazly later complained, as proud as if he were the author.

Waters ran swift in the Suez Canal. Navigation would always be tricky. But there were variables. At the southern end of the canal, the currents rushed by at nearly 100 yards a minute. While at the opposite end, up north from Port Said to Ismailia, the currents traveled at the rate of 20 yards a minute, brisk but certainly slower. Tides, too, could be both dramatic and erratic. With the phases of the moon, they rose and fell as much as six feet. The locations where the currents would not be a hindrance, and the nights with low tides, would need to be calculated.

Another requirement was for a "long" night, a time of the month when the moon shined brightly, then quickly set. That way, engineers could assemble and lay the pontoon bridges in moonlight, and hours later tanks could sneak across under the cover of darkness.

Israel's religious holidays were also studied. In the event of war, the Zionists called up reserve troops by broadcasting code words on radio and television. But there were eight official religious holidays, and weekly Sabbaths, when many people would be in synagogues, not at home or in cars.

Even Israel's election schedules were researched. In the midst of a campaign, in the heated flurry of charges and countercharges, the Jews would be too preoccupied to focus on any buildups along their borders. Also, their politicians would be wary about mobilizing troops in response; a false alarm would anger the voters.

On the Syrian front, the problem was winter. Up in the Golan, snow fell as early as November. The first wave of tanks might charge across the border, only to bog down in mud or snow.

When all the variables and requirements were itemized, then weighed, juggled, and debated, the conclusion was definitive: an autumn attack. In September and October the nights were long, moonlit with still ten to twelve hours of darkness. The canal tides, except when the moon was full, would be relatively calm. And in the north, snow would not be a consideration.

Of the two months, October seemed better. Not only was the weather favorable, the nights long, and the tides low, but, as if predestined, every other possible requirement fell into place with a reassuring thud. The Israeli Knesset elections were on October 28. The Jews celebrated three separate official religious holidays that month. And on Yom Kippur, October 6, the national radio and television stations did not broadcast at all. Calling the reserves would be even more difficult on the holiest day of the Jewish religious calendar.

October offered still another advantage. It coincided with the sacred Muslim month of Ramadan. It was a propitious time to launch a jihad, a holy war of revenge. And the enemy would be less likely to expect an attack during a month of fasting.

After midnight, the council held another vote. The fourteen men agreed to recommend two periods—either September 7–11 or October 5–10—to presidents Sadat and Assad. The final decision belonged to their political leaders. But either way, they knew, war was only weeks away.

As the meeting broke up, Yusuf Shakoor, the Syrian chief of staff, took his Egyptian counterpart aside. Shazly instinctively liked the man. He was handsome, smiling, and always confident. He could imagine fighting alongside him.

"We must start by taking the strictest security measures for the fourteen of us in the room," the Syrian said.

Shazly agreed. "The plan, the date—all our work is unimportant if we can't keep it secret from the enemy."

Shakoor asked, "How long do you think it'll be before the enemy knows our intentions?"

The Egyptian Defense Intelligence Department, Shazly told him, had estimated Israel would know the attack was coming a full fifteen days before H-hour, the time of the assault.

"The director of the DID is just guarding his rear," Shazly said. "If anything goes wrong, he doesn't want to carry the can."

"So you believe—"

"They won't suspect a thing until forty-eight hours before H-hour. And then it will be too late."

Both men agreed that if they could prevent Israel from discovering their preparations until only forty-eight hours—two short days!—before the attacks, it would determine everything that followed. They would be surprise the Jews, catch them unprepared. And victory would be theirs.

In the days after the meeting in the Ras el-Tin Palace, two seemingly unrelated events occurred.

The first was secret, and certainly more historic. President Sadat traveled to Saudi Arabia and then on to Qatar. He informed the governments that within weeks Egypt and Syria will be going to war. From Qatar, he flew on August 28 to Damascus to see President Assad. The two men met to review the council's recommendation and select one date.

They decided on October 6. It was Yom Kippur, the Day of Atonement on the Jewish calendar, the holiest day of the year. For Muslims, it was the tenth day of Ramadan. During Ramadan in the year 624, the forces of the Prophet Muhammed won their first victory in the campaign that would take them in triumph to Mecca. This was the Battle of Badr.

On the plane ride back to Cairo, Sadat spoke of this fateful coincidence to the Egyptian diplomat who had accompanied him on the trip to the three countries. It was a good omen, he said. Ismail was already calling it Operation Badr.

"*Inshallah*," agreed the man who was married to Nasser's daughter. We shall succeed.

The second event was less secret, but no less solemn. In a ceremony at a base in the Golan on September 4, Yossi Ben Hanan handed over command of his tank unit to Lt. Col. Oded Eres. He had headed the battalion for the past year and a half, and it was not easy to let go. His eyes teared as he returned Eres's salute.

But in nine days he was leaving on his honeymoon. "Nati and me are going to be two Marco Polos," he told his friends. They planned to travel to Iran, then on to India, over to Nepal, and finally by motorcycle across the Himalaya passes and into China. Each leg of the three-month journey required careful planning, and as the summer passed and the arrangements were finalized, their anticipation built. The wedding had been for the parents; the honeymoon, he promised his bride, would be for them alone.

But after the military ceremony, Yossi was depressed. He had not expected saying good-bye to his men would be this difficult.

"You think it's okay to go?" he asked Yanosh Ben Gal.

"Climb a mountain. Make a baby, Yossi."

"Now's a good time, right?" Yossi pressed. "Everything's quiet."

"Of course it's quiet," Yanosh teased. "Except for all the women bawling because their Yossi has gone and got married."

Yossi laughed.

"Go ahead, laugh," said Yanosh. "Go off and have fun, my Yossi. Don't worry. Israel will manage to get by until you return."

Part II

DECEPTION

Israel/Egypt/Syria
September 1–October 6, 1973

Who shall come to his timely end . . .

ELEVEN

Nizanim Beach, Israel/ 8 September 1973

Shabtai Brill pulled back on the stick, and the model plane climbed higher. It flew on a steep diagonal across the clear blue sky, gaining altitude as its speed increased.

When it finally leveled off, about 300 meters above the beach at Nizanim, he told his son and daughter to look up and wave. As they did, he switched the controls to channel four, activating the tiny 35-mm camera he had attached to the belly of the miniature Piper Cub aircraft. He waved, too, face lifted toward the sun as the plane passed overhead, and its motorized camera clicked off shot after shot.

He steered the plane in a looping circle above the orange tent farther down the beach. His wife was removing plastic-covered bowls of salads from the picnic basket and setting them out on the blanket. "Wave," he yelled to Talim. "And smile." As the small plane buzzed overhead, she obeyed, vamping outrageously all the while.

After directing another pass over the beach, he switched back to channel three and began to guide the plane down for a landing. Its wheels bounced as they hit the sand, and it continued on for another hundred feet or so, heading precariously close to the water's edge before, with a small sputter, the engine shut down and the plane stopped. The kids raced barefoot down the beach to retrieve it.

Brill followed more slowly, deep in thought. As soon as he arrived at the unit tomorrow morning, he'd have a photoint tech develop the film. With any luck, the images would be clear, the detail as precise as in all the other tests. Then, once again he'd try to persuade Military Intelligence that his invention, this mini remote-piloted vehicle—the MRPV, he christened it, hoping the initials would convey an appropriately martial pedigree—was an ingenious solution. Without triggering a thunderstorm of enemy SAMs, without putting a reconnaissance jet and its pilot in harm's way, without provoking a political incident, it could fly below radar over the Golan and Sinai. It could provide photographic evidence of what the Syrians and the Egyptians were up to.

And this, he was convinced more than ever, was vital. He needed to see across the borders. Lt. Col. Shabtai Brill desperately wanted to be proven wrong.

"You'd be surprised at the ideas you get when someone's shooting at you," Brill would respond when asked how he came up with the MRPV. But like many good stories, this one, too, was only partially true.

In 1969 the Egyptians *were* shooting at Brill.

An Aman intelligence officer stationed at a Bar-Lev Line fort, part of his job as the War of Attrition entered its bloody, final months was to monitor enemy deployments on the opposite side of the Suez Canal. The Egyptian engineers, however, made this difficult: They had piled ten-meter-high sand walls around their troop and artillery positions. To see over these barriers, Brill and the other *kamanim*—their official Military Intelligence designation—climbed to higher ground.

Armed with 120 × 20 field glasses, they perched on top of armored personnel carriers, half-tracks, and, in a pinch, the fort's ventilation systems. The ordinance corps even rigged up a Sherman tank with a platform attached to the turret that could rise, like a cherry picker, sixty feet into the air. But this was dangerous, often lethal duty. The desert sun bounced off the lens of the field glasses, and signaled the Egyptians. Their snipers were experts. Each day's duty brought the same fear: that at any moment a bullet would drive straight through the binocular lens, and slam into his skull.

The obvious solution had its own obvious danger. A photoreconnaissance flight above the Suez Canal would find dozens of telephone-pole-thick surface-to-air missiles zooming its way. Brill had no choice but to stand tall, look across the canal, and pray.

This was his motivation. The actual idea didn't occur to him until, on leave, he attended a friend's son's bar mitzvah party. A relative just back from the United States brought the boy a remote-controlled model airplane for a present. As the delighted child flew the toy high above the lawn and the guests looked up, Brill began to think.

Col. Avraham Arnan, the head of Aman's collections department, loved the idea. A field agent stationed in New York bought three model planes at a total cost of $850 and sent them on to Tel Aviv in the diplomatic pouch. Aman's technical department fitted cameras to the undercarriages, and a test flight was arranged.

The model flew over an isolated stretch of the Sinai desert as Israeli gunners opened up with a ZFU23, a four-barrel antiaircraft machine gun left behind by the Egyptians as they fled in the Six Day War. The plane's first run was at 300 meters above the desert. Then it dived to 200. Finally, it tried 100. And each time the gunners never came close. "If we can't hit it," they confidently told Brill, "neither will the Egyptians."

The Egyptians didn't even try. When the plane circled the canal-front city of Ismailia, not a single shot was fired. The photographs were excellent. A flight over an eastern portion of the Jordan Valley was also encouraging. Antiaircraft artillery ignored the small plane, and the photographs revealed the Arab Legion's covert firing positions. On orders from Maj. Gen. Aharon Yariv, the head of Military Intelligence, a top secret model airplane squad went to work. Its goal was to develop a prototype.

Two years later, in 1971, Aman abandoned the project. As the technicians labored to design their own remote-controlled plane, the original inspiration—a low-cost model from a hobby shop—gave way to something more ambitious. And much more expensive. In the end, they decided that it really should be an air force project. But the air force was already working on a technologically sophisticated pilotless drone, the Mabat. They dismissed Brill's clever, inexpensive spy plane as a child's toy, while at the same time ignoring that this was precisely its virtue.

Brill could not get the MRPV program reactivated. "I talked to all the district Command officers, but it was like talking to the wall," he complained. Frustrated, yet still careful, a career intelligence officer mindful that his superiors promoted men who obeyed rather than argued, Brill decided to give in. He threw his energies into his work, and never again mentioned his invention. And in time, like so many things that had once seemed important, it receded from his mind.

His career flourished. In July 1973, now a lieutenant colonel, he became Operation officer of the top secret Aman unit 848.

Unit 848 listens. Its ears—massive, multipronged arrays of antennas and radar dishes—are located at covert surveillance stations near Israel's borders. On Mutzav 104, the code name for the installation atop snowcapped Mount Hermon in the Golan Heights, rose a high-tech forest of devices aimed at Syria. The Um Hashiba base, surrounded by stone walls and sandbags, was situated thirty kilometers from the Suez Canal. A futuristic oasis in a biblical wilderness, this facility targeted Egypt. And everything that was heard, every scrap of intelligence that was collected, made its way back in real time to unit 848's (later redesignated as unit 8200) windowless, subterranean headquarters in a green and leafy suburb outside Tel Aviv.

There was a treasure trove of information. "Signit" was the curt, comprehensive term Aman officers used for their daily catch of electronic signals intelligence, and it came in a variety of forms.

The communications intelligence—comint—intercept specialists listened to the known frequencies of enemy military and government communications. Whatever they heard—troop movements or ammunition shipments, for example—was immediately filed as a "spot report." The comint operators also had the ability to eavesdrop on telephone conversations throughout Egypt and Syria, and they constantly monitored the phones of key military and political leaders: The whispered midnight call to a mistress while the wife obliviousy slept, the banker politely requesting payment of his loan before further action would, unfortunately, be necessary—all was recorded, transcribed, and passed on.

The electronic intelligence—elint—technicians monitored the bristling flutter of electronic pulses generated by radar and missile installations, as well as from ships and planes. This was Brill's specialty and it was an intense, focused pursuit. Operators spent entire eight-hour shifts listening to the "signatures"—precise frequency emanations—from a multitude of surface-to-air missile sites. And, more painstaking work, each SAM installation had two separate and distinct radars: One searched for enemy planes, the other targeted them. Nevertheless, the dogged elint teams had compiled a meticulous inventory of every radio frequency at each Syrian and Egyptian missile site. And they updated this EOB—electronic order of battle—daily.

After his first month as Operation officer, the third-highest-ranking position in the signit unit, Brill decided he hated the work. He spent his time sitting in front of a computer screen watching the rising and falling spikes of radar pulses and listening to high-pitched, whining electronic screeches.

He preferred a job where he could interact with people, one that required more flexibility of mind. Here he watched, listened, and recorded. Day after day the routine was the same, and he was trapped inside it.

The long, intense hours wore on him. More and more, he looked forward to the weekends. The prospect of going to the beach and playing with the kids loomed in his mind all the dreary week. It was his chance to clear his brain, and his reward for having done another hard week's work.

His son was nine, but the child already was quite skilled at *matkot,* a racquetball game that everyone on the beach seemed to be playing that summer. Brill imagined it wouldn't be long before the boy beat him. With a father's pride, as well as a philosophical sigh of resignation, Brill acknowledged that in its small way the victory would mean his son was becoming a man, and that he was growing old. For both of them, the entire summer seemed to be building toward this one milestone.

But as September began, the contests stopped. There was no longer any time for games. His son was disappointed, but Brill had to focus on other matters.

Reports were coming into the unit, and they were not at all routine.

The tanks first prompted his suspicions. Normally, the Syrians deployed three infantry brigades, including about 400 to 450 tanks at the Golan front. When Brill arrived at the unit in July, the armored line was below its usual levels; in the spring the Syrians had withdrawn forces. But starting August 7, tanks had begun to roll into positions along the border. Each week another fifty or so arrived, mostly Soviet T-55s with 100-mm cannons. The Syrian Command had decided to restore its previous deployment levels.

But what troubled Brill was that the tanks did not stop coming. Many now were the new Soviet T-62s, squat, compact killing machines with the most powerful armored cannons in the Middle

East—115-mm guns whose shells could blow a hole through a thick, reinforced concrete wall and still keep going. By the first week in September, Syria had massed more than 600 tanks close to the Purple Line, the northern border with Israel in the Golan Heights. And each day more tanks arrived.

Curious, Brill checked the intelligence reports along the Egyptian front. What he read, he would say, "made me weak in the knees." Five infantry divisions had been deployed. About 80,000 men. The size, he realized, of an invading force.

"Nothing has changed," his commander, Col. Yoel Ben Porat told him. His tone was indulgent, not confrontational. The two men were old friends. They had gone to university together, and then worked in the Syrian branch of Aman's Research Division.

The size of the Egyptian or the Syrian border forces, the colonel explained, was unimportant. They were defensive forces deployed, according to standard Soviet doctrine, in an offensive formation. Neither of the two countries had any plans to go to war.

Brill listened. Clearly, the commanders were privy to more information than he was. If they weren't concerned, it would be presumptuous for him to be.

Then, on September 3, the comint specialists intercepted a message raising the level of readiness of the Syrian air and land forces. Four days later, Brill came into work to learn that overnight the Syrians had nudged the level up a further notch. An official war alert seemed imminent.

Brill anxiously cornered Ben Porat for another talk. Now the colonel turned testy. His voice was high and tight, and Brill thought: If he pushed his commander any further, the situation might get dangerous.

You're not the only intelligence officer in Israel monitoring the situation, Ben Porat admonished. Higher authorities had looked at the "whole picture" and decided there was no reason for concern. The front line's reinforcement was a response to terrorist activity. And now that the tanks had been deployed, they would remain along the border for the annual Syrian training exercises; the war games were running late this year, but undoubtedly would start before winter. The increased state of alert was also easily explained: President Assad was about to leave for a scheduled summit conference in Algeria, and it was standard procedure to increase the level of preparedness before and during his trips.

Brill felt foolish. The answers were so reasonable, so logical, that he should have deduced them on his own.

"You worry too much," Ben Porat said. Brill's wife, too, had always complained that he was a worrier. Perhaps they both were right. And, more distressing, he did not miss Ben Porat's tacit warning: Nerves were not a good trait in a lieutenant colonel who still dreamed of a colonel's chevrons.

But soon Brill's suspicions solidified. Once Brill began monitoring the missiles, he knew he was was on the trail of something very ominous.

During the next three weeks, Brill tracked the Syrians moving thirty SAM batteries to the Golan Heights front. Half of these were SAM-6s, state-of-the-art missiles newly arrived from Russia. Next, the Syrian Air Command brought their antiaircraft formations close to the edge of the border, barely beyond the range of Israel's mortars. Once these guns were in place, they moved their SAM batteries forward, just ten kilometers from the line separating the Syrian and Israeli forces.

Aman was unconcerned. Though the installations were near the border, the missiles were pointed west, over Syrian territory. They protected strategic sites in the basin between Damascus and the Golan Heights from Israeli jets.

Brill conceded that this was one way to evaluate the situation. According to the prevailing theory, it was the only way. But if the Concept was wrong, then another possibility suddenly jumped up: The missiles pointed west. *Toward Israel.*

Syrian doctrine required that a thirty-kilometer-wide shield of infantry and tanks protect a missile battery. The sites were ten kilometers from the border. The Syrians could get the additional twenty kilometers protection—by charging across the border and seizing the Golan Heights.

As the scattered pieces merged, a distinct, recognizable pattern took shape. And there was only one conclusion: The enemy was preparing to attack.

This incredible idea fixed in his mind. It welled inside him like an unexploded bomb. He couldn't sleep. Anxiety became a constant, stalking presence. But what could he do? No one would listen.

Reluctant to challenge his superiors, to jeopardize his career without irrefutable proof, he found himself thinking again about his MRPV. Yet as he caught up with his children that September afternoon on the beach and retrieved the plane, he could not help but fear that even if he somehow persuaded Command to give his invention another try, it might already be too late.

On Sunday, September 9, Brill returned to work. First thing, he sent the film to the Aman lab. Then he put his headphones on and began listening. More tanks were moving to the border. More troops were being trucked to frontline camps.

It unnerved him, and he was completely caught up in his work. There was so much to monitor that on Thursday, September 13, when a clerk brought him an envelope containing his developed photographs, he had to pause for a moment to remember what he had sent out. As he looked at the photos, as he recalled with pleasure the day at the beach, part of him perceived an urgency in the room. Then operators began shouting, calling to him.

He rushed over. In stunned silence they watched the screen.

TWELVE

Northern Syrian Shoreline, near Latakia/13 September 1973/0640

Coming in high over the gleaming Mediterranean, the rising sun a blinding screen in front of them, the two Israeli F-4 Phantoms moved into Syria. These were heavy planes, large and mighty, and as they sped above the coarse, rocky terrain their afterburners flamed a distinctive pink and purple against the blue sky.

The pilots in the Israeli Air Force who flew these beasts called them "Hammers"; they were designed to hammer away at the enemy, to pound and to destroy. Their armaments were formidable. They delivered 2,000-pound-deep penetration bombs, radar-guided Sparrow missiles, and napalm canisters; their multibarreled 20-mm Vulcans spewed 6,000 rounds per minute. But this morning the mission above northern Syria was reconnaissance.

In the Sinai air base's subterranean ops room before the predawn takeoff, Flight Operations had told the two-man Hammer crews it would be an easy flyby, as trouble-free as a training exercise. They'd come in over the sea, and cross into enemy territory through the north, above Damascus. The SAM batteries had been relocated south, near the Purple Line. Without the missiles, the Syrian air defenses in this part of the country were negligible. Keep the cameras on auto, bear northeast, and then turn and head on home. It was a perfect day for flying, calm and clear. Enjoy it, gentleman, the squadron leader said.

But as the lumbering Hammers continued into Syria, green lights flashed on their instrument panels: radar lock-ons.

Closing from three miles off were MiGs, with Syrian markings.

An extremely light fighter, less than half the size of the Phantom, the MiG-21 was a very agile, single-man craft. Its wings were small, and they stood out in profile against the sky like the telltale fin of a shark. Beneath each wing were the shark's sharp, glinting teeth: long bullet-headed air-to-air missiles.

Four MiGs streaked toward the Phantoms. And nearly parallel to this formation was another quartet: eight fast attack jets closing in at Mach 2 on the two intruders.

At this point, the outnumbered Hammers could still disengage. Cut loose, dive, and the monster plane's superior acceleration would do the rest. They'd zoom low and fast back over the Mediterranean before the MiGs could get off a shot. But the Phantoms did not run away. They did not evade. They charged on.

Their radars switched to tracking mode and illuminated the MiGs. Their "Shafir" air-to-air missiles armed for launch. The Vulcans went "hot," primed for fire. The closure rate was a thousand miles per hour, intruders and the defenders coming straight at one another. They were in each other's sights, roaring closer and closer each second.

Suddenly, out of the west, coming down high from the clouds were more invaders. Israeli Mirage jets, fast single-man attack planes, had been over the Mediterranean when they saw the fight taking shape on their radars. Light cavalry, armed with American Sidewinder missiles, they charged to the rescue.

While from the east, another flock of MiGs appeared. Four more. And then another four. A force of sixteen MiGs, angry and determined, now spread out in two lines to meet the invaders. The blaze from their engines streaked the Syrian sky, a trail of brown-and-orange vapors. From below, it looked like a giant tiger's pelt stretched across the blue heavens.

All at once, missiles rushed through the air. Planes veered, breaking left and right for miles over the sky. Cannons fired. The Vulcans rattled. At such close quarters it was more a shoot-out than a conventional air battle.

Training helped the pilots, but mostly they fought on instinct. Whoever scored first, won. There were no second chances.

The Hammers were relentless, the big planes shaking as they gathered speed and moved in. The Mirages were more athletic, mischievous, and cruel. They set traps for their prey. Climbing high and then streaming out of the clouds at full throttle, cannons blasting, heat-seeking missiles zeroing in. They chased, targeted, and hunted down the MiGs.

Pillars of black smoke clouded the sky. Flames rose from sputtering engines. Finally there would be a terrible noise, a bursting, explosive boom as the tiny jets blew apart. Eight MiGs were killed. In minutes, it was over.

Gloating, confident they had taught the enemy a lesson, the Israeli fighter jocks banked into a sharp turn. In formation, the planes headed back toward the sea.

But the Syrian pilots had watched their friends die. They gave chase.

A MiG closed in behind a Mirage, its nose tight on the intruder's tail. The pilot brought the enemy in his sights and held steady, waiting, marking. Then he fired. An Atoll missile shot across the sky.

The Mirage tried to maneuver, but it was futile. The missle honed in, and hit.

"Fire in the engine," the pilot screamed over the radio. "Fire in the engine."

Quickly, the Israeli jets organized a defense around their crippled comrade. But there was no hope of leading him home. The Mirage whined like a dying animal, its engine ruined. The pilot descended, gliding toward the Mediterranean, the plane weaving and shaking. "Mayday, Mayday," he shouted over the radio.

Hold on, he was told. Try to get out of Syria before ejecting. A rescue helicopter was on the way.

The pilot, both arms taut, took the plane low, letting the air currents carry it along. It required all his strength to steady the wildly vibrating rudder. It seemed an eternity passed before he was out of enemy territory, and over blue water.

He pulled the ejection lever. The canopy exploded overhead, and an instant later he was hurled into the air. His comrades watched helplessly as he dropped through space. But then his parachute opened and he floated down toward the sea.

He struggled to stay afloat in the cold water as the Evacuation Helicopter approached. He waved, and the chopper moved into a hovering position, and prepared to lower the hoist.

But the MiGs wanted revenge, and they came in with guns rumbling, forcing the helicopter to retreat. A frustrated crewman dropped a dinghy to the pilot as the MiGs closed in on the slower rescue craft.

On the flight leader's command, the Israeli fighter jocks rolled their Mirages ninety degrees toward the sea, and then came up and out of this maneuver with their cannons firing. Four MiGs splashed into the sea. The rest scattered.

A Syrian pilot managed to eject, his orange-and-white-striped chute billowing as he drifted down. He landed a few hundred yards from the Israeli, his body floating inertly in the smooth water.

The helicopter returned and pulled up the Israeli pilot. Then they winched up the Syrian. A medic started an IV, as the formation of Phantoms and Mirages surrounding the Evacuation Helicopter returned home.

Throughout the Middle East, heads of state, ministers, and generals quickly learned of the dogfight. Radar tapes of the aerial battle were replayed in Tel Aviv, Damascus, and Cairo. And in each apprehensive capital they asked the same question: What will happen next?

* * *

Success had been so close, Shazly brooded. H-hour was a little more than three weeks away. If only the Syrians would wait before retaliating. If only they would let Operation Badr move ahead according to the schedule, they would catch the Zionists by surprise and have their revenge.

This morning he had received a report that the secret desert training of the R-17 E Brigade was moving forward. The Scuds that had arrived in Alexandria weeks earlier had been hidden in ancient caves; even the American satellites could not spot them. Now thirty-seven Soviet advisers were instructing his men how to launch these terrifying missiles. The arrangements for the crossing, the deception plan—everything was moving ahead. Three more weeks, and his army would be ready.

But Shazly feared the humiliated Syrians—twelve splashed jets!—would rush to respond. In April 1967, after six Syrian jets were downed in a dogfight, they had shelled settlements in the Golan. The Jews had retaliated en masse. If Syria struck back now with their missiles or their artillery, the Zionists would call up their reserves, and fortify their front lines. The opportunity to catch Israel unprepared would be lost.

Shazly waited. Three days passed, and Syria had still done nothing more than issue an angry protest. Using an assumed name and a false passport, Shazly flew to Algiers. The next morning he met with Pres. Houari Boumedienne and informed him that there soon would be a war. Could Egypt and Syria count on Algeria's military support?

"And the combat readiness of your forces?" the president asked.

Shazly answered that it had never been so high.

"What about the Syrians?"

More or less the same as ours, Shazly carefully said.

"If that is so," Boumedienne challenged, "how come the Israelis four days ago shot down twelve Syrian aircraft at the loss of only one of their own?"

Shazly was frank. "My own opinion is that the Israelis have air superiority not just over the Syrians but over us as well. Our plan is devised to operate within that constraint."

When the talk ended, Boumedienne announced, "The decision to go to war is a hard one. But the decision to remain in our present humiliation is just as hard." His country would help.

Encouraged but still on edge, Shazly flew later that day to Morocco to inform King Hassan. He still did not know what Syria would do. But only nineteen days remained. And every day without a Syrian response brought them closer to war.

President Assad wanted to attack. In a rage, on September 14 he had telephoned President Sadat insisting that they move up the launch date. The Israelis had ambushed his planes. The Phantoms were the bait, and his MiGs hungrily took it. Then the enemy Mirages appeared and slammed the trap shut.

Sadat agreed; perhaps he even believed this interpretation, too. But by the time the phone call ended, Sadat, with the shrewdness of a statesman and the persistence of a general, had persuaded Assad to wait.

Moreover, the Israeli aerial victory, however hard to take at the time, had sweet consequences neither man ever contemplated. The loss of the twelve jets gave their preparations just the blustering, logical cover they needed.

In Israel, the leaders debated how Syria would respond. On September 16 Dayan told an anxious cabinet meeting that he suspected Assad would order the shelling of the Golan Heights settlements, and that was just for starters. Dado, the chief of staff, disagreed. Syria wouldn't dare threaten the kibbutzim, he said. An attack on Israeli citizens would provoke a massive air strike. Instead, the Syrian president would do something more measured. Perhaps he'd order his SAMs to shoot down an Israeli plane. There were a dozen officials at the boisterous session, and afterward it seemed there were as least as many grim predictions swirling around the room. But one things was agreed: Syria would act.

On the following day, September 17, they learned how. Eli Zeira, full of his typical granite confidence, told Dayan and the general staff of further reinforcements along the Syrian border. Additional tanks and troops had been moved over the past three days to these frontline positions. But, he said, these were *defensive* deployments. The Syrians wanted to be prepared in case the air battle was the start of an Israeli offensive.

Similarly, he dismissed the reports coming in of an Egyptian air force war alert. Sadat simply wanted to be ready if Israel, full of swagger after the easy victory in the sky over Syria, launched a surprise attack.

But Israel was not going to attack. And the official Aman position was that there was a "low probability" of the Arabs even considering war for at least another five years.

Brill was unpersuaded. The lack of a significant Syrian response gnawed at him. Reinforcing the front line? They had been doing that since August 7, a month before the dogfight. He was convinced that the longer Syria delayed its retaliation, the more dangerous the situation became.

"There's a Sherlock Holmes story," he told his wife one night as he lay in bed unable to sleep, "where the clue is the sound of the dog *not* barking."

Late in afternoon of September 13 after the jets had returned to their underground hangars in the Sinai, Nati and Yossi departed on their honeymoon. Nati's parents drove the couple to the airport and on the way the car radio broadcast a report about their country's latest victory. With that news, any lingering misgivings Yossi had about leaving vanished. This was the confirmation he needed. There was nothing for him, or for mighty Israel, to worry about.

THIRTEEN

GHQ, Cairo/ 22 September 1973/0900

Along the bank of the Suez Canal, the Egyptian troops sat and fished. They wore soft knit hats, not helmets, and they did not carry rifles. Nearby, others sat and chatted, their laughter carrying across the undulating hills of pale sand. On the flat higher ground, squads played soccer. Despite the punishing sun, these were fast, high-spirited contests. Boisterous shouts celebrated each goal.

Shazly often drove down from Cairo to watch his men, and he hoped the Israelis were watching, too. He wanted the enemy to think his frontline soldiers were loafing.

But fishing, soccer, even the shouts and the laughter—they were all part of the plan. These troops were members of what he called "the lazy unit." Their assignment was to lull the enemy into thinking the Egyptian canal forces were doing easy, relaxed duty.

He also hoped Israeli intelligence collection units were avidly reading the newspaper dispatches filed from Cairo. All summer the British papers ran a litany of contemptuous Soviet complaints about their incompetent ally. The Russians had shipped high-tech missiles, sent advisers to train the operators, and still the inept Egyptians were incapable of maintaining the missile batteries in working order. It was doubtful if the SAMs would ever launch, let alone hit a jet flying at Mach 2. The *Washington Post* in an exasperated, hand-wringing news analysis piece declared that "Arab unity was more a myth than a reality." And the *New York Times* reported that the Russians were so disillusioned with both their Egyptian and Syrian allies that the relationships had deteriorated beyond repair.

The articles dutifully quoted several officials, as well as unnamed government contacts. But the reporters did not know that their "sources" disseminated these tidbits on Shazly's instructions. Or that they were also his inventions.

In the western part of the Canal, the land was hot and dry and bare, but there was a loop where both banks run through Egyptian territory. El Ballah island, a five-mile-long sandbar, floated in the dark hollow of this quiet stretch of racing water.

Shazly had become familiar with this empty corner of the Canal during his time in the Red Sea Command. Now nightly, its sandy ridges teemed with men. On the shore, in the gray water, throughout the length of the island, the covert shadows of combat soldiers fell across the grainy, starlit darkness. Far from the enemy's watchful eyes and unnoticed by the vigilant foreign press, Shazly's troops prepared for war.

Its varied topography—boot-sinking sand, miles of steep shore, fast-moving currents, a wide expanse of water—offered the perfect training ground. It was a microcosm of all the daunting natural obstacles his invading army faced.

For the initial assault to succeed, there was one fundamental problem: They needed a way to get across the Suez Canal. So Shazly and his engineering staff reviewed the science of military bridge-laying. According to standard doctrine, alloy pontoons were transported to the shoreline, pushed into the water, and then men working from a flotilla of barges struggled to connect the floating, disparate sections. Well-trained engineers could lay six feet of bridge a minute. At that rate, it would take two hours to construct a bridge across the Canal.

But Shazly's invasion plan required a total of twenty-five bridges—all constructed under fire. He pictured a two-hour barrage of Israeli artillery; he pictured diving Zionist jets firing their rapidly pulsing 20-mm machine guns; and the final image in his mind was one of a disaster: besieged engineers, loose pontoons drifting away with the current, rolling tanks splashing into the water, and his exposed infantry strafed and bullet-riddled. His army would drown, as Pharoah's had; and the war would be over before it started.

He needed a better way, and the Russians helped him find it. In anticipation of the need to cross the rivers of Western Europe, Soviet engineers had developed a revolutionary fording technique. Along the shoreline, soldiers would unfold large, boxlike pontoons, push the pieces into the shallow water, and then connect the parts; the segments fit together like pieces in a child's Lego kit. This PMP bridge, as it was called, grew rapidly, at a rate of twenty-one feet per minute. And it took little effort to glide one end of the completed bridge through the water and anchor it to the opposite shore. In less than half an hour, a bridge could be assembled and stretched across the Canal.

Or, at least that was the promising theory. Construction had never been attempted under intense fire. But Shazly decided his soldiers could be trained to do it. He created forty new engineer battalions and, driven by Gen. Gamal Ali, they set to work.

Methodically, Ali divided the twenty-five bridging teams—one for each bridge—into specific units. One did nothing but practice backing trucks to the water's edge. Another made sure the heavy pontoon sections moved quickly out of the truck and into the water. There were also units specifically taught to connect the sections, and others that swung the completed bridge into position.

Night after night along the El Ballah loop, they drilled. Each soldier had a single task, and with repetition, duty became a reflex. In time, Shazly's confidence grew. The bridges would be ready.

But after the troops, tanks, and heavy artillery crossed the Suez Canal, they'd run straight into the Israeli sand ramparts. A single tank required an opening twenty feet deep. That meant removing, the engineers reported to Shazly, about fifteen hundred cubic yards of sand. His bold invasion plan called for sixty passageways through the east bank. Shazly, jolted, did the rest of the mathematics on his own: Ninety thousand cubic yards of sand would have to be cleared.

The Israelis had boasted it would take an invading force at least twelve hours to blast through the barriers—long enough for their armor and troops to be mobilized for a counterattack. With the bulk of Shazly's force stranded on the east bank shore, the large advantage of surprise would be squandered. His men would be forced either to retreat over the bridges, or be annihilated. Victory depended on finding a way to smash through the enemy's wall.

Across from El Ballah island, his engineers constructed their own sand barriers. In a nearly deafening series of demonstrations that began in the afternoon and continued late into the night, Shazly watched with increasing frustration as they attempted to destroy them.

Even the placing of an explosive charge was an exasperating, time-consuming drama. The engineers would hollow an opening, only in the next instant to watch it fill again. The loose sand ran like a downhill stream. Digging a large hole was impossible. Shoveling quickly, the engineers finally managed to insert a small charge. After detonation, a brief shower of sand cascaded down the slope. But the mountain remained standing, a high, solid impenetrable barrier.

In the end, near midnight, the best a resolute team of sixty engineers working in tandem could do was blow a surface hole about three yards square. Using this method, it would take five, perhaps six hours to create a tank-wide passageway. But that was only an estimate, and an unrealistic one. In wartime, the squad of engineers would be working in close proximity under savage fire. A single well-placed mortar round from the elevated Bar-Lev sites could wipe out an entire team of engineers. Then the massed power of the Israeli artillery would turn on the infantry rushing across the bridges. He envisioned his packed, huddled men stranded on the far shore, torrents of gunfire pouring down on them.

"Enough!" Shazly finally shouted at General Ali. "This is futile. There must be another way." The words were almost a prayer.

His disappointment consolidated into the realization that he was leading his country toward another tragedy. For the first time he felt inadequate to the responsibilities he had assumed, to the mission he had accepted.

So he was surprised when, after only a moment's pause, General Ali said perhaps there was. One of his young engineers, a veteran of the Aswan Dam construction, had an idea.

Shazly listened. At this point, anything was worth a try.

Three days later, engineers aimed fire hoses attached to British-made water pumps at the barriers—*and the blasts of water ate away at the sand.*

Shazly grew excited. What if Ali's engineers could find super pumps, machines capable of booming truly powerful jets of pounding water?

They found them in Germany. Magirus Deutz Fire Protection Techniques Ltd., in Ulm, sent two T.S.T. 40/7 pumps to Egypt on trial. These were portable, turbine-driven machines, capable of pumping an impressive 1,000 gallons of water a minute. Egypt, Magirus was told, was considering reequipping its fire brigades.

Five months later—after a secret series of tests off El Ballah island—the Egyptian government informed the company it wanted to purchase 150 pumps. A cagey Magirus executive tried demanding an inflated price of $1.875 million for the order. The Egyptians, to his delighted surprise, agreed. But with one condition:

The pumps must be shipped immediately; the modernization of the country's fire-fighting was a national priority.

In June 1973, the pumps arrived. Ali had already designated eighty pump teams, and now their training began. They worked day after day, in the mornings and at night, logging 348 sessions that summer. When they were ready, Shazly arrived for a demonstration.

From pontoons floating in the Suez Canal, the turbine pumps fed water to the hoses. Four-man teams held the hoses and aimed pounding gusts of water at the sand barriers. Thirty minutes, and there were deep, strategically placed holes dotting the mountain. Another unit ran in and placed the charges. Moments later, the blasts echoed in rapid succession. A beaming Shazly watched as the wall came tumbling down. He had his secret weapon.

His tanks, his artillery, his infantry outfitted with thousands of handheld Sagger missiles, could storm the Bar-Lev Line. If the surprise held, nothing would stop them.

All these thoughts, all the months of covert preparations, raced through Shazly's mind on the morning of September 22 when he met with his staff and field commanders. Hours earlier he had returned from his secret conference with King Hassan of Morocco, but he was reluctant to reschedule this 9 A.M. monthly staff meeting. He did not want anyone to ask where he had been, or why he had traveled. The enemy had long ears.

Yet as Shazly spoke with his commanders, he began to feel guilty for not sharing his secret knowledge. In fourteen days many of them would be crossing into the Sinai. It would be the most difficult mission of their lives. And for some, the last.

But, he told himself, they would know soon enough. In the meantime, secrecy was essential. Besides, there was nothing more to be done. The crossing would pass into the annals of war as a historic triumph. And every officer and soldier who charged into the Sinai would talk of it with pride for the rest of his days.

Shazly ran the meeting briskly. Still, it was 4:30 before he finished, and then he left to confer with General Ismail. The Syrian air force's final plans had just arrived.

In Israel, there was talk of Syria, too. On September 24 the general staff met, as they did each Monday. The discussion centered on the possible procurement of the F-15 fighter. Fresh in the generals' minds was how easily their Phantoms and Mirages had swatted away the Syrian jets eleven days earlier. But, they agreed, there never could be too much air power. The more muscle Israel flexed, the more wary its enemies grew.

When it was General Hofi's turn to speak, however, he ignored all the grandiose talk about future plans. Hacka was a soldier, not a deep thinker. He was uncomfortable with visionary ideas. Bluntly, without prelude or apology, he moved the discussion to a more urgent concern. He was in charge of the Northern Command, and he did not like what was happening up there.

"I would like to first emphasize something that is well known, but, in my opinion, is serious," he said. "Perhaps even very serious. We have no warning at all in this sector. The Syrians have lately got out of their layout. There is here a danger of a sudden attack. In my opinion, the conclusion from all that we have seen is that the Syrians constitute a greater risk to Israel than the Egyptians."

The generals ignored him. The discussion quickly returned to new jets, and to the future. It was only as the meeting ended that Dayan revisited Hacka's concern.

As a teenager, mounted on his sorrel horse Tauka, the defense minister had guarded the fields of northern Israel. A threat to the Golan farms affected him personally. He challenged, "If it is true that the Syrians can, without prior warning, advance tanks and take two or three settlements in the Golan Heights, perhaps even more—this would be an unprecedented catastrophe."

Gen. David "Dado" Elazar did not like Dayan's alarmist tone. He was a handsome man; Golda Meir often joked that she appointed him chief of staff because she liked to look at him, his brooding eyes, his mountain of thick, wavy black hair. But despite his good looks, Dado possessed none of Dayan's celebrity. Dayan had a restless, self-conscious style. He was an exuberant figure, at home in the political marketplace. Dado was a private man. His was a calmer, heavier presence. And responding to Dayan, he often spoke, perhaps even unconsciously, as if setting out to emphasize the contrast between them. The more histrionic or provocative Dayan's words, the greater the flat, level authority in Dado's retort.

"I do not accept the assumption that the Syrians are capable, today, of conquering the Golan Heights," he responded, sounding almost grouchy.

When Dayan pressed on, Elazar interrupted. "Under no circumstances do I think they can prepare a surprise attack without our knowledge. We have in the Golan Heights enough force that can, within a reasonable amount of time, block an attack," he added with confidence.

"If it's a question of war, then, in my opinion, this [SAM] layout will make no change in the ability of the air force to finish off Syria *in half a day*."

FOURTEEN

Mossad Safe House, Herzliyya/ 25 September 1973/1800

The ground radars picked up the Bell 206 helicopter as it flew over the Jordan River, and entered Israeli air space. A track number was immediately assigned, and a computer automatically labeled the radar blip with enemy designator graphics. Air defense operators watched their consoles intently as the flight path veered west toward Tel Aviv.

But no fighters were scrambled. No missiles were launched. Earlier in the day, a top secret flash had been sent to Air Command stations alerting them to the intruder's flight. Its message was succinct and emphatic: Do not take any action.

The helicopter touched down shortly after 8 P.M. on September 25 in a heavily guarded compound in Herzliyya, just north of Tel Aviv. The landing pad was well lit, and the helicopter's markings had been purposely concealed. However, when the pilot shut down the engine and exited the craft, its origin became apparent. The short, well-built man with his ramrod military gait was immediately recognizable.

Two days earlier he had sent a message: A matter of considerable urgency needed to be discussed. Quickly, schedules were juggled and with great secrecy this nighttime meeting had been arranged.

Followed by several of his aides, the pilot approached a line of waiting cars. All the cars had blackened windows. Standing beside them was Zvi Zamir, the head of the Mossad.

The prime minister is waiting, he told the pilot. King Hussein of Jordan hurried into the car.

The translators were unnecessary. From the start, they spoke to each another in English. The king had been educated in England, and the prime minister had lived in the United States. And in another unacknowledged yet tacit agreement, concealed Mossad microphones recorded their entire conversation.

Sitting across the table from Golda Meir in the conference room of the Mossad safe house, King Hussein began with an uncharacteristic hesitancy. He had thought long and hard about what he was about to do, yet apparently needed to build to the moment. These were extraordinary circumstances. Israel and Jordan were officially at war.

Perhaps that explained the prime minister's rigid demeanor. She did not interrupt. She allowed his rambling, tentative monologue to wander. She did not want to deter him. Each small story he shared, no matter how irrelevant on its surface, was an offering, and a confidence. She followed it with her full attention, knowing that it brought her closer to the larger, still hidden reason they were in this room.

At length, King Hussein described the meeting he had in Cairo on September 12 with Sadat and Assad. Both men, he lectured the prime minister with a didactic, rude insistence, could no longer accept the "neither war nor peace situation." He agreed with them. He hoped that "before the patience of the Arabs expires completely, something will happen to prevent war."

If the king was trying to provoke the prime minister, it failed. She chose to ignore the tone and the insinuation. After all, how could an Arab monarch meet with her, *in Israel,* and not offer support, however perfunctorily, for the Arab cause?

After firing off his volley, all the initial belligerence subsided. He did not want to fight another war, he confided to the prime minister. He had told his fellow Arab leaders, "Leave me alone. I had already paid a high price for such a partnership in 1967."

King Hussein had spoken almost nonstop for nearly an hour, but now he came to an abrupt halt. It was as if he needed to find the courage to continue.

The room went completely quiet. The prime minister let the silence build. A full minute ticked away. And Hussein still hesitated. Betrayal, no matter how lofty the motivation, was a hard, ruthless enterprise.

At last, he revealed why he had risked this clandestine journey to Israel. He gave a warning.

King Hussein: From a very, very sensitive source in Syria, that we have had information from in the past and passed it on . . . all the units that were meant to be in training and were prepared to take part in this Syrian action are now, as of the last two days or so, in position of pre-attack. . . . That includes their aircraft, their missiles, and everything else, that is out on the front at this stage. Now this had all come under the guise of training, but in accordance with the information we had previously, these are the prejump positions [to attack Israel], and all the units are now in these positions. Whether it means anything or not, nobody knows. But I have my doubts. However, one cannot be sure. One must take this as a fact.

Golda Meir: Is it conceivable that the Syrians would start something without the full cooperation of the Egyptians?

King Hussein: I don't think so. I think they are cooperating.

The prime minister was rattled. An enemy monarch, his kingdom still at war with Israel, had revealed Arabs were preparing to attack. No less astounding, Syria and Egypt were united in this imminent invasion. If this were true, then Military Intelligence's assessment was completely wrong. And, the entire foundation of her government's long-term strategic faith—the Concept—was an illusion.

Golda Meir hurried from the room.

Alone, sequestered in an office in the safe house, Golda picked up the phone. It was after midnight, but that was irrelevant. She needed clarification. Hussein's words contradicted all she had previously known. It was as if she had learned that black was really white, or up was really down. And so much—her very nation!—hung in the balance.

"Moshe," she said into the receiver, rousing the defense minister from his sleep.

Yet even as Moshe Dayan listened to the prime minister, even as the king waited for her return, elsewhere in the safe house another meeting continued without interruption.

Zamir and his assistant for Operations, Col. Aharon Levran, discussed the specifics of the king's message with two Jordanian intelligence officers.

The Israelis asked for more information about the king's source. With apologies, the Jordanians insisted that this could not be revealed.

The Israelis relented. But this exchange was all theater. The Mossad already knew the source: A major general in the Syrian army had also approached Israel. He had offered Syrian invasion plans detailing the identical "prejump positions" Hussein had found so disturbing and conclusive. But the Mossad was not interested. Disinformation, the agency analysts decided. Besides, they already had an agent deep inside the enemy camp. And the In-Law, with his files of purloined documents and cabinet room gossip, had convinced them that war, especially a two-front war, was an impossibility.

With Colonel Levran's leading the assault, the Mossad officials launched into a skeptical critique of Hussein's warning. The process of dismissing all the king had said, all the risks he had taken, had begun.

When Golda Meir returned, she seemed more at ease, more confident. She and King Hussein talked for another hour, until after one in the morning. Still, the meeting ended without the prime minister's asking when they would attack. After her telephone call to the minister of defense, she decided that this information was unnecessary.

Just hours later, in a succession of early-morning high-level conferences, Israeli officials assessed the secret discussion between the two leaders. It was a short working day, the eve of Rosh Hashanah, the Jewish New Year, and the start of a three-day holiday. Things moved quickly.

Military Intelligence's review convened first, and it was a shouting match. Brig. Gen. Arieh Shalev, director of the research division, was furious. The head of the Jordanian branch had been an observer at the safe house last night. When he left, he was so concerned that he violated protocol as well as security: He telephoned his colleague on the Egyptian desk. Without naming the source, he shared the king's warning. This morning when the general learned of this "unauthorized distribution of sensitive material," he lost control.

Neither the developments on the Egyptian nor on Syrian front, Shalev bellowed at the brash intelligence officer, were his concern. Jordan was his sole responsibility. Ferocious with anger, the general called the officer an "alarmist" and accused him of unnecessarily generating panic. Shalev's temper rode on, trampling the junior officer.

Finally, after all the hard words, all the spent emotion, Shalev concluded that the warning was both vague and unimportant.

At 8:15, just as the intelligence meeting ended, the chief of staff's began. Among the assembled officers were the heads of the air force, Military Intelligence, and the commander of the northern front.

"A serious source," Dado announced both grave and deliberately cryptic, warned last night that Syria was preparing to attack. Then, either he misinterpreted a vital part of the king's clearly articulated message—English was not Elazar's native tongue—or, perhaps he simply refused to believe what he had read in the transcript earlier that morning. But for whatever reason, he told the officers, "It is not known if [Syria's war preparations] are in cooperation with the Egyptians."

With that distortion thrown out, Eli Zeira took over. As head of Aman, he was the only other man in the room who knew the identity of the "serious source" and who had read the transcript. He began by conceding that the Syrian army was in a state of alert. It was now capable of starting hostilities at short notice. However, Syria would not go to war without Egypt, and Egypt was not going to war. He seemed exasperated, as if he was trying to teach a simple fact to a particularly slow student. Further, he cavalierly dismissed the source, without revealing the name to the other generals. The quality of the warning was not high, he said definitively.

Dado agreed. War was not at all likely. But he still expected the Syrians to retaliate in some way for the downing of their twelve jets earlier. They would shoot down an Israeli plane, or bombard a settlement, or perhaps even dare a "land grab." The upcoming three-day holiday, the Golan countryside filled with travelers, gave them a tempting opportunity. Therefore, as a precaution against a limited Syrian reprisal, he upgraded the level of preparedness along the northern front, reinforcing the line with one 175-mm artillery battery and two tank companies—thirty tanks—from the Seventh Armored Brigade.

"We'll have one hundred tanks against their eight hundred," Dado told the officers. "That ought to be enough."

Satisfied, the chief of staff headed down the hall to a 9 A.M. meeting in the minister of defense's office. As soon as he arrived, his mood dipped precipitously.

Dayan, to Dado's surprise and anger, announced that he intended to fly to the north. He would meet with the settlers and hold a press conference, personally warning the Syrians not to attempt anything.

Dayan paced as he spoke. He was openly racked. The prime minister's anxious late-night call, as well as the indisputable evidence that Syria had increased its attack readiness, filled him with concern. Like Dado, he did not expect a war. But he, too, believed the Syrians would retaliate for the humiliating downing of their planes. And the tank reinforcements gave him only small confidence.

"We must remember," he told Elazar, "that [in the Golan] there is no Suez [Canal] that you need to cross. All they have to do is cross the no-man's-land, and get in with tanks." It was as if he was viewing a clear image in his mind: settlers fleeing in panic, chased by relentless Syrian tanks.

Dayan's words angered Dado. Fifteen minutes earlier he had dispatched tanks and artillery to the front. Now in response to Dayan's hyperboles, in reaction to his proposed press conference and public meetings, to the defense minister's aggrandized sense of the impact of his own celebrity, Dado pulled back.

"I don't think this is a serious matter," he said. "We know that the Syrian army is deployed in an emergency deployment. And it is a deployment from which you can attack and do other things—it is true. . . .

"Still, it seems to me that we do not face war with Syria. I think that nothing can be more idiotic on behalf of Syria as attacking alone. I think we have all the indications that there is not going [to be] a war of the two [Egypt and Syria] of them. And, therefore, I would not make preparations to prevent a war in the Golan Heights."

His certainty placated Dayan—a bit. Nevertheless, the minister of defense still insisted on making a personal tour of the border region. Immediately after the meeting, Dayan, accompanied by Dado, departed for the Golan.

It was a successful trip. As he shook hands with the settlers and drank New Year's toasts, the defense minister's his spirits rose. "I hope the Syrians realize that any blow they land will hurt them more than it will us," Dayan told one reporter. While to another he confided, "I don't see any special reasons in recent time for warning."

And so within just twenty-four hours, Hussein's facts were undermined and rationalized until, finally, they meshed with the prevailing assumptions. The Concept remained impregnable.

But even while the generals and ministers moved on to other matters, the small consequences of the king's secret visit reached down into the ranks: Thirty tanks had been ordered to the northern front.

At about noon on September 26—approximately the hour when Dayan and Dado's helicopter landed in the Golan—Lt. Col. Avigdor Kahalani was on the roof of his farmhouse in Nes Ziona. He had a hammer in his hand and a pain throbbing in his head.

Last night his brother Emanuel had gotten married, and at the festivities he'd drained a second—or was it a third?—bottle of wine. Now he regretted his indulgence. He was on leave from his tank battalion in the Sinai for only the three-day New Year's holiday. It would be his last home leave for months. And the roof had to be shingled before the winter rains.

The ringing of the phone was an unwelcome noise. "For you," his wife, Dalia, called.

"Who is it?"

"Yanosh!"

Avigdor hurried down. Brigade commanders did not call on Rosh Hashanah eve.

"Kahalani?" said Col. Yanosh Ben Gal. "What are you doing right now?"

Avigdor explained about the roof, and about the hangover.

"Jews don't drink. Didn't anyone ever tell you that, Kahalani?" Yanosh teased. Then he turned serious.

"Your battalion is on alert. Part of the battalion is moving north in a few minutes."

"North?"

"Your duty officer has the details. Nothing to worry about."

"Something special up there?"

"Yes, but not over the phone."

"Okay."

"I'll be there in the morning. You'll be representing the brigade till I get there."

Avigdor's mind was already working out how he'd tell Dalia that he would not be home for the holiday. So, he did not follow when Yanosh said, "Maybe the problem is weddings. You should stay away from them."

"Huh?"

"At Yossi's. You had too much to drink."

Avigdor shot back, "We all did."

"Never enough," his commander corrected. Yanosh's laughter roared across the line.

"Where the hell do you think our Yossi is right now?" Yanosh said. "Probably screwing his brains out. I just hope it's with his pretty new bride."

Avigdor could still hear Yanosh laughing as he hung up the phone.

FIFTEEN

Victoria Station, Bombay, India/ 28 September 1973/1100

The best way to get to know India, Mahatma Gandhi had suggested to visitors, was to travel in a third-class railway car. Nati had read this in a guidebook as she planned their honeymoon and offered it up as a challenge to Yossi. It was just the sort of high adventure the Indian leg of their eastward journey needed. And so carried along at a sedate twenty-five miles per hour, nestled side by side on austere wooden seats, they rode across a vast, complex country in trains packed beyond even their previous imagination.

What a daily spectacle! Their compartment burst with people, a hectic, rolling, exotic world. One day they'd be crammed next to a group in boldly colored muslin saris, scarlet powder and sandalwood paste decorating their faces, and chattering with the high, unnatural voices of eunuchs. Another day the jostling sea of humanity was less curious but more affecting, a cajoling flock of beggars, untouchables, lepers, and mothers nursing vacant-eyed infants. Or it might be a fairground: conjurers, puppeteers, and men leading goats or hauling cages with squawking parrots. Once even a cobra charmer who, in return for a few of Yossi's coins, brought the entire compartment to a sudden, transfixed quiet as he coaxed his snake to perform. There was always noise, a grueling cacophony of people and animals, of hectoring voices and low-pitched sobbing. And the smells, a high, noxious mix of urine, spices, heat, curry, and unwashed bodies, the odor thick and pervasive, pressing constantly. Every day they lived with India, and the experience was both intense and demanding.

Nati, as they returned to Bombay to catch the plane that would take them on to Nepal, told Yossi she had one regret. "We should have bought a monkey." Whenever they had left the train, Nati would be drawn to the packs of monkeys that screeched and scampered over the ancient temple stones and along the parapets of crumbling Mongol fortresses. To Yossi's dismay, she would feed them nuts from her outstretched hand. And now as they prepared to leave India to pursue their next adventure, Nati, with a playful longing, wanted one for a souvenir.

"A monkey," answered Yossi. "What are we going to do with a monkey in Israel?"

Nati knew he was right, of course. It was just that she was not thinking of home. Israel was another world, a land and a life she had stepped out of. Travel encouraged her fantasies, though she knew they were short-lived and illusory. With her Yossi, bound by love and their strange, exciting journey, Israel seemed very far away.

For Shabtai Brill, there was no escape. He no longer left the unit to go home. The little sleep he required, he reluctantly grabbed on a cot in an adjoining room. Whatever small opportunity there might have been to lead a campaign to resurrect his MRPV had passed. Things now were moving too quickly.

Each day he was a detective building his case. He never knew when the next clue would appear. His mission was to find the evidence that would prove, once and for all and beyond a shadow of a doubt, his worst suspicions.

So, a solitary hunter, he listened, and he searched. He pored over all the reports that arrived daily from the Sinai stations; and each one sounded a shrill alarm in his mind. The ground forces at the Suez Canal, the Egyptian air force, the naval forces in the Red Sea—all were on raised alert. A division stationed in Cairo had joined the Second Army sector near the Canal. Amphibious armored fighting vehicles (AFVs) were headed there, too.

Yet while he looked at these activities as preparations for war, Branch-Six, the Egyptian desk of Aman, had another view. Their assessment appeared in the *Likem,* the daily *Intelligence Digest:*

"Egyptian fears of an Israeli offensive action, which started after the air battle of September 13, when 12 MiG-21 planes were shot down, continue. These fears were intensified because of the annual anniversary of Gamal Abdel Nasser's death [September 28], and possibly the Ramadan feast. . . . In light of these apprehensions, the state of alert in all arms of the Egyptian army was raised."

He read this with a growing bewilderment and frustration. Couldn't they understand what was really happening?

And when a disturbing CIA flash arrived on the night of September 29–30, this report, too, was ignored with a similar cool nonchalance. Brill was incredulous. The CIA warned that as of the end of September, Syria, according to "highly reliable sources," planned a massive offensive to occupy the Golan. Three infantry divisions would attack at twilight, and, in a second stage, armored divisions would move to establish a bridgehead at the Jordan River.

But even though the vaunted CIA supplied this intelligence, even though the war warning reenforced with additional detail the one delivered to the prime minister on September 25, the Aman military intelligence analysts dismissed it. Lurking behind the CIA's "highly reliable" source they recognized King Hussein, and they already had concluded he was distributing tainted gifts. The Americans, they believed, were simply the inadvertent middlemen in another shifty Middle East con game.

Then, even as analysts were writing a report to defuse the CIA information about Syria, Aman began to monitor transmissions detailing new activity in the Egyptian army.

"Between October 1–7, 1973, a large-scale staff exercise on the occupation of Sinai is going to take place. Its participants will probably be the headquarters of the air, antiaircraft, and naval arms, and the headquarters of the armies, the divisions, and the special forces. Because of the exercise the state of alert will be raised (as of October 1) to highest in the air force and all units which participate in the exercise, and all leaves will be called off."

As Brill read this, he experienced a sad yet at the same time satisfying confidence. Surely his superiors would now deduce what was clearly happening. The Egyptians' "Tahrir 41" exercise was not a war game deployment but the real thing. And, as both the activity on the Golan and the CIA report further confirmed, Syria was preparing to join in, too.

But to his astonishment, after a few dense paragraphs providing impressively precise details of the Egyptian mobilization, the report concluded:

"The information about the expected exercise and the call of reserve soldiers for a limited time . . . and the additional preparations that are underway or will be done in the coming days . . . *are, in actuality, solely connected to the exercise.*"

Such unqualified certainty left Brill undone. He considered the rigid minds he would need to persuade, and he lost all hope. With a stern, rebuking bark, his superiors would scatter all the small clues he had assembled.

And let him just dare to suggest his new suspicion: The recent terrorist hijacking of a train in Austria of Jews immigrating from Russia was a deliberately well-timed distraction. That the prime minister was extending her trip to Europe for an urgent meeting on October 2 in Vienna with Austrian Chancellor Bruno Kreisky meant she was falling for the bait. She would be out of Israel just when her presence, her decision-making authority, would be essential. Brill could envision the effects of his presenting such a speculative hypothesis to his commander. Colonel Ben Porat would first dismiss it, and then, with even greater alacrity, dismiss him. His hard-won career, his cherished life in the army, would be over.

Yet despite all his growing suspicions, Brill knew he still needed one piece of incontrovertible evidence. An event that could not be rationalized away. His proof.

Then he found it.

Shabtai Brill's eureka moment snuck up on him. He was considering a small, seemingly inconsequential bit of information Aman had collected on September 28. Two Sukhoi fighter squadrons had moved from their base in northern Syria—designated T-4 on Military Intelligence maps—to an airfield closer to Israel in Dmeir. Aman's analysts had made quick work of this development:

"The advancement of the Sukhoi planes . . . enables them to attack targets in northern Israel, in a low-altitude profile. We estimate that this move was taken as part of a defensive state of alert—whose goal is to prepare [a] means to attack Israeli targets in response to a possible Israeli action—and also for warning purposes."

There was, Brill conceded, a logic to this reasoning. If Israel attacked, the jets would be in the air and flying over the Golan to retaliate a full twenty minutes sooner than if they had taken off from T-4. But if Syria was truly afraid of an Israeli first strike, why should they position their planes twenty minutes closer to the enemy?

As he struggled to answer his own question, Brill thought back to the Six Day War. In a surprise attack, Israeli Phantoms had demolished formations of Syrian planes lined on the runways. After the war, a wiser Syria moved their fighters far north of Damascus; alerted by the border radars to enemy invaders, the planes would have time to scramble. As a further precaution, the Soviets had constructed fortified bombproof underground jet hangars at the T-4 base.

In an electrifying instant, Brill realized he had his proof: *the hangars.*

There were no bombproof hangars at the Dmeir base. The Sukhois would be vulnerable to an Israeli attack. But Syria was not apprehensive. Why should they be? They never believed the enemy intended to attack. This deployment was not a defensive precaution. It was preparation for a surprise first strike. It meant war.

Now certain he had found the strong rope that enabled him to tie the incriminating pieces into a hard, tight package, he once again confronted his commander. With a showman's timing, Brill presented his case, saving his new, unimpeachable discovery until the very end. "Look," he said, "it's war. I'm sure of it. You understand this, don't you?"

"No," Colonel Ben Porat answered, "I don't."

Brill tried to argue, but his emotions overwhelmed him. His voice rose in loud bursts of conviction. Even as he went on, he knew he had lost everything.

This is completely unprofessional, Colonel Ben Porat announced. Brill tried to recover, to regroup his argument. But it was futile. With icy, dismissive fury, Ben Porat turned and walked away.

For two unsettled days, Brill considered his situation. If he let the matter drop, he could salvage his career. Ben Porat was an old friend. With time, he would forget Brill's rashness.

But as he lay awake, unable to sleep, an image, strong and clear, appeared in his mind and took hold. It lodged in his thoughts, firm and indelible. And became a call to action.

In the country's pioneer days, *hashomrim* had climbed wooden towers, standing guard, ready to alert the farms and settlements to an Arab attack. With his tens of millions of dollars of fantastic electronic equipment, with this power to listen and even see the enemy in its own lair, what was he after all, but another *hashomer.* Another watchman: the eyes and the ears of his people. And like the *hashomrim* of another age, he, too, had his duty.

And so early on the morning of October 1 he filled his briefcase with forty separate clues, a thick collection of underlined Aman assessments, frontline observation reports, and raw pieces of intercepted intelligence. The case bulged, and he had difficulty closing it.

A half hour after leaving his office, he arrived at the Sde Dov military airport outside Tel Aviv. The Cessna had already begun boarding, and he hurried on to the plane. Brig. Gen. Zvika Lidor, the director of Military Intelligence's deputy for Organization and Management, sat in the front of the ten-passenger plane. Adjacent were the two aides accompanying him on this long-scheduled inspection of Bavel, Aman's code name for one of its most sensitive Sinai listening posts. As Brill passed down the narrow aisle to take a seat in the rear, the general looked up.

"Didn't know you'd be joining us, Brill," he said.

"Last minute, sir," Brill answered as he took his seat.

As the small plane leveled off at its cruising altitude on its way south to the Sinai, Brill unfastened his seat belt, grabbed his briefcase, and approached the general.

"Sir," he began, "I have something very important to talk to you about."

A surprised General Lidor turned toward the major sitting next to him. "Sit here, Brill," he said, as the aide immediately rose and moved to the rear of the plane.

SIXTEEN

Bavel Base, Sinai/ 1 October 1973/1000

Brill understood the chance he was taking. The turbulence tossing the light plane about as it crossed the Sinai mountains was only a small annoyance compared to the heaving in his own uneasy stomach. His direct appeal to General Lidor was entirely out of line. Soldiers did not scamper up the chain of command several rungs at a time. And certainly not to protest an immediate superior's decision. It was insubordination, and men had been court-martialed for less. But what choice did he have? He could think of no other way.

Once he had made up his mind, Brill plotted with an instinctive cunning. His first step was to pick his target. Lidor not only worked in the Kirya, the military headquarters in Tel Aviv, but also his office was, literally, right outside the door of Zeira's. He had daily access to the men who guided Israel. And Lidor had worked with Brill in the War of Attrition. The general had always been, albeit in his reserved, formal way, friendly.

When Brill read the internal Aman memo announcing Lidor's

inspection of the Bavel base, that clinched it. He would be able to meet Lidor away from the crowded, always political corridors of the Kirya; the risk of Ben Porat's learning of his misconduct, would, for the time being at least, be minimalized. And for the plane ride he would have a captive audience.

But as Brill began his presentation, his analyst's mind could not help focusing on what, in just a sudden irreparable moment, could go wrong. Lidor worked with Zeira, Shalev—all the steadfast architects of the Concept. Why shouldn't he be another true believer? Even as he presented his case, producing document after document, he kept expecting Lidor to burst in. *Enough!* he could hear Lidor growling. We know all this, and it is inconsequential. You have added two and two—and come up with five. Does Ben Porat know you're here?

But General Lidor did not interrupt except to ask, on occasion, a probing, follow-up question. Mostly he listen in stunned, shocked silence as Brill's recitation continued over the drone of the plane's engines. The general seemed incredulous. When the plane landed, a room on the base was quickly found, and Lidor, trailed by his aides, led them inside.

Brill went on for four hours. Carefully, this time controlling his emotions, he shared all the disparate pieces in the puzzle and, with precision, fitted them together.

When the general finally spoke, his voice was weary, even mournful. "Look," Lidor said, "I share an office with all of Aman's top brass. With Zeira himself. And I never heard there was any reason for concern. Everything was normal. And now somebody from outside comes in and tells me everything is not the way it seems."

He paused. Brill understood the full significance of the moment: A verdict was about to be delivered.

"But," Lidor decided, "you convinced me. Egypt and Syria are going to attack."

Lidor abruptly called to an aide, "Zuska, make me a meeting with Zeira. Get me in his office as soon as we return." Then his attention focused on Brill. "I'm going to tell him everything you told me," the general promised. "He'll have to make a new evaluation."

Brill felt the pride of a man who had set out on an impossible mission and, against all odds, had seen it through in triumph. The Watchman had sounded his warning, and as a consequence the future would be rewritten.

On the bright morning of October 1, as the Cessna flew toward the tip of the Sinai, Shazly and his staff traveled in a procession of jeeps across miles of sandy, rugged terrain. They were not far from the bustle of Cairo, but the land, barren, somber and primitive, belonged to ancient Egypt.

The vehicles stopped in front of a massive sand dune. It seemed an arbitrary destination; a broad, humpbacked pile rising up in the bleached, forlorn landscape. But on closer inspection, an opening stood in the center of the dune.

Shazly went first. The passageway was a narrow, hidden trail, long and dimly lit. It ended at a giant steel door guarded by armed soldiers. Even as Shazly approached, the door creaked open on heavy hinges.

Shazly entered, and it was as if he had entered a tomb. Another lengthy, silent corridor illuminated by the anemic glow of overhead tubes of electric light stretched ahead. He followed it to a metal staircase. The stairs snaked down, and down, and still farther down; the boots of Shazly's group beat a steady tattoo throughout the long descent. With the last step, Shazly felt he had reached the earth's core.

But there was another steel door. And behind it, another long dim corridor ending in still another heavy door. It opened into a secret world.

A vast, brightly lit hall bristled with activity. Men in uniform rushed about. Telephones shrilled. Telexes clicked. A series of oversized yet precisely detailed maps of the Sinai, the Suez Canal, as well as the Golan Heights had been drawn on glass panels filling a long wall. Color-coordinated markers indicated the deployment of troops, armor, and artillery. A flock of harried soldiers updated the positions constantly.

When Shazly entered, things quieted. He, too, was caught up in the momentousness of the occasion. He took the chief of staff's chair on the dais of Center Ten, the Egyptian Operations Command, with the knowledge that the final countdown to war had begun.

The enemy would learn of his presence in the center, but he was unconcerned. He had moved to Center Ten during last year's annual exercise, and the methodical Jews would expect his arrival here for Tahrir 41. Perhaps he should make certain they found out. He would ask Mohammed Heikal, editor of *Al Ahram,* to run an item—one more bit of decoy news the editor published as "a patriotic duty"—to lull the Zionists into complacency.

Over the past nine months, Shazly had called up and then demobilized the reservists a numbing twenty-two times. Reports in *Al Ahram* had explained that this activity was an attempt to modernize the army's mobilization system. So just days earlier, when the twenty-third call-up was announced along with the promise to release 20,000 of the reservists on October 7, Shazly was convinced Israel would pay little attention. And this would be a fatal mistake.

Tahrir 41 was another large part of his deception plan. As widely announced, the exercise had a single goal: to train troops to liberate the Sinai. Hundreds of vehicles carrying amphibious and bridging equipment were already traveling toward the Suez Canal. Camouflage nets were being removed from the field guns. Soldiers in full combat gear assembled in frontline camps. It did not matter that the enemy watched. It was all part of the exercise. *The Jews expected it.* Just as they anticipated Shazly's presence in Center Ten.

But from his command desk, Shazly prepared for war. For months he had lived uncomfortably in two worlds. One was filled with routine and public duties. The other carried his secret. Now he was free.

He summoned his two key field commanders, Gen. Saad Mamoun

of the Second Army and Maj. Gen. Abdel-Moneim Mwassil of the Third Army. "Prepare to carry out Operation Badr on October 6," he told them. He reviewed the communiqués to be released when the invasion started. The texts accused Israel of starting the hostilities. The lie bothered him, but then he told himself the Zionists had issued a similar fabrication after their surprise attack in '67. He gave the order for the submarines to sail to their battle stations. The captains had been instructed not to open their sealed orders until an hour before the attack, but they sailed under strict radio silence. They could not be recalled, their mission could not be canceled. War, he realized solemnly, had become irrevocable.

There was, however, still one last formality. Later that day Shazly and nineteen other members of Armed Forces Supreme Council convened as President Sadat read the War Order aloud, then signed it. "I bear responsibility before history," Sadat declared in a booming, confident voice.

D-day was in five days.

In Israel, General Zeira was amused. On his way to that Monday morning's general staff meeting, he stopped the chief of staff in the corridor outside Dayan's office. As if sharing a coy joke, he told Dado that he should thank him. He let the chief of staff get a good night's sleep.

It wasn't until the meeting began and the other generals were present that Zeira delivered the punch line. Late last night he had received a report from a Mossad agent that the Tahrir 41 exercise would end today with an invasion across the Suez Canal. But after reviewing the information, Aman decided it was unreliable. So, Zeira concluded brightly, since there's no war today, I think you will agree that I did the right thing by not awaking anyone in the middle of the night.

Dayan was not so sure. Even as the meeting went on, he passed Zeira a curt note demanding to know why he had not been informed of the warning as soon as it had been received.

Zeira wrote back:

Moshe,

1. I received the message by phone at 0230.

2. The message was a first version and, so far, we do not have a complete version.

3. Throughout the night we made an assessment, checked all the information that arrived last night and in recent days . . . and toward the morning hours we reached the conclusion that the message was baseless and that it was an exercise.

4. Hence, I did not report anything to the chief of staff and the defense minister. In order to avoid telling you: "There is information, but I don't trust it." (By the way, in recent days we have had a number of such messages.)

5. I reported the information this morning, during the general staff meeting, and distributed it through regular channels.

6. In principle, I do not think that information, which by our assessment is baseless, should be disseminated during the night. This can be done in the morning, together with its assessment.

And with that explanation, the incident ended. The head of Military Intelligence was not reprimanded. Instead, a principal had been established: A good night's sleep was not to be rashly interrupted.

Only now that he had spoken with Brill, General Lidor was not sleeping either. On his return from the Bavel base, he walked directly to Zeira's office.

"He's home. Sick with the flu," General Shalev told him.

Lidor considered what to do. Shalev was head of research for Military Intelligence. He would understand the irrefutable logic of

Brill's deduction. And he was Zeira's right-hand man. Flu or not, he could help get to the director. So, Lidor laid it all out for Shalev just as Brill had done for him.

"Do you read everything?" Shalev challenged after Lidor finished.

"No."

"Who is responsible for evaluation here? You or me? It's my responsibility. So why don't you just let me do it."

Lidor walked away from Shalev's desk. Down the hall was the chief of staff's office. He and Dado were old friends. He could knock on his door, tell him everything. And he had an excuse to justify his boldness: Zeira was out sick. Surely, Dado would listen.

He started down the hall, but then stopped. The chief of staff could not be bothered with every dispute. He couldn't impose on Dado's friendship this way. Lidor turned around, and went back to his own office.

He sat pensively at his desk. Tomorrow he would go to Zeira's home, he finally decided. Even if the director was sick in bed, he would talk to him and present Brill's evidence.

And as Lidor continued to think it all through, he came up with an additional plan. Later that day, he called Brill and told him he had ordered a photo-reconnaissance flight for the next morning above the Suez Canal. "If the photos show anything like I expect they'll show," Lidor explained, "Zeira, Shalev—they'll all have to wake up."

Brill agreed. But he could not help thinking that this is what he had been saying all along. And that if they had developed his MRPV, the model plane would already be flying above the front lines, its 35-mm camera clicking off incriminating shot after shot.

SEVENTEEN

Nafekh Camp, Golan Heights/ 3 October 1973/ 0900

Just outside the town of Kuneitra, Yanosh Ben Gal and Avigdor Kahalani wandered through the rocks and crevices along Booster Ridge. They moved silently, observing, tabulating what it would take to defend this stark promontory against a rush of Syrian tanks.

The Golan was hard, nearly treeless country, slick plateaus and brittle ledges molded centuries ago from streams of rushing, foaming lava. Sharp, conelike *tel*s, craggy pillars of ancient volcanic rock, shot up like raised, angry fists from the dark basalt. Day or night, this was nasty, inhospitable terrain. It did not seem worth fighting for.

But this northern territory, 480 square miles elbowing up against Syria and nudging a corner of southern Lebanon, was vital. It was the threshold into the rich, green heart of Israel. And its sustenance.

High up in the snowcapped Hermon Mountains were the first, faint drizzles of water, natural springs that fed into the mighty Jordan River and then rolled on to empty into the Sea of Galilee. The water that nourished the nation, that made the deserts bloom and the crops grow, flowed down from the north.

While just below its foreboding volcanic escarpments, lay the fertile Huleh Valley and the busy Galil towns and settlements. Beneath the Golan's gloomy shadow, a lush, brimming countryside of fields and orchards, prosperous and fecund, a biblical dream made real, had spread out.

The two men knew what was at stake. For four years, the Seventh Armored Brigade had been based in the Sinai sands. This was a new battleground, a sector with new dangers. Orders, if they came, would arrive while they were on the move. They had to be prepared. Each day they went off on foot, scouting, sensing, looking at the unfamiliar terrain with tankers' eyes.

They searched for fast, direct routes that would lead their Centurions from their new base near the central Nafekh crossroads to the enemy deployments. They studied the land for firing positions, looking for boulders or hills they could hide behind while taking aim with their 105-mm cannons. They learned the locations of the antitank ditches, the minefields, and the nearly two dozen bunkers along the border. A mere dozen infantrymen, they discovered with some concern, manned each bunker, with only a chain-link fence separating them and the Syrian forces. Yanosh walked up to the fence, grabbed it with his two big hands, and rattled it to its foundations. A thirty-six-ton Syrian T-54 would drive through as easily as a speeding car through a red light.

When they were back at camp, they busied themselves calibrating the barrels of their heavy guns, checking the tracks and drivetrains of their tanks, loading ammunition, making sure all the radios were tuned to the battalion net. The battalion's mission in the Golan was to serve as a counterstrike force, twenty-two tanks waiting in the rear, ready to run to the rescue if the Syrians broke through the seventy tanks of the frontline 188th Brigade. On full alert, they were ready to go operational at a moment's command.

Kahalani doubted anything would happen. The Syrians periodically flexed their muscles, and then the Israelis flexed theirs. Intelligence had reported there were 800 Syrian tanks along the fifty-mile front line, with another 460 in reserve. The numbers were daunting. Still, he believed, finishing the tiling of his roof before winter posed more of a problem than did the Syrians crossing the Purple Line.

Last night the sergeant in H Company had complained to him. "We're fed up with shooting at barrels," he said.

"There's an advantage in barrels," he had pointed out. "They can't shoot back at you."

The sergeant was young, and very eager. He didn't appreciate a veteran's cautious wisdom. In the Six Day War Kahalani's tank had been hit by a well-aimed shell. Instantly, it became a furnace. His body caught fire, his flesh burned. The miracle was not just that he survived, but that after more than a year in the hospital and a dozen operations, he was still a soldier. He ended the discussion abruptly. "You've got a lot more years to live, and statistics say that there's a war every ten years, so don't worry about it."

But Yanosh could not relax. Something was coming soon. At night he would walk alone through the camp, a solitary brooding figure. He heard the men in their tents, but he also listened to the silence moving over the cool lava plains. Something was out there. He could feel it.

By nature, he was a pessimist. He attributed this, in his rare moments of introspection, to his difficult childhood. He was born in Poland, and when the Nazis marched his parents off, he ran with his brother and sister to the Red Army to find protection. They sent him to a camp in Siberia, where he watched his brother die. But Yanosh managed to escape. Ten years old, he began a desperate and circuitous journey, each leg its own trial, that took him to Baghdad, then Bombay, and finally Cairo, where the Jewish Agency found him. They placed him in a kibbutz in Palestine. He hated it, and ran away. A family in Tel Aviv took him in and, still unhappy, he bided his time until he was eighteen and could join the army.

He did not fit in there, either. A natural outsider, he did not take well to orders or discipline. His hair was deliberately too long, falling in a straight curtain over his eyes. He was never deferential to rank, always determined to get in the last, cutting word. Even to his friends, his style was a sly, jokey irony.

Yet in the relatively freewheeling informality of the Israel Defense Forces, Yanosh not only found a home, but prospered. A few senior officers were determined to run him out, but most of the others enjoyed him. He was their defiant iconoclast, a winking rascal, intuitively smart, always prepared, and, as he had demonstrated in combat, as brave as a lion. The men found it easy to follow a commander who gave them orders with a straightforward reasonableness, and yet didn't hesitate to scream back at the brass.

This morning as Yanosh wandered along Booster Ridge, a tall, slim figure still limping from a fall off a tank turret years ago, he was moodily silent. His vague feeling—"the rumble in my soldier's gut," he called it—had become a certainty.

"Kahalani," he finally asked his lieutenant colonel, "are you completely ready? We're going to have a serious war here.

"The generals think," Yanosh went on, "that David is such a better fighter than Mustafa. That we can do with three tanks what they need three hundred to do. The generals seem to forget that during the Six Day War, Nasser gave the Egyptians the order to withdraw. They listened to him. They weren't running from us.

And as he spoke out loud the words that had been slowly forming in his mind since he had arrived up north, Yanosh had another intuition: His country was in danger.

In Tel Aviv that morning, the chief of staff was busy convincing the minister of defense that there was no danger. In a meeting in Dayan's office, Dado insisted, "We checked it again and concluded—and we can say it definitely—that what we have in Egypt is an exercise. . . . In Syria, my assessment is that they are not going to open fire."

He had good reason for such unwavering conviction. Yesterday he had given the order to activate the crown jewel of the nation's electronic espionage network.

In Aman's carefully veiled, euphemistic parlance this device was always referred to as "the special means of collection." The few cabinet-level people—the prime minister, the minister of defense—aware of its existence called it "the national insurance policy."

In reality, it was a series of battery-operated devices attached to phone and cable connections buried deep in the sand outside Cairo. When Brill's unit 848 sent the signal to a separate transmitter hidden underground not far from the cables, the devices went "hot." In real time, operators in Israel could hear not only what was said over the telephone and cable lines, but could also eavesdrop on conversations in the rooms where the telephone and telex consoles were located.

There were, however, risks involved in using such electronic bugs. A diligent enemy might "sweep" the premises, discover the microphones, and rip them out. Or if they were cagey, begin planting disinformation. Another problem was that these high-powered bugs ran on a battery pack that had a relatively short life. Replacing the batteries in enemy territory would be a technically complex and dangerous mission and would need to be done by a special commando force, the *sayaret tzanhamin*. Success could not be assured.

Given the risks, Israel activated these devices only in times of great emergency. It was the ark they had built for dreaded rainy days. The last time they had gone operational was in May after the In-Law had warned that war was imminent. They had proved invaluable. Israel had listened to what was being discussed, on phones, in telexes, and in conversations, throughout Center Ten. They monitored the entire subterranean Egyptian war operations room. All the activity in Center Ten was broadcast live back to Tel Aviv.

Now Israel was caught up in a new crisis. They had clear evidence of the enemy's preparations, but they still did not know its intentions. Was it a training exercise? Saber-rattling to discourage an

Israeli attack? Or was it war? Despite the risks, the time had come to listen in on the secret conversations of the Egyptian High Command.

Yesterday, October 2, the chief of staff had asked Zeira if the devices had been activated. An anxious Dayan also inquired. On both occasions Zeira had led the men to believe they were.

This was not true.

Later, Zeira would insist he believed Ben Porat had ordered his unit to turn on the transmitters. Ben Porat, however, contended he never received any instructions to do so.

The misunderstanding had irreparable consequences. Israel's key military decision makers, the chief of staff and the minister of defense, were certain their analysts had access to Egypt's closely held secrets.

This false knowledge firmed their own unshakable confidence. And sealed the nation's fate.

If the Israelis had been monitoring Center Ten that day, they would have learned that Shazly's carefully orchestrated world was in turmoil.

His problems began in the morning after a cargo plane had taken off from Cairo. On board was a three-man delegation headed by Ahmed Ismail, the minister of war. They were going to Damascus to deliver the final orders of war.

Traveling by cargo plane was one more attempt to protect their secret. They had decided the Zionists would pay no attention to a seemingly routine flight. Still with so much at stake, the journey was tense and wearing.

"What happens if the Israelis catch us and they find us with the order of war?" Ismail asked.

Bahieddin Nofal, head of Egypt's operation general staff, said, "I will simply eat the piece of paper. It is small and easy to swallow."

But the plane arrived in Damascus without incident, and the delegation proceeded to the office of Mustafa Talas, the Syrian minister of defense.

Their arrival surprised Talas, who had not been informed of the trip. He immediately summoned his generals to headquarters. When the two groups faced each other, Talas revealed his own surprise: Syria wanted to postpone the attack for forty-eight hours. It needed the additional two days to empty the oil refineries. The Syrians were certain the malicious Israelis would target them in their counterattack.

Ismail was taken aback. The date had been carefully chosen. The moon, the tides, the Yom Kippur holiday—all made October 6 the optimal day. Shrewdly, hoping to deflect the blame if he ultimately lost the argument, he invoked Shazly's predictable anger.

"You must think of the Egyptian front," he explained. "Think of General Shazly's position if we agreed to a postponement. We cannot hope to keep the secret much longer. He would lose the surprise we have been working so hard to achieve. Before any decision we would have to seek Shazly's military opinion, and I simply do not think he would agree."

But there was no need to contact Shazly. With a weary resignation Talas agreed he would accept the previously established date—if they set a new time for the simultaneous invasions.

Months ago, the Egyptian High Command had decided that their troops would cross the Suez Canal in the late afternoon. If they began the initial fording preparations at six o'clock, the October sun would still be in the eyes of the Israelis. And by the time the assembled PMP bridges swung across to the enemy's side of the canal, it would be dark. The infantry and armor could charge across shielded by the desert night.

General Talas, however, wanted his troops and planes to invade the Golan at dawn. With the sun rising in the east and shining bright into the Israeli's eyes, the enemy artillery would be blinded.

Ismail listened to the Syrian argument, but continued to insist on the later time. Talas, too, was adamant. It seemed as if the Syrian invasion, along with the advantage of a two-front war, would be canceled. But just when the meeting threatened to dissolve in anger, Talas suggested that both armies attack at two o'clock.

Later that afternoon back at Center Ten, Ismail re-created the rocky day for Shazly. The tale was a testimony to the war minister's level manner, quiet charm, and forceful authority. He had beaten back Talas's attempt to change the date of the invasion. And then he had engineered an artful compromise on the time.

Shazly listened patiently. He had read Talas's book on guerilla warfare, and had paid close attention to the general's appreciation for diversionary tactics. But he did not find it necessary to suggest Talas never had wanted to change the date. Or that two o'clock was no doubt the hour the Syrians had preferred all along for the attack.

Instead, Shazly buoyed himself with the fact that even after the eventful trip to Damascus, D-day remained only three days off. And resigned, he hoped that the Canal could be crossed just as easily at two in the afternoon as it might have been four hours later.

Gen. Zvika Lidor's long day brought him neither comfort nor hope. It moved steadily from one disappointment to another.

He arrived at his office to learn that the reconnaissance flight he had ordered above the Suez Canal had been canceled. Cloudy skies, said the intelligence officer at the other end of the phone. The air force, he was reassured, had scheduled another flight for this afternoon.

Lidor had spent a torturous night deciding over whether he should confront Zeira. This latest disappointment made up his mind. He would go to Zeira's home in Zahalaya and, even though his superior was bedridden with the flu, demand an audience. If Brill was right—and the more Lidor replayed the evidence in his mind, the more convinced he became—then there was no other choice. The well-being of the nation took precedence.

Wrapped in a robe, Zeira met with Lidor in his living room. Light streamed in through a row of patio doors, and revealed his watery eyes and a gray, unhealthy pallor. Zeira seemed smaller, almost fragile as he listened to Lidor's recitation. But illness had not weakened the director's sting.

"You don't understand," Zeira said, hot with indignation. "This is not your job. This is not for you." He continued, but Lidor had stopped paying attention. It had been a mistake to try to persuade Zeira, and now he just wanted to get out of the house as quickly as possible.

Lidor returned to his office in the Kirya, holding on to the small consolation that while Brill's evidence could not persuade the director, the reconnaissance photos would provide incontrovertible proof. Aman could not ignore them. Dayan and Dado, too, would read the reports. In a sudden rush of panic, he phoned the Sinai base to make sure the plane had taken off. Yes, he was told. And today there was hardly a cloud in the sky.

So he waited. At nearly seven that evening he still had not heard from the base. He was about to call when his phone rang. It was the photo technician. They had the film, but there was a problem. The camera's shutter failed to open. Tomorrow they would install a new camera and try again.

General Lidor was not alone in thinking Israel was running out of time. That evening, Wednesday, October 3, in his home in Al Gezira, President Sadat sat with his friend Mohammed Heikal, the editor of *Al Ahram.* Sadat rejoiced:

"Whatever they do . . . even if they know tonight. Even if they decide to mobilize all their reserves. And even if they think of launching a preemptive attack. They have lost the chance to catch up."

EIGHTEEN

Office of Defense Minister, Tel Aviv/ 4 October 1973/0830

Moshe Dayan wished it was winter. Its arrival in the Golan was just a month away, but for him the cold and rain and mud couldn't come soon enough. He needed time, and when the weather changed he would finally have it. There were no wars in winter.

"If the Syrians get to our settlements, it will be calamitous," he had warned in a sudden burst of anxiety at a general staff meeting earlier in the week. Winter, he thought, would give him a second chance. It would be the opportunity to make sure the Golan farmers would never again be placed in such jeopardy.

Dayan revealed his newly found resolve early Wednesday morning at a meeting in his office. Present were the chief of staff, the commander of the Syrian front, and the head of Aman's Research Division. The defense minister began earnestly, as if sharing a nightmare that had plagued him during a restless night:

"I have a trauma, not of the Heights, but of the settlements there. . . . I think it is necessary and worthy for the state of Israel, for the IDF, to invest a lot of money and a lot of work . . . to create a situation in which they [the Syrians] cannot start to move, and which they'll just have to deal with."

He was not worried about the short term. "If the Syrians dare now—we will destroy them." Similarly Egypt, despite the buildup of forces along the Suez Canal, was not an immediate threat. "Egypt does not [intend] to fight now," he asserted.

Nevertheless, in the year ahead there would need to be a serious redefinition of the plans to protect the settlements. More minefields? An artificial lake as a barrier? He threw out these ideas, and also suggested that perhaps an ingenious deterrent would simply have to be "invented." But something must be done.

"This month we will not make drastic changes. After this month, winter starts. In the winter it is clear that a serious war won't be inaugurated. . . . I summarize: What can be done during this month—should be done. What can't be done—make a plan to see how much it should cost. . . ."

The men agreed. In two days it would be Yom Kippur, and the holiday was a sure sign that cold weather neared. Everyone believed they would have the time to make things right.

While in the Kirya there were no apparent concerns about Egypt, Amnon Reshef looked west across the Canal from the turret of his M-60 tank that morning and was less certain. His men had been stationed in the Sinai, living with its sand, dust, and sun, since the Six Day War. They had fought in the War of Attrition. But he had never seen anything like this. The activity on the west bank—Africa, the men called it—was unprecedented. In the past week, the number of Egyptian artillery pieces had grown from 800 to 1,100. Tanks had moved into firing positions on the bluffs. Amphibious equipment and mobile bridges arrived daily in each sector. And, he estimated, there must be five combat-strength infantry divisions—perhaps 80,000 or even 100,000 soldiers—massed in the enemy camps.

Intelligence insisted that the Egyptians were ending their Tahrir 41 exercise. But despite the burning sun that already rose high and bright in the sky, Amnon looked across the Canal that morning and shuddered. The possibility that it was not a training maneuver unnerved him.

On his own initiative, Amnon's tankers in Brigade Fourteen slept with their boots and overalls on. For the past two days, they'd been on full alert.

If an attack came, their mission was to rush to the front line. According to *Shovach Yonim,* the army's Dovecote war deployment plan, two brigades—220 tanks—would be in position along the water line or about 1,000 meters back to repel the invaders. Another brigade—120 tanks—waited eight kilometers away in reserve.

But the plan's logic, Amnon knew, existed only on paper. His brigade was not up to strength. They had only 90 of their normal compliment of 111 tanks. Yet they still were responsible for 130 miles of frontline defense along the center of the Canal. If there was a widespread invasion, his force would be spread dangerously thin.

Another concern was the Bar-Lev Line forts. Amnon had personally supervised the building of many of these fortresses, and it disturbed him that even with the massive increase of the Egyptian forces across the Canal these positions remained undermanned. Most had only about thirty soldiers, and some had as few as seven. And none of these men belonged to the crack paratrooper battalions that were supposed to man the strongholds in case of war. These troops were *jobniks*, reservists from the Jerusalem Territorial Brigade doing their mandatory annual thirty-three-day service. A few had seen duty during the Six Day War, and then returned to their jobs as shopkeepers, kibbutzniks, and university professors. Others were Orthodox Jews, serving grudgingly at the front during a period that included the most sacred religious holidays. And there also was a group of new immigrants who had never been in the regular army, and had only a brief period of basic training before being assigned to the reserves.

At least, Amnon told himself, now that Gonen was in charge of the Southern Command there was the prospect that the fortresses would soon be improved. In July, when the general learned that the system that turned the Canal into a fiery moat had become inoperable, he had ordered repairs. Clogged sand was to be removed, bent, rusted pipes replaced, and the oil tanks refilled. An engineering team would tour the forts in two days, on Saturday, October 6, to begin the process of getting the systems up and running.

Encouraged by this prospect, Amnon hurried back to camp and a farewell luncheon for Gen. Albert Mandler. On Sunday, he would move on from commanding the armored forces in the Sinai to become chief of the Armored Corps. And as Amnon traveled across the desert, he found additional comfort in his certainty that his brigade had been well trained. They had practiced the Dovecote deployments countless times, and could move rapidly into their designated firing positions above the Canal. Of course, he realized, if there was a war, speed of deployment would never be his primary worry. Even in Dovecote, the grim scenario designed to hold off a "surprise" invasion, the Armored Corps was certain they would have at least forty-eight hours' notice of the enemy's attack. And that would be more than sufficient time to travel the few kilometers across the desert, set up on the high ground, and catch the invaders as they moved unprotected across the Canal.

His confidence was short-lived. When the good-natured luncheon toasts ended, the general rose to offer his parting words. "I am supposed to be taking leave of you," Mandler said, looking down the table and fixing each man with a long stare from his piercing blue eyes. "But I am here to tell you that we are not about to part yet. We are in a period of top alert, and we are about to go to war."

As Mandler spoke his harrowing words, in the sky above the base an unmanned plane headed west over the Sinai. Three days after General Lidor had ordered the mission, an Israeli Air Force Mabat, a drone capable of taking photographs from high altitudes, had finally been sent across the Suez Canal.

* * *

That evening Shabtai Brill, in his underground room outside Tel Aviv, and Saad el Shazly, deep beneath the desert in Center Ten, were awakened by aides alerting them to the same news.

Brill had been waiting all day for the results from the Mabat's flight. When the report had not arrived by eight o'clock, he decided to grab a quick nap. It would be a long night, and experience had taught him to take advantage of the lulls. So he was already dozing when his unit began to intercept the first reports. A sudden evacuation of Soviet military families and civilian personnel was underway in Syria. They were being taken in buses to the port of Latakia. A little after ten, further intercepts revealed that Soviet families in Egypt were involved, too. And that it was no longer a naval evacuation. Eleven Aeroflot planes were on their way. Five headed to Damascus, and the remainder were scheduled to land in Cairo.

With that last news, an excited lieutenant woke Brill up. Minutes later, Brill was in the main hall of unit 848 demanding his men get the answer as soon as possible to one question: Were military advisers *and* their families being evacuated? If everyone was leaving, that would mean it was another rift between the Soviets and their tempestuous allies. But if it were only the women and children, it was more ominous. Moving families out of the line of fire meant just one thing. It was a final step before war.

As unit 848 tried to find the answer, Shazly was awakened after midnight with a call from an angry General Gamasy announcing the evacuation. "Until now the enemy failed to guess the truth," he complained. "If there's one thing that can open their eyes, it's this frightening desertion."

Shazly agreed. "If anything would now persuade the Zionists," he said, "this panicky action would." He could no longer count on Israel's being taken by surprise.

But a quick series of calls restored his spirit. Many of the Russian military experts were staying, including the advisers who trained the Egyptian R-17E Scud missile brigade.

Brill, however, had not been able to learn who was being evacuated. Yet even as his unit hunted for more definitive information, the Aman analysts in Branch Three (superpowers) were rushing to distribute a hedging, scrupulously careful either/or assessment. He read their initial explanatory brief with dismay:

"One. A Syrian decision to expel the Soviet experts and advisers, as Egypt did [in July 1972].

"Two. An emergency evacuation of Soviet women and children from Syria, in light of a Soviet assessment or information that a military clash between Syria, and possibly also Egypt, and Israel is expected. This possibility gains strength from information (not yet verified) about a flight of six Aeroflot planes to Egypt, in parallel to the flight of planes to Syria."

Gains strength? Brill felt like shouting. What else could it be when looked at in conjunction with all the supporting information from the Egyptian and Syrian fronts? It was as if Aman still remained convinced there could not be a war, and therefore the facts, however reliable and frightening, were to be ignored.

Brill raged with renewed frustration. How many days had passed since Lidor had ordered a reconnaissance flight? Command's failure to take advantage of his MRPV just when the nation needed it most was more salt on his wounded mood.

A summons to the phone interrupted his anger. A photo interpreter in Branch Six, an old friend, was on the line.

"We got the shots processed. Each one's a gem. We'll be up all night drawing everything on the maps."

"And?" Brill demanded impatiently.

"—The brass is going to shit."

Later, at about midnight, an encrypted flash message marked with the director's code name arrived at Mossad headquarters. Freddy Einy, the agency's Bureau Chief, rushed from his home to "unbutton" it.

It was slow, laborious work, and it required all his concentration for the next two hours. It was half past two in the morning when he was done and read back the plain text of what he had deciphered. He picked up the phone.

The ringing of the red telephone on his night table awoke Zvi Zamir. The head of the Mossad listened on this secure line as Freddy announced that the In-Law's case agent had sent an emergency message. The In-Law needed to meet with Zamir tomorrow evening in London. The message had included the word "radish": He wanted to talk about war.

Get me on a plane in the morning, Zamir ordered.

He had just fallen asleep when the red phone rang again. This time it was Zeira. The director of Military Intelligence informed him about the rushed evacuations of Soviet families from Egypt and Syria. Still, Zeira announced, his evaluation remained the same. War was a very low probability.

Perhaps, Zamir agreed. But he would know more tomorrow. After a moment's pause, he revealed the summons from the In-Law.

"Let me know what you learn as soon as possible," Zeira requested before he hung up.

Zamir put his head back on the pillow, but then leaned over to grab the phone. He called Freddy.

Make sure the prime minister knows I'm meeting with the In-Law, Zamir ordered his bureau chief. Call Golda Meir's military secretary first thing in the morning.

With that done, Zamir at last tried to fall asleep. It was useless. He got up and began to pack. Perhaps he would be able to sleep on the plane.

NINETEEN

West Bank of the Canal, Egyptian Third Army Field HQ/ 5 October 1973/0830

Shazly also had a fitful night. He tried to go back to sleep after learning about the unexpected Soviet evacuations, but he could not. The prospect of the enemy's grasping that war was imminent kept rushing through his mind. Would Israel call up its reserves? And if it did, could it mobilize in time? His troops were assembled at the front. And D-day was only one day away. Perhaps it was already too late.

The realization electrified him, and with it sleep was impossible. He rose from the cot in his small office and entered the Operations Room of Center Ten. Even before dawn, it hummed, a jumbled commotion of phones, telexes, and harried military clerks. Suddenly, he felt trapped and isolated. He had to clear his mind for all that lay ahead. He could not remain hidden away in this airless room deep below ground while his men were out there, assembled on the steep banks of the Canal, preparing for battle. For many of them, it would be the last day of their lives. He needed to see them; and he wanted them to see him, too. "Get me a car," Shazly ordered.

He went first to Third Army Field HQ by the southern end of the Canal and saw the troops staring at him. Immediately he was glad he'd made the trip. Good, he thought. They should know I'm here, that I'm with them. Tomorrow on his order, their blood would be shed. Intelligence had estimated that 10,000 men would be killed and another 20,000 wounded in the crossing alone. Shazly looked at his men and said a silent prayer.

In the command post, Shazly found Maj. Gen. Abdel-Moneim Mwassil busy writing. The general handed the pages to the chief of staff. Shazly read a long, emotional address meant to inspire the troops as they rushed across the bridges into battle.

Shazly had been in combat. He knew what it was like to charge ahead under fire, running in a screaming wave through a hail of bullets, exploding artillery, and the men around you crying out as they were hit. The experience was packed with an infinity of overwhelming moments, all a lightning blur. Chaos provided the only coherence. Racing minds and hearts could not, *should not,* be slowed by words. Mwassil's speech was an irrelevancy. "I don't think anyone would actually listen," he politely told the general.

At the same time, the idea of giving the troops one final push forward as they took part in this historic moment appealed to him. And, the momentousness of what they were about to do should be made clear. With these thoughts, the chant of the Muslim warriors in the early days of Islam rose up in his mind. "*Allahu-Akbar,*" God is the Greatest, he suddenly said out loud. The vision of his men going off tomorrow, tens of thousands of voices shouting in unison the same inspiring battle chant, a homage to their ancient heroes and their God, filled him with awe.

"I suggest we distribute transistor loudspeakers the length of the front," he told Mwassil. "During the assault they broadcast only one phrase—*Allahu-Akbar.*"

By the time Shazly arrived at Mamoun's Second Army headquarters in the north, the Armed Forces Public Relations Department had found fifty loudspeakers. By tomorrow morning, ten would be delivered to each crossing station.

After conferring with Mamoun and learning that everything was proceeding according to schedule, Shazly realized there was nothing more for him to do at the front. Still, he was reluctant to leave. He asked the general to accompany him on a last look at the Bar-Lev Line.

Hidden behind a sandbag at a forward observation post, Shazly raised his head carefully and focused his telescope. Three hundred yards across the canal was what the Egyptians called Fort Ismailia East, one of the largest enemy strongholds. It protected the vital road east across the Sinai leading to the enemy's air base at Bir Gifgafa. Tomorrow the Egyptian flag would fly above it.

Unless, he worried, Israel was already shoring up its defenses. After the impetuous, panicky Soviet evacuations, the Zionists had to know that an attack loomed. Yet as Shazly searched for evidence of increased activity, he found none. He did not see tanks on the firing ramps, or troops in combat dress at the lookout stations. Camouflage nets covered the artillery. Could they really not know?

"Well, Saad," he said as he handed the telescope back to Mamoun, "it looks as if the enemy is still not alerted." And amazed by the effectiveness of his deception, Shazly could not help but wonder: If I were the chief of staff on the other side, what would I be feeling now?

For Dado, the Israeli chief of staff, it was a day of meetings. He was beginning to have second thoughts. At 5:45 A.M. he had received Branch Six, Aman's Egypt desk's, analysis of yesterday's photo sortie along the Egyptian front lines. It began: "From the findings it can clearly be deduced that the Egyptian army on the Canal front is in an emergency formation, the magnitude of which we have never seen before."

It went on for several pages, full of details about the deployments of armor, troops, and artillery. The review carried no concluding assessment. But perhaps that was unnecessary. Dayan finished the report, and said, "You can get a stroke from just reading the numbers."

This report coupled with the news of the Soviet evacuations began to erode some of Dado's previous certainty. At an 8:25 session with his commanders he conceded:

"If I were a military commentator or a member of the Knesset, I would say this is not an attack. But since I am neither . . . I need to look for proof that we are not going to be hit. I don't have enough evidence that all these signs do not signal an intention to attack."

So he issued a series of orders. Leaves on the southern and northern fronts were canceled; the air force was placed on full alert; the entire Seventh Armored Brigade was to join the tank battalion that had been sent two weeks ago to reinforce the Golan Heights, making a total of 177 tanks on duty near the Purple Line; an additional armored brigade was to be airlifted to shore up the southern front; and, for the first time since the Six Day War, a "C State of Alert" was declared. The administrators needed to summon the reserves would be on duty. Once the prime minister gave her formal authorization, a general troop mobilization could, hopefully, be completed within forty-eight hours.

Now more at ease, Dado went to inform the minister of defense of the steps he had just taken. "Everything you did for this Yom Kippur is fine," he agreed. But Dayan's praise only stirred the chief of staff's anxieties. He worried that on Yom Kippur it might be impossible to alert the country to a mobilization because "during the holiday the entire country was dead." Perhaps, he suggested, the army radio should continue to remain on the air. It could broadcast Psalms every two hours.

"If so we tell everyone that now they need to listen to the IDF radio," an exasperated Dayan said. "It will cause a great panic."

That settled the matter. No one wanted to alarm the nation on the eve of the holiest day of the year. And neither of them raised the possibility of immediately calling up the reserves. If that were necessary, both Dayan and Dado believed Military Intelligence would give them sufficient warning.

Accompanied by Zeira, who had recovered from the flu, they proceeded on this preholiday morning to the prime minister's office in the Kirya. They needed to inform her of what they had learned the previous night, and what they had decided to do about it.

Zeira gave his usual unruffled assessment. The likelihood of an Egyptian–Syrian attack "is entirely improbable," he said. "But perhaps the Russians think that they are indeed going to attack because they do not know the Arabs very well." His implication was clear: We, however, *know* the Arabs.

Dado, too, tried to put the crisis into perspective for the prime minister. There was reason for concern, but not for drastic measures. And there was absolutely no need to call the reserves. "If they are going to attack, we will receive better indications."

Dayan spoke last and was more philosophical. "Preparations have been made. . . . We are not worried about the Egyptian front, and of the Golan Heights we are worried all the time."

Still, in light of the Soviet evacuations, Dayan believed that the time had come to inform the cabinet. This would be their first intimation of the crisis that had been building along the fronts since Rosh Hashanah, nearly two weeks earlier. Most had already left for the holiday, but the prime minister agreed to hold a meeting at 12:30 for whomever was available.

To this audience, Zeira described the situation with candor, conceding that there were "things for which we have no explanation."

Dado, however, was reassuring. "In my mind," he said, "Aman's basic evaluation that we do not face a war is the most probable estimate. It is very possible, since the deployment and preparations we see are also characteristic of a defense formation. . . . If they seriously intend to do something, we will know more than what we do at the moment. I am saving the mobilization of the reserves and other measures for further indications."

But Yisrael Galili, the minister without portfolio who was one of the prime minister's close advisers, had lived through too many wars to be comforted by these predictions. "On May 15, 1967," he said, "all the clairvoyants and astrologers said that we can count on having two years without a war, and at the beginning of June it broke out. . . . There is something in the air that loosens the belt, and therefore there can be surprises."

Such a vague, intuitive approach to military intelligence angered Zeira. It was an absurdity to sit with the prime minister and listen to nervous old men rumbling poetically about "surprises." With its investment of hundreds of millions of dollars, the state knew precisely what was "in the air."

There was a "low probability" that anything would happen, Zeira stated, hoping to end the matter. But if fighting did start, "the least probable move is the crossing of the Canal. And the highest is raids and perhaps shooting here and there."

Golda Meir relied on her generals, but nevertheless she was worried, too. "I would like to say one word: There is something."

Her intuition, however, was not strong enough to order Dayan or Dado to call up the reserves. She never asked if the army's forces as they presently stood could repel an invasion on two fronts. The prime minister was simply troubled. Absorbed and uneasy, she concluded the meeting and wished the cabinet members a good fast for tomorrow's holiday.

And the day ended without the prime minister's learning about the emergency meeting in London with the In-Law. As instructed, the Mossad Bureau Chief had telephoned Golda Meir's military secretary. But when Gen. Yisrael Lior was unavailable, Freddy Einy simply left a message asking him to call back. Since there was no apparent urgency and there was so much to do before the holiday, the general never found the time.

* * *

In Nepal, Yossi and Nati suffered through their own inadvertent foul-up. That morning they had rented a Honda 750-cc motorcycle and zoomed up the Katmandu road. The ride was a thrill, with the cool, crisp wind whipping their faces, and their eyes focused on the snowcapped Himalayas rising majestically in front of them. Nati had her arms wrapped tight around Yossi's waist, but they were already bounded together in a giddy, self-satisfied pact. There was no other couple like them on the planet. So blessed. So beautiful. So adventurous. But when they reached the border station, things fell apart.

The Chinese guards stamped their passports, but would not allow them to cross. Only Chinese citizens could enter at this location. Nati and Yossi argued, then pleaded, but it was useless. They had no choice but to turn around.

On the way back to Katmandu, they stopped in a village for some lunch. They bought round, hard loaves of bread and a strange cheese, and used Yossi's army knife to make sandwiches. Nati sat stubbornly by the motorcycle as she ate. She did not want to be in this godforsaken place. She wanted to be in China.

But Yossi was determined to make the best out of it and set off to explore the town. As he worked his way through the busy marketplace, something in a stall caught his eye. Without even arguing over the price, he bought it.

"Still disappointed?" he asked Nati when he returned.

She answered with a muffled silence. Her heart had been set on touring China.

"Well," Yossi announced, revealing what he had been hiding behind his back. "Maybe this will cheer you up."

In his hands was a large, stuffed white monkey with a grinning face and an absurdly long tail.

"We didn't get one in India," he reminded her. "Well, at least you'll be able to say we got one in Nepal."

Nati erupted with delight. She hugged the monkey, and then she hugged Yossi. Soon the three of them were on the motorcycle returning to Katmandu. If they hurried, Yossi told her, they would be in the city before sunset and the start of Yom Kippur. Nati, as happy as she could ever imagine being, held on to her husband all the way back.

At eight o'clock that evening in Israel, Dado had still not left his office, despite the holiday. His apprehensive mind kept mulling over whether he had done enough.

Should he mobilize the reserves? With the C Alert mechanism in place, if he pushed Golda to give the order *now,* the troops would be in the Golan by tomorrow afternoon. The Sinai deployments would take longer. But the regular army could move into Dovecote—a paratroop brigade airlifted into the strongholds, tanks sent to the firing points above the Suez Canal, additional artillery batteries rushed to the water line.

But was this really necessary? A full mobilization required a staggering expenditure. And what if it was a false alarm? Last spring's had cost $35 million, and the Treasury was still complaining about the expense. An unneeded call-up on the holiest day of the year would have other, even costlier consequences. It could bring down the government. This was not the time to act with rashness or on intuition.

On his desk was the assessment dated October 5 that Military Intelligence had distributed just before two this afternoon. It concluded:

"Though the mere taking of an emergency disposition in the Canal front allegedly implies the existence of warning indicators for an offensive initiative, to the best of our knowledge no change took place in the Egyptians' estimate of the balance of power between them and the IDF forces. Consequently, the probability that the Egyptians intend to renew fighting is low."

When the analysts looked to the north, they made a similar judgment:

"There is no change in our estimate that the Syrian moves are caused by fear, which even increased during the last day, of an Israeli action. The probability of a Syrian independent action (without Egypt) remains low."

And this afternoon before they left to join their families for the holiday, Zeira had addressed the GHQ officers at their final staff meeting. A coordinated attack by Egypt and Syria was, he said, "in low probability. Even lower than low."

Perhaps, the Chief of Staff began to think, issuing the C Alert had been unnecessary. This was Dado's hope as near 10 P.M. he at last left the office and, exhausted, went home.

In London, it was two hours earlier than in Israel, but at ten o'clock Zamir was still waiting. The olives were in a bowl on the living room table in the house in Mayfair. A fresh bottle of ouzo was opened. And the recorders were running. But the In-Law was uncharacteristically late.

Just before midnight, London time, the spy rang the front doorbell. The In-Law spoke to Zamir for about a hour, then he left.

As soon as he was gone, Zamir began condensing the agent's message into a short coded report; the details could follow in a cable in the morning.

When he was done, he called the embassy switchboard and asked an operator to place a call to Israel. She made the connection, but there was no answer on the other end.

No one will pick up, the operator insisted. It's a holiday.

Zamir ordered her to keep trying.

Finally, Freddy Einy answered. When he heard Zamir's voice, he grabbed a pencil. The coded message was only a few sentences. Translation took only minutes.

It was twenty to four on Yom Kippur morning, but he immediately placed a call to General Lior, the prime minister's military secretary.

"This evening," Freddy said, "they'll start firing." The Egyptians and Syrians, he explained, will attack simultaneously on both fronts at sunset.

TWENTY

Chief of Staff's Residence, Zahala/ 6 October 1973/0430

Yom Kippur, tradition has it, is a day when what is done can still be undone. It is a day of last chances. A person's fate has been determined, but it is not sealed. There remains the possibility of escape. But it is a fleeting promise; and, therefore, every moment is of great consequence. When the day ends, the judgment is final.

The day is lived with this solemn, fearful knowledge. In prayer, voices soar in resigned confirmation of the tenuousness of existence, and crack with the urgency of a final appeal. They chant:

> *On Rosh Hashanah their decree is inscribed, and on Yom Kippur it is sealed.*
> *How many shall pass away, and how many will be created . . .*

There was still time. That was Dado's first thought after his aide, Lt. Col. Aryeh Shalev, telephoned at 4:30 Yom Kippur morning with the Mossad agent's news: Egypt and Syria will launch a simultaneous attack at 6 P.M.

But that was not what the In-Law had reported. He had told Zamir the invasions would be launched at "sunset." The sun fell that day at 5:20 P.M. Freddy Einy, the Mossad bureau chief, had first passed Zamir's message to the staffs of both the prime minister and the minister of defense. Then Dayan's military secretary had called Shalev. And in the rapid series of tense predawn phone calls, a mistake had been made. An additional forty minutes had been granted. Six P.M.—1800 military time—became H-hour. But Israel did not have the power to give itself more time. In a day where every moment led to an irrevocable deadline, this error affected the choices the decision makers made, and the outcome of their endeavors.

But at 4:30, with seemingly an entire day stretching before him, the chief of staff felt liberated. War was now a certainty, and there was no longer any reason, military or political, for restraint. Plans had to be formulated, and it would not help to agonize over why he had been forced into this situation. With a commander's decisiveness, he swung into action.

Ten minutes later, shaved and in his uniform, he telephoned the home of the head of the air force, Benny Peled.

In the gravest of all the general staff's war scenarios, Israel had forty-eight hours' notice of an enemy attack. It would be sufficient to mobilize the reserves and deploy a reinforced standing army along its front line. In all the planning, however, the necessity for such a hurried, last-minute response was always viewed as improbable. The IDF counted on its having five to six days' notice to prepare for war. Today's reality was desperate beyond even any previous hypothetical: In thirteen hours war would break out *on both fronts.*

Dado was convinced that the only way to disrupt the enemy's attacks and for Israel to gain the time it needed to get its forces to the battlefields was for the air force to launch a preemptive strike.

Israeli jets must hit airfields and missile batteries inside Egypt and Syria even as the first calls went out to the reserves.

The air force's attack plans were ready, formulated and approved last June. Tagar (Challenge) outlined the attack on Egypt's antiaircraft and missile array along the Suez Canal. Dugman (Model) targeted the Syrian air defense layout between the Golan Heights and Damascus. Negiha (Butt) destroyed the Egyptian and Syrian airfields. Dado's first question to Peled was how quickly could the operations be launched.

By eleven o'clock, Peled answered confidently. It would take about an hour to destroy the Syrian air force. The SAM layout would require several additional hours. If there was still light, the jets would fly south to concentrate on the Canal defenses.

Dado asked much time did he have before the order for a preemptive strike needed to be given.

"Now," Peled said. "I must start preparing immediately."

The chief of staff knew that only the cabinet could authorize a first strike. But given the circumstances, he believed, their approval was simply a formality. "You have an order to make preparations to attack," he told Peled.

He hung up the phone and his wife, Talim, accompanied him to the door. The look on his face was grave yet focused and determined. In their long marriage, she had seen a similar expression only on rare occasions. And she knew without asking what the early morning calls meant: Her husband was going to war.

After a high-speed drive through the empty early morning streets of Tel Aviv, the chief of staff arrived at the Kirya to discover that Dayan did not share his sense of danger. Or his resolve.

"Even if it earns us a ticket to paradise," Dayan announced at the crowded 5:50 A.M. meeting in his office, he would not authorize a preemptive air strike.

Dayan did not want to anger the Americans. According to Zeira's latest information, the CIA was still not convinced that the Arabs planned to attack. And as long as the White House doubted the inevitability of war, Nixon and Kissinger would not condone a first strike by Israel. "Even if the Americans were one hundred percent sure," Dayan said, "they would say, 'So what? Let them fire the first shot!'" The prime minister, Dayan insisted, would also refuse to authorize a first strike. For her, the risk of losing the support of the United States was too great.

Dado was astounded. In less than twelve hours Israel would be in a war for which it was unprepared, and the minister of defense was worried about being rebuked by the White House. The future of the state, the lives of its soldiers and citizens, were at stake. In Dado's view, the air force gave Israel its best chance to lessen the sting of the initial invasions. Perhaps massive air attacks could even deter the Arabs. Yet Dayan would not allow a first strike for political reasons. It was absurd.

But rather than prolong an argument he knew he could not win, and aware that each moment was crucial, Dado moved on. He called for a general mobilization. The IDF's entire reserve fighting force—200,000 soldiers—must be called up immediately.

Once again, Dayan disagreed. "On the basis of messages from Zvika [Zamir] you do not mobilize a whole army."

Dado, ignoring the baiting tone, explained that he needed a maximum force to enter the battle. Already he was considering what it would take to win the war. He needed to be able to counterattack as quickly as possible. He wanted to destroy the Syrian army.

"The chief of staff wants to mobilize troops for a counterattack in a war that hasn't even begun?" Dayan taunted.

Dado struggled to keep his anger in check. He pleaded, one soldier to another. Finally, Dayan offered a compromise. There were only 177 tanks on the Golan and this, he agreed, was "not a setup for war." He would authorize the call-up of 20,000 to 30,000 men in the Armored Corps. With their arrival, the troops at the Golan front would be brought to divisional strength.

Dado pointed out that even if the armored division mobilized at once, it would not be in position near the Syrian border until the next morning. And the line would still be dangerously weak. To hold the two fronts, to defend against an invasion, would require an additional 50,000 to 60,000 soldiers.

And what about the rest of the war? he asked. "If the Arabs do attack today, we should be thinking about how we'll fare tomorrow morning. Tomorrow morning we will want to attack."

Dayan cut him off. He would consider "tomorrow" only when it was here. Mobilization for a counteroffensive would begin "only after the first shot."

Back and forth they went at one another. Dayan hard as cement, intransigent. Dado, his desperation almost tangible. The generals in the room witnessed this unique bargaining session with silent amazement. Meanwhile, the day moved on.

Finally, Dayan offered a new compromise. He wanted to present the prime minister with a joint proposal: Mobilize one division for the north, another for the south, and the entire air force. In total, about 50,000 to 60,000 men.

Dado argued that they'd need at least twice that number. But Dayan would not hear it. Eager to be done, he sent Brig. Yehoshua Raviv, his military secretary, to telephone the prime minister and obtain her approval for his compromise.

Raviv was unable to reach her. And so despite all the bargaining, the long, hard-fought meeting ended without a resolution. A decision was postponed until later that morning when they would meet with the prime minister.

Furious and despairing, Dado left. The enemy would attack in less than eleven hours. And Dayan was still not convinced there would even be a war.

As they waited for the prime minister to arrive from her home in northern Tel Aviv, Dayan instructed an assistant to find out what effect the mobilization of 100,000 reserve soldiers would have on Israel's economy.

Dado, meanwhile, held a war council. He met with the commanders of the Northern and Southern fronts to inform them war would break out at six o'clock. Afterward, General Hofi returned to the north, and General Gonen to the south. They would begin the tactical deployments according to the prearranged battle plans.

"Be seated. We haven't got much time," Yanosh ordered the Seventh Armored Brigade company commanders and their deputies. The room in the army's Nafekh Camp had holes for windows; no one had gotten around to putting in the glass and the October Golan chill swept through. It was nearly 10 A.M.

"Kahalani—what's the state of the tanks?"

"All are deployed under nets in my area."

"Good," Yanosh answered. "Now let's get down to business. Gentleman, war will start today."

Kahalani's first reaction was not to believe him. It would be like Yanosh to joke about something like that. He waited to hear his commander's hearty, irreverent bellow. But Yanosh remained grim and silent. Kahalani suddenly felt all the cold air drain out of the room; and fear rushed in to fill the vacuum.

Yanosh continued. "Yes, there will be war today, coordinated between Israel and Syria. We don't yet know the precise hour, but it will start this afternoon or evening. This is verified information from top sources."

Yanosh reeled off instructions: Check machine guns. Zero sights and adjust barrels. Stow ammunition. The men scribbled in their notebooks. As Kahalani wrote, the routine steadied him. It required all of his attention. Everything else receded. He was a soldier and he had a job to do.

Battalion commanders, Yanosh ordered as he ended the meeting, were to report back to him at two o'clock. He wanted an update on their preparations.

* * *

Six kilometers south of the Nafekh Camp, at a gloomy spot near the front called Hushniya, Shmuli Askarov leaned against his tank. Whatever burst of excitement he had felt when he first heard the news had passed. In its place was a newfound calm. The weight of all the wondering was gone. Now there was no choice. And he would do what had to be done. In his mind, it was that simple. They had told him nothing would happen before six o'clock, but he had already changed into his battle overalls. And he stayed close to his tank. There was always the possibility that the Syrians would move earlier than the generals in Tel Aviv expected. Someone should be ready.

In the Sinai, Amnon Reshef began Yom Kippur morning racked with guilt. Last night he had told the rabbi his men would not be able to attend the Kol Nidre services, which opened the sacred holiday.

"Amnon, is it worth it to break Yom Kippur with all this driving about? All this activity?" the rabbi had chastised.

"Ephraim," he had yelled, "There's going to be a war."

All night he had brooded about the exchange. He had raised his voice. He had called the rabbi by his first name. A week ago such conduct would have seemed impossible. He would have to apologize, and blame the disrespect on his nerves. The situation along the Suez Canal, the tremendous massing of Egyptian soldiers, tanks, and artillery, had left him more frayed than he had realized.

His apology would have to wait. That morning General Mandler had summoned his armored commanders to a meeting; he was determined not to leave for his new post until after the situation stabilized. In the midst of the meeting, at about 10:30 A.M., the general was called away. Gonen wanted to speak with him. Immediately.

The general hurried off, and there was a moment of unexpected quiet. Along with the other battalion commanders, Amnon focused on the single question running through his mind: What was so important that the head of the Southern Command needed to speak at once with his deputy on Yom Kippur? And like all the other men in the room, Amnon believed he already knew the answer.

Mandler returned fifteen minutes later. Full of the occasion, he announced that the Egyptian H-hour was today. At 6 P.M. But, the general went on to explain, according to General Gonen, it was not clear what was to happen. Was it simply the end of the Tahrir 41 exercise? A small skirmish? Or were the Egyptians launching an all-out war? But war, Gonen had emphasized, was only a remote possibility.

Amnon found his orders—"Avoid breaking routine activity until 1600"—even more surprising. He had assumed his ninety tanks supported by another armored brigade from the division would be sent immediately to their Dovecote firing positions along the waterline. Gordish, however, did not want to reveal to the Egyptians that his troops suspected an attack. Nor did he want the sight of his tanks rushing to the Canal to provoke an incident. He was convinced that if his armor began to deploy two hours before H-hour, they would have more than enough time to travel the eight kilometers to the Canal.

Further, Gordish had decided on his own to change the Dovecote formations. Only Amnon's brigade would move to the waterline. In this new plan, two brigades—not one—would be held in reserve. That way, the bulk of armor could be dispatched where they were needed.

The plan made sense, Amnon thought, but only if the enemy struck with a concentrated force in a single sector. A simultaneous invasion at several sites along the water would be disastrous. Reserve tanks would not be able to respond quickly enough to multiple breakthroughs along the Canal. By the time they arrived, the Egyptians would be dug in.

And the delay? Routine activity until nearly the last minute? Amnon believed it was imperative that his brigade be deployed as soon as possible. The enemy's most vulnerable moment was as they crossed the Canal. The Fourteenth Armored Brigade needed to be in position, locked and loaded on the ramps high above the Canal, ready to fire down on them.

But his tanks were still under their camouflage nets. A journey of even eight kilometers on tank treads through sand dunes and across the Sinai wadis could be problematic. He requested permission to move forward as soon as his men were ready.

"You are not to move. Period," Mandler told him. "You will deploy later this afternoon. There will be plenty of time."

Amnon hoped the general was correct. Just three tanks were garrisoned at the waterline firing positions. And they were grouped together, near the northern sector of the Bar-Lev Line. If anything happened before six o'clock, they would be the only armor along the Suez Canal. Three tanks to hold off an invasion.

Dado had no idea that Gonen had misinterpreted their briefing, revised the battle plan, and delayed its deployment. As the orders were given that sent the Sinai forces into a state of suspension, Dado was meeting in the prime minister's office. He found the unhurried, desultory pace maddening. It was as if he could hear each steady tick, each lost second, as the day moved toward sunset.

The mood, too, troubled him. Golda Meir and her staff acted as if they were already in mourning. In his warrior's world, the time for tears was when the fighting's over.

But, a soldier among politicians, all he could do was listen to the infuriating debate over whether it was too soon to evacuate thirty children from the Golan settlements. *What is there to discuss? Do it!* he wanted to shout. And Zeira made things worse. Although Egypt and Syria were technically ready to attack, the head of Military Intelligence reported, war was still not a certainty. Sadat knew that he would be defeated and therefore might hesitate at the last moment.

The chief of staff could not bear to hear any more hedging analyses. With the In-Law's warning, plans had to be made based on what the enemy had the strength to do. The time for analysis, for predictions, had passed.

Then—at last! Dado silently cheered—Dayan turned to the questions of a preemptive strike and whether to mobilize the reserves. "On the basis of the information we have now," Dayan said, an attack "is impossible. We cannot fire before they do." And he remained adamantly opposed to a general mobilization. The call-up of a division for the north, another in the south, and the entire air force would be enough manpower. "If fire starts, we'll mobilize the rest in the night. Otherwise, it would signal that we go for war."

When he finished, it was Dado's turn. He understood that he had to appeal directly to the prime minister. It was his last chance. As well as the nation's.

His words rushed out in a torrent. Even as Dado spoke, he appreciated that the tone, the emotion, was more like Dayan's than his own. But his logic was pragmatic. Rather than demand a general mobilization, he took Dayan's compromise figure, 50,000 to 60,000 soldiers, and used this as his starting point. Only now he argued for an increase to four armored divisions—a total of about 120,000 men. "If we don't mobilize on a large scale, I don't see how we can manage," he said, nearly pleading.

Dayan interrupted. He wanted to cut the total call-up of reserves to half, to his 60,000 figure.

Now Golda Meir intervened: "If war breaks out, better to be in proper shape to deal with it, even if the world gets angry at us."

Yet despite her own argument, she would not allow a first strike. Israel could not jeopardize its relations with the United States.

And so at 9:20 it was settled. Not the 250,000 men the chief of staff had originally wanted. But within minutes 120,000 men would be called to the front from their homes and synagogues.

Dado had no sense of triumph. He had done his best, yet he was not sure it was sufficient. H-hour was less than eight hours away.

At eleven o'clock the subterranean High Command post—the Pit, it was called—beneath the Kirya was operational. Updated maps of the Egyptian and Syrian fronts hung in the cavernous War Room, and officers were at their desks. Cigarette smoke swirled about in a thick gray haze. The silence was deliberate and anxious. Everyone waiting, wondering.

As Dado crossed the room, the minister of defense blocked his way. "What if the Arabs don't open fire?" he asked. "When will the reserves be released?"

"If it's really canceled, not just postponed for a day or two, we'll send the reserves home."

"But what will happen if at midnight it turns out there's no war?"

"The men won't be released for forty-eight hours," Dado reiterated.

"A hundred thousand men will hang around for a full day before they're sent home?" Dayan still could not believe the call-up was necessary. Or that war was imminent.

At one o'clock Shazly watched as President Sadat, accompanied by Minister of War Ismail, entered the Operations Room of Center Ten and took a seat on the dais. Sadat, wearing a military uniform, looked toward Shazly and read the tension etched in his chief of staff's face.

"Why aren't you smoking? Why isn't anyone having a drink of some kind? This operation requires your utmost attention and concentration." Sadat pointedly lit his cob pipe, and ordered tea for himself and for Shazly.

Shazly sipped the tea absently. He thought of his men waiting at the ramparts. He watched the row of clocks high on the wall opposite the dais. The hands did not appear to move. Time had stopped. He had been waiting since 1967, but now the delay was excruciating.

Then a voice from the air force command desk shouted out, "They're preparing for takeoff."

It was ten minutes to two.

In the Syrian operations bunker, President Assad sat by a phone, his hand resting on the receiver. A huge white clock hung on the wall. The generals stared at it: two o'clock.

The president's phone rang and Assad picked it up on the first ring. He listened for a moment, replaced the receiver without saying a word, and nodded toward General Talas.

A cheer went up. Then it was as if every phone started ringing at the same time. Activity charged through the room.

Golda Meir was meeting with her cabinet in her office in the Kirya. Sirens began to whine, but she talked over them. "If they don't start war by four-thirty, we can vote again. I would like to know the situation and if by four-thirty they start . . ." More sirens joined in, and she stopped.

"What is this?" she asked.

The cabinet's stenographer answered. "It seems that the war has begun."

"*Nor dos felt mir,*" the prime minister moaned in Yiddish. This is all I lack.

Kahalani was walking from his jeep, heading to the meeting with Yanosh, when he heard the whine of low-flying jets. He looked up to see four MiGs on a bombing run above the camp. He started to run toward a barracks, then dropped to the ground, and covered his head with his hands. The explosions were deafening. It was as if bomb after bomb were bursting right above him. He was stunned. Syrian jets bombing at will.

Yanosh ran out of his office. "To your tanks!"

Avigdor raced toward his jeep. The road out of the camp was clogged with vehicles, so he headed toward the chain-link fence, gunning the engine as he smashed through.

As soon as he heard the MiGs, Shmuli ran for his tank and, without breaking stride, called to his men. At that moment, he heard a terrifying, high-pitched boom. The Operations sergeant flew into the air. No, Shmuli realized, it was only the sergeant's head and torso. The man had been cut in half at the waist. The sergeant's legs, or what remained of them, were splayed on the ground. There was nothing to be done, so Shmuli kept running to his tank. But he thought: This is bad. A very bad omen.

Amnon heard the sirens, and then the ground started shaking. The Sinai Desert quaked under his feet as 2,000 Egyptian artillery pieces opened fire. The thunder was relentless. He hugged the ground and prayed. His tank was parked in its shelter, under its camouflage netting, its motor cold, six miles from the Suez Canal.

"Put it on the speakers," Brill ordered.

In the Operations Room everyone listened to the pounding bombs, the stuttering antiaircraft fire, the wail of sirens, the shouts of men as the Egyptian jets attacked the Bavel base in the Sinai.

Brill had predicted it all. But being right was no consolation. He stared at Ben Porat with hatred.

Without warning, Ben Porat hurled a book from his desk, then another. He knocked over a lamp. He sent a radar console crashing to the floor. A wild swing of his arm, and files and folders took flight.

The men stared at their commander. But no one tried to stop him.

Then Ben Porat began shaking. He dropped to his knees, and then started to crawl. But he could not stop shaking. Finally he lay down, stretched flat out, convulsing.

Someone yelled for a stretcher.

Brill watched silently as they carried his commander away. But there was no compassion, only an icy, hard anger.

"You're Israeli, right?"

Nati nodded to the hotel clerk in Katmandu. She had come down from the room to ask if he could recommend a place to eat. She wanted to break the Yom Kippur fast with a special meal.

"I just heard something on the BBC . . ." he said.

Nati raced up the stairs to find Yossi.

In London, the In-Law enjoyed the satisfaction that came with the successful completion of his long-running, complicated mission. He had been living by his wits for so long, juggling both sides, that he marveled that he had pulled it off.

Just two days ago, the Egyptian High Command had been convinced the sudden evacuation of the Soviets had wrecked any chance of surprise. They feared the awakened Israelis would attack before the invasions were launched. His mission had been to lull the enemy into believing they had more time.

And despite the rush to center stage in the living room in Mayfair without the usual preparations or rehearsals, his performance had pleased both audiences. He gave Egypt four more hours. And no less gratifying, the shrewd Israelis still did not suspect his motive. Or that from the beginning he had been sent to deceive them.

Part III

"THE DESTRUCTION OF THE THIRD TEMPLE"

Sinai/Golan Heights
October 6–9, 1973

. . . and who to an untimely end

TWENTY-ONE

Center Ten/6 October 1973/1400

At two o'clock, the Arab armies went to war. Egypt attacked from the south, and Syria from the north. The strategy on both fronts was to overwhelm the surprised enemy with colossal, disproportionate force.

Along the west bank of the Suez Canal Egypt had deployed five infantry divisions, two armored divisions, and three mechanized divisions with a total of about 100,000 men and 1,550 tanks. These forces were supported by 1,850 artillery pieces. Israel faced them along the 110-mile Bar-Lev Line with 436 soldiers and three tanks; another 277 tanks remained further back in the Sinai. Seventy artillery pieces were dispersed near the line.

In the Golan, the Syrians had three infantry divisions massed by the border, a total of 45,000 men and 540 tanks; directly behind them, second line armored brigades with an additional 960 tanks were ready for battle. Artillery consisted of 942 pieces. Israel had two infantry regiments, about 175 men, and 177 tanks in the region. There were eleven artillery batteries for support.

The Arabs attacked in wave after wave. Their onslaught was massive. Jets and artillery. Infantry and armor. The battles continued all day and through the night.

Shazly knew he was sending men off to risk their lives, but he could not help thinking, What a glorious moment! What a momentous day! After the humiliation of 1967, there would be honor. He sat on the dais in the Operations Room and as scurrying clerks updated the progress of the invading army on the glass screen that covered the huge map wall, it was as if he was there. In his mind, every terse telex, every battalion flag making its way across the map's absurdly sky blue Suez Canal water, was transformed into something vivid and significant.

At H-hour, as the plastic arrows signifying squadrons of planes moved west across his glass screen, Shazly streaked low and fast with the task force into Israeli territory. Two hundred twenty-two bombers blanketed the three enemy airfields in the Sinai, their Hawk surface-to-air missile batteries, command posts, and radar stations.

The artillery barrage began the moment the planes passed over the Canal. Concealed behind the sand ramparts, 1,850 Egyptian guns opened up in near unison on the Israeli forts. Mortars thudded. Howitzers hurled 96-pound shells. FROG-7 missile installations launched devastating 1,000-pound warheads. In the first terrifying minute alone, 10,500 shells fell on the Bar-Lev Line, 175 explosions every second. It did not stop. For fifty-three brutal minutes three tons of thunder crashed down on the strongholds along the east bank. Shazly tried to picture what it was like for the helpless enemy soldiers caught up in this sustained inferno: Doomsday, the very planet exploding into searing orange balls of fire.

But it was only prelude. Even as the artillery roared, as the Egyptian T-62 tanks on the ramps above the waterline aimed their long 115-mm cannons across the Canal, as commando teams scurried into position on the east bank, the order went out to send off Wave One. At 2:20, 4,000 infantrymen headed over the ramparts.

Throughout the summer Shazly had watched the rehearsals, and each time he left more impressed. Now that it was real, the crossing of the Suez Canal loomed in his mind as something magnificent, a work of art.

He saw rifles glittering in the high afternoon sun, as men swarmed down the steep dunes and flowed into the prearranged paths, 8,000 boots marching as one. All had been marked: The approach to each boat was numbered and color coded, and a corresponding luminous sign stood tall in the hull. The men had practiced so often that the trek to the waterline was mechanical. They stepped into the rubber boats as if going off for an afternoon's fishing. But now as the 720 dinghies shoved off and the men paddled furiously, each stroke a counterpoint to their war chant of "*Allahu-Akbar,*" as clouds of covering smoke drifted over them, it was as it had never been before. Training belonged to another lifetime. This was the moment they would have with them forever. Today they were making history.

Deep beneath the desert in Center Ten, tension built as they watched the boat markers progress across the map from west to east. Then as marker after marker was fixed on the enemy shore, cheers broke out. The first wave had landed! They had accomplished what the Zionists had said could never be done. Sadat and Ismail left to celebrate.

It was 2:45. Shazly, puzzled and disapproving, didn't dare leave. The operation was just beginning. As the boats recrossed the Suez Canal to pick up Wave Two, the engineering platoons ferried the German water pumps to the opposite shore. Seventy breeches, each one wide enough for a tank, had to be made in the sand ramparts over the next seven hours. Ten heavy bridges had to be assembled and stretched from shore to shore. Five infantry divisions waited to be moved across; the Second Army would deploy north of the Great Bitter Lake and the Third Army to its south. Armor, artillery, and mobile SAM-6 missiles would follow. In the morning, men and equipment would still be pouring into the newly established bridgeheads.

He stopped before he got too far ahead of himself. A life spent fighting against the Jews had taught him about the resilience of the enemy, and the mercurial fortunes of war. He focused on what had to be accomplished now. If the first wave did not succeed, the Zionists would reclaim the front line, and repel the invasion.

So he was with the infantry assault teams as they jumped from their boats and raced, under fire, to the shore. He pictured the scene: swaying ladders dangling from the pale artificial cliffs for miles and thousands of men in gray uniforms, climbing hand over hand up to the summit. It was if they were storming a castle. But Shazly knew these assault teams had no interest in the Bar-Lev forts; the strongholds, what was left of them after the artillery pounding, would be dealt with later. Instead, the troops charged through the wide, undefended stretches of land that lay between the fortifications. There would be no resistance as they headed into the desert.

Yet as the initial confirmations came into Center Ten, as teams raced to their assigned positions, another report arrived. Clouds of dust had been sighted deep in the Sinai, moving toward the waterline. Enemy tanks were charging to their firing positions.

The real fight would soon begin. Shazly could only hope his men had found hiding places. That they were pressed flat behind arcing sand berms or crouched in the steep crevices of the wadis. And that they were already taking the heavy hexagon-shaped cases they had lugged like knapsacks from their backs, and were clicking open the metal latches.

Through the echoing thunder of artillery fire, Amnon Reshef's tank rushed across the desert to the Canal. "Move it," he shouted to the driver. "Move it!" The enemy was on Israeli soil. If he could get his tanks to their firing ramps above the waterline, he could drive them away. Bridges across the Canal were not in place, and the Egyptian armor remained on the other shore. There still was time to hold off the main invasion and pray for reinforcements. But he had to get there fast.

As the tank raced on, he received frantic reports from Command. In his central sector, two major crossings were taking place. He got on the brigade network and, deciding quickly, split his force to into three thrusts. When they reached Artillery Road that paralleled the Canal, one tank company would swing north toward Firdan, another south to the other crossing site near Ismailia. His company would defend the Hizayon stronghold near the northern crossing site.

The news from the fort was desperate. The bombardment had taken the men by surprise. Many were dead, others badly wounded. And the few who fired machine guns out of their shooting holes saw the Canal blanketed with black boats. Their pleas for help screamed over the radio: "Egyptians are putting in boats directly below us . . . they're crossing now . . . full of crowds of infantry. . . . More boats crossing . . . they're fanning out in our area. . . . Egyptian infantry is all around us. Send reinforcements and help extricate us. . . ." Amnon was determined to rescue these men.

As he neared the water, he tried to remain calm, to rein in his anger. There was no point in raging about the foolishness of the orders that had kept his tanks parked back in the desert or that manned the forts with a token force of poorly trained reserves. The time for recriminations would come. Now he had fifty-six tanks under his direct command, and they had to stop the invasion.

He crested a long rise, standing tall in his turret, the way Israeli tank commanders went into battle. From this vantage point he could begin to see out across the water. There were boats everywhere and soldiers running from the cliffs, a spreading swarm of gray uniforms. "Oh, my God," he said. Then he thought: The men in the forts, the nation, were not counting on God, but on me. He ordered the company to proceed at full speed to the firing position adjacent to the stronghold.

* * *

Through the V-shaped viewfinders, the Egyptian soldiers hiding in the sand watched the tanks approach. They had worked quickly. From their suitcases, they had removed the two-foot-long Soviet Sagger missile from its compartment and attached the fins. The two halves of the case became platforms, one for launching, the other for guidance. Within minutes, the rocket, with its high-explosive warhead, lay horizontally in its cradle, ready to fire.

Hands gripped the joysticks that controlled the guidance system, as the soldiers tracked the tanks' progress. The faces of the officers standing in the turrets grew distinct. Still the Egyptians waited. If the enemy suspected anything, the first clue would be a tank's machine gun swinging toward them. The next would be a hail of 7.62-mm bullets ripping through the wadi. Excitement and anxiety charged through them. Yet they were patient, disciplined. They let the tanks approach, until they were about a quarter mile away. They could hear the treads grinding over the sand and the rumble of the heavy engines. When the long cannons seemed to be pointed directly into their hiding places, they fired.

The missiles leaped from their launchers, speeding toward their targets at 450 feet per second.

The percussive whoosh of the rocket launchings alerted the Israelis. The tanks accelerated, hoping to outrun the missiles. Machine guns firing, they charged toward the Egyptians.

But the exposed soldiers stood their ground. Fine electrical wires ran from the missile chassis to the guidance platform, and the soldiers needed to "gather" the Sagger to its target. Under fire, steeled with a sense of mission, they directed the missile with the joystick. Either the tank would be stopped, or fifty tons of steel would grind them into the sand.

Amnon's two lead tanks exploded into flames. As dozens of men in gray uniforms rose from the desert, he realized the enemy had been waiting by the ramps the whole time. They had been ambushed.

And in that same horrifying instant he saw a dense, whining flock of Saggers speeding toward him. The Egyptians had used the weapon in the War of Attrition and he had seen what the rockets could do: They'd cut through the armor of a Centurion tank and ignite a 1,000-degree blast. A crew would be incinerated in a swirling fireball.

Amnon sprayed the wadi with the turret-mounted machine gun. He was firing wildly, full of fury. Over the rattle of the bullets he heard the explosive thump of RPGs—rocket-propelled grenades—landing all around him. The Saggers closed in, too. His company was pinned in a cross fire. Another tank was hit, and its hydraulic fuel ignited. Flaming pillars geysered into the desert sky. In minutes, he had lost five tanks and their crews.

"Get out of here!" Amnon yelled to the driver. "Now!"

He couldn't get to his firing position. He couldn't reach the stronghold. Now all he could do was pull back from the Canal, and hope to find another approach to the waterline.

As he retreated, frantic messages crossed the battalion net. Near Ismailia four tanks were killed. The entire force he had sent to Firdan was wiped out.

His voice hoarse from shouting to his men over the explosions, Amnon radioed Southern Command and pleaded, "Where is the air support? I need air support. I'm by myself out here facing the entire Egyptian army."

That afternoon as the first flurry of reports came into the Pit, the chief of staff was also wondering what had happened to the air force. Earlier in the day Dado had ordered Benny Peled to prepare for a preemptive strike. Yet the planes, incredibly, were still not ready for war on the Sinai front. But then again, just four hours ago the probability of war was "less than low" or "almost zero."

Finally, at four o'clock Israeli jets took off. They came in over the dunes, saw the ground level off beneath them, and crossed over the Suez Canal. It was a hasty, thrown-together mission. There were no assignments, no attack coordinates. The orders were to acquire targets visually, and open fire.

The SAM-6s slammed into the jets as soon as they neared the west bank. There was no warning. The electronic counter measure pods on the jets' underbelly were not tuned to the SAM-6 signal. The pilots never heard the shrill "Sam Song" that usually sounded in the cockpit when the ground radar locked on. Their only hope was to spot the puff of white smoke that signaled a missile launch. With the rocket's heat-seeking sensors relentlessly homing in on the exhaust from the jet's engines, the pilots had forty-two seconds before impact. Forty-two seconds to twist and turn frantically, to climb and dive across the sky. Twelve Phantoms were shot down before the mission was scrapped.

The air force would concentrate for now on intercepting enemy planes and helicopters flying into the Sinai beyond the missile umbrella. But at dawn tomorrow, the IAF squadrons would return. After a night of careful preparation, they would try again to destroy the missile batteries.

In Shazly's subterranean room, there was only artificial light, but at 5:30 P.M. he could imagine dusk beginning to shade the Sinai. The daylight phase of the invasion had been a complete success. In three hours, five reinforced infantry divisions—30,000 men and 2,000 officers—had crossed the Canal. Each division now controlled a bridgehead that ran five miles along the waterline and stretched in a semicircle between two to two and a half miles deep into the Sinai. Egyptian flags few above the fallen Bar-Lev forts. Casualties were minimal—about two hundred men. A day ago, he had expected thousands.

In the last shadows of daylight, the engineering battalions began assembling the sections of the prefabricated pontoon bridges bobbing in the water. The high-powered hoses continued to blast away at the enemy sand barriers. It was all going according to his plan.

But Shazly knew that enemy jets could return at any moment.

And certainly would the next morning. Before first light, the bridges had to be in place, and passages cut through the sand barriers. Until then, his infantry was in enemy territory without armored support, heavy artillery, or mobile SAM batteries. If the Zionist reserves arrived and they counterattacked swiftly, all could be lost. Everything depended on how quickly weapons and equipment could reach his men. Tonight would be crucial; and then if all went well, there would be more battles to fight.

His eyes settled on the large map of the Golan Heights across the room. The war was going well there, too. He silently urged the Syrians to continue to push forward, to apply even more pressure on the Jews. He wanted Israel to feel besieged, for its leaders to divert men and planes from the Sinai to the north. It would make his tasks easier. He prayed for Syria's success.

TWENTY-TWO

Mount Hermon, Golan/ 6 October 1973/1445

Gazing out from the top of Mount Hermon, a height of 6,600 feet, the view was often dazzling: the roofs of Haifa spread in a multicolored patchwork to the west, and the minarets of Damascus rose to the east. But by 2:45 on Yom Kippur afternoon it was impossible to see more than an arm's length. The smoke from the Syrian artillery barrage poured out as if from a furnace and swallowed up the panorama.

Wedged into the mountain's crest was the target: Mutzav 104, the code name of an Israeli top secret electronic listening post. Using advanced eavesdropping equipment supplied by the U.S. National Security Agency, a team of about thirty intelligence specialists from Brill's unit 848 pulled vast quantities of information out of Syria. If President Assad sneezed, a signit operator in the Mount Hermon post would be the first to say "gesundheit," or at least that was the confident belief in Tel Aviv, as well as in Washington.

The Syrian barrage continued, yet the men in the post were not alarmed. The boxy, concrete fortification had been designed to stand up to howitzers and aerial bombardment. The young lieutenant in charge of the thirteen soldiers assigned to protect the installation and its Aman specialists sent a routine telex to the Northern Command: Heavy shelling, but situation under control. Will repair damage to aerials soon as guns stop.

But at 2:55 four MI-8 helicopters dropped teams of Syrian commandos near a ski lift about a mile away. The commandos advanced toward the post in two columns.

Armed with Uzis, the Israelis barricaded themselves behind the fortress's heavy steel doors. For several hours, they held off the attack. Explosives finally blew down the doors, and hundreds of Syrians poured in. The firefight in the narrow, winding corridors was swift and murderous. Syria now controlled Mount Hermon. Its troops quickly went to work gathering up its great treasure: rooms crammed with America's most ingenious and secret electronic intelligence equipment. Gleeful Russian technicians would soon arrive to inspect the plunder.

By four o'clock the clouds of artillery smoke had floated away. The view to the border revealed column after column of Syrian tanks driving into Israel as if on parade. The Syrian armor attacked in two formidable thrusts, dividing the Golan along the central Nafekh Road.

General Hofi's Northern Command had been reinforced in recent weeks, but like the Sinai front, it was unprepared for such a powerful invasion. "I never knew there were so many tanks in the world," one stunned tank commander said as he stared at the long, dark river of enemy armor. Bunkers all along the Purple Line besieged Command headquarters in Nafekh with urgent calls for help. It was chaos.

At 2:45, just forty-five minutes after bombers flew unchallenged over his base, as ferocious artillery blasts exploded along the border, and tanks smashed through the chain-link fence, forded antitank ditches and entered Israel, Hofi formulated a strategy to deal with the invasion. The shortest route into Israel's farms and cities went through the town of Kuneitra and across the Bnot Ya'akov Bridge, so the general decided the enemy's main push would be in the north. He ordered Col. Yanosh Ben Gal to rush the three battalions of the Seventh Armored Brigade, 101 tanks, to the hilly triangle between Kuneitra and the mountains. The weaker 188th Barak Brigade, 76 tanks under the command of Col. Yitzhak Ben Shoham, would deploy around Rafid. They would defend the open plateaus of the southern sector.

Shells passing over his tank, the enormous sounds of war bursting all around him, Maj. Shmuli Askarov hurried in the late afternoon sun from the Hushniya base to the front. He led a platoon of three Centurions, and they were to join up with another armored platoon from the Barak Brigade already near Bunker 111. Heavy artillery fire poured down on this fortification protecting the southern Kudne Road, and the initial agitated reports indicated that Syrian tanks were moving forward under its cover.

The barrage was still intense when Shumli reached the bunker, and the dark, wafting smoke obscured his view to the border. Reports on the intercom net, however, were encouraging. The line here was holding; and, more, there were no signs the enemy intended to challenge it. A few Syrian T-55s had made tentative thrusts through the smoke, but the three tanks deployed around the bunker had been brutal. Shooting from long range, they had scored four kills. "Scared them off," a lieutenant bragged over the net. "Except for the artillery, nothing's happening here. War will be over by sunset."

Shmuli hoped this was true. Meanwhile, his tanks were exposed on flat ground in a stationary line. He ordered his two platoons to mount the tank ramps surrounding the bunker. From the top of these five-foot-tall gradients, his 105-mm cannons would be able to fire down on the Syrians if they crossed the valley to attack the bunker. The risk was that parked atop the ramps, his tanks would be unprotected targets. But he was confident in his gunners. Seven Centurions firing high-explosive antitank rounds in rapid succession could drive back a company, or more, of enemy tanks.

Soon the artillery subsided, and from the top of the ramp Shmuli could begin to look out across the valley. The thick smoke had dissipated into a gray haze. Eyes straining through his binoculars, he spotted a large mass of indistinct forms in the distance. Supply trucks? he hoped. Armed personnel carriers, perhaps? Then a sudden gust of wind cleared the air. And he saw the valley was filled with tanks. An entire Syrian armored brigade, at least 100 tanks, was about two miles away and moving toward him.

In that awful and hopeless moment Shmuli realized that Hofi was wrong. Syria's main thrust was not coming through the north, but through Kudne in the south. They planned to outflank the Israeli defenses, penetrate through the level Rafid Gap, then make the seventeen-mile dash to the roads that led deep into the nation.

He had to stop them. With seven tanks.

In the north, moments after the jets attacked, Col. Avigdor Kahalani's jeep sped out of the Nafekh Camp. His was the only vehicle on the road and he knew he'd make an easy target. But there was nothing to be done about that. The thought of his battalion going into combat without him forced aside all his fears. Driving wildly, he yelled into the radio mike, "All policemen, this is the battalion commander. Stand by to move."

Not until his jeep pulled alongside his Centurion parked at the Nafekh crossroads and he leaped up to the turret did his mood steady. He was with his men, ready to go to war.

The radio bristled: "Yanosh stations—this is Yanosh."

"Kahalani here. In place at the crossroads. Deployed and ready to move."

"Stay there, ready to move."

Kahalani waited. When an hour passed and he had not received his orders, he finally turned off the engines. There was no point in wasting fuel. Artillery shells landed nearby. But he had still not seen the enemy. Perhaps this wasn't a full-scale invasion. Maybe it was only a raid. He continued looking east, but saw nothing coming. So he waited. Where's the war? he asked himself.

From his position on top of the ramp, Shmuli looked out over the valley. Six Syrian T-55s had begun to drag portable bridges over the five-meter-wide antitank ditch that ran parallel to the border. They worked slowly, but expertly; the operation had been well rehearsed. The massive tank force stood farther back, their idling engines a grinding, impatient roar. Once the bridges were secured, they would move.

Shmuli sighted his targets. He would work left to right down the line. He instructed the other six tanks to work in the opposite direction. His force had the high ground, and with good marksmanship they could hold off the fording operation for a while. Tomorrow the reserves would come. He tried to convince himself it was that simple.

He picked his first target and passed the information to his gunner. The turret swiveled toward the enemy tank. The mechanical range finder judged the distance, and simultaneously factored in the slight side winds blowing across the valley.

"Target acquired," Yitzhak Hemo, the gunner, announced.

"Fire at will."

The gunner pulled the twin triggers. The tank jolted, the breech kicked back, and an armor-piercing shell shot out of the 105-mm cannon. Traveling down the valley, the sabot flew off the speeding shell. A bright tracer, the tanker's "silver bullet," illuminated the path of the sharp, penetrating tip as it continued streaking downrange.

The moment of impact was surprisingly quiet, like the solid thud of a well-thrown punch. Then the turret of the Syrian tank caught fire. The shell had hit the diesel fuel line that ran around the base of the turret and the flames spread quickly. All at once a spectacular explosion erupted.

Shmuli, however, did not pause to admire his kill. On his command, the gunner moved to the next target. Firing rapidly, he scored another hit. This time there was no explosion. The T-55 simply sat immobilized, like a large wounded beast.

Shmuli saw tanks dragging bridges move up to take the place of the two that had been hit. Awakened, the mass of Syrian tanks began shooting toward his position. But they were firing from long range, and were too far off to be effective.

Soon Shmuli knew the tanks would be rolling out. Streaming into Israel. He had no hope of holding them back. But he did not know what else to do, so he chose one target after another.

He worked rapidly, too quickly to think about what he was doing. A routine took hold: Acquire target. Aim. Fire. He kept at it, sending off round after round. Then gradually, despite his absorbed state, it came to him that he was alone. His other tanks were not shooting.

Had they been hit? He turned toward his force and saw they were not on top of the firing ramps. His six tanks were parked behind them—hiding.

He screamed over the radio net: "This is war. Get on the ramps."

After a moment, an officer explained that his cannon was not working.

"Reverse," Shmuli ordered his driver. The tank backed down the ramp, and stopped alongside the Centurion that claimed to have a faulty cannon.

Across the valley, the Syrian brigade had begun its advance. The first companies crossed over the ditch and their guns found their range. Shells rained down, a steady, lethal torrent falling about the ramps. Oblivious to the danger, Shmuli jumped down from the turret and ran to the nearby Centurion.

He climbed up and stood very close to the tank commander. He did not speak. He stared fiercely, as if still undecided about what he had to do. Then Shmuli drew his revolver and placed it against the man's temple. When Shmuli spoke, his words were measured, full of the perfect calm of resigned anger.

"You join me," he said. "Or I shoot."

Those were the only choices. No discussion, no debate. As a child, Shmuli had been raised on stories of hard-pressed Israeli soldiers fighting against impossible odds to protect the state. Now a man, he had inherited those same responsibilities. But he fought out of a spiritual duty, too. A binding covenant had led him to this battlefield.

At the same time, he understood the man's fear. Shmuli, too, was terrified. Yet he accepted what was about to happen. He knew they would all die today.

A moment passed. Then the tank commander slowly nodded. With great relief, Shmuli holstered his gun.

Within minutes seven tanks were atop the ramps and firing down at the Syrians. The Barak Brigade gunners were expert, and they hit dozens of Syrian tanks as they crossed into Israel. But there were too many of them. They couldn't stop them all.

Suddenly, Shmuli's tank buckled, and he was thrown hard to his knees. His entire body shook from the force of the unseen blow.

"We took one in the hull," his driver shouted. But the shell had not pierced the tank's armor, and the Centurion was still operational. Very slowly, Shmuli managed to stand. And as he got to his feet, he heard a tremendous explosion.

The tank to his right was on fire. Draped over the lip of the turret, laying inert was the tank commander he had forced into battle. Bright flames danced over the man with a consuming fury. It was a vision that might have been pulled from a biblical Hell.

A nearby Centurion backed down its ramp and hurried over to rescue the men. But as the tank pulled alongside, it, too, was hit. It ignited in a terrible whoosh and instantly was transformed into a vicious ball of fire. Then the tank exploded.

The stench of burning flesh and diesel fuel bit at Shmuli's nostrils. Awful screams reverberated in his ears. All he could do was watch them die. He had been prepared for his own death, but he was not ready for all the other deaths he would have to face. It took all his discipline to keep his mind from running to a desperate, forlorn place.

At last, he got on the intercom and ordered the five remaining tanks to prepare to deploy on the ground. When the charge came, they would form a line and hold off the enemy. The fight, he assured them, was not over.

He spoke confidently, but he knew his words were unreasonable. There were too many enemy tanks. All they could do was fight with honor. And that, he consoled himself, was not the worst way to die.

"Brigade commander to Kahalani. Start moving east. Over."

"Where to? Over."

"Move to take position on the ridges north of Kuneitra facing east. A large Syrian task force is approaching the town."

Late in the afternoon, endless hours it seemed after the jets had strafed the camp, Kahalani and his tank force finally rolled off to face the enemy. The quickest route was through Kuneitra, but he decided not to lead his battalion into the northern town. A Syrian bazooka team could be crouched on a rooftop or hiding in a doorway. Cripple the lead tank, and the whole column would be strung out on a narrow street, easy targets. Instead, the battalion crossed the fields of Kibbutz Merlon Golan. Wherever Kahalani looked he saw deep craters gouged out of the farmland by the afternoon's incessant shelling. The clawed, ripped earth affected him beyond any actual damage that had been done. It connected him directly to his own home, his own family. "We are going off to defend our nation," he told the men over the intercom. "We will protect Israel."

In the evening's first shadows, Kahalani deployed his tanks on top of Booster Ridge. He knew the position well, having scouted it days ago with Yanosh. In his mind was a map of its *tel*s and its ravines. The ramps were arranged too close together to suit him, but if the tanks had to come down from the firing positions, there were plenty of places to hide. It was not the worst ground to make a stand.

As darkness spread over the ridge, his tanks mounted the ramps. To the east, Kahalani saw pillars of dust moving toward him.

"Keep moving," Shmuli ordered his driver. "Back and forth. Fast."

Darkness blurred his position, and his plan was to kick up sand, to try to convince the enemy that reinforcements had arrived. After nearly five hours of constant fighting, he now commanded only two tanks. Between them, sixty-nine antitank rounds remained. His tank had been hit four times, and he did not doubt they'd find him again. He could only hope that the next shell would not be the crippling one.

It had been an odd battle. He was alive, an exhausted Shmuli realized, because the Syrians were more intent on plunging through the Rafid Gap than in pausing to deal with the small annoyance on the ridge. All afternoon and into the evening, he had taken ruthless advantage of their strategy. Shooting from the high ground, he had knocked out, by his own count, thirty-five tanks, as well as six armored personnel carriers loaded with infantry. Yet the Syrian invading force swerved around the crippled, burning vehicles and continued on. Occasionally they'd fire toward his position, but they did not charge. They rolled on, steady columns of tanks determined to outflank the Israeli line before the day ended. To his surprise, he found himself admiring their discipline and courage under fire. But he also knew his time would come. Once the main force reached Rafid-El Al Road, they would deal with him.

At 7 P.M. Shmuli watched as two companies, about twenty tanks, detached themselves from the columns moving on to Kudne. They proceeded slowly, but without hesitation. The force ignored the bunker and split into two wings. One circled to the east, the other to the west. Both headed up the rise, preparing to converge on the ramps in a classic pincer movement. And Shmuli understood his time had come.

* * *

As evening fell in Tel Aviv, the shofar sounded in synagogues through the city and the fateful Yom Kippur holiday ended. The outbreak of the war had been a shock, but as people returned to their homes they felt certain the situation would be quickly normalized. A battle against the Arabs could hold no unexpected outcome. Today would play out as the seventh day of the Six Day War.

The prime minister reinforced this confidence in her evening television and radio address to the nation. In a firm, unwavering voice, she announced: "Citizens of Israel, at around two o'clock today the armies of Egypt and Syria launched an offensive against Israel. . . . The IDF is fighting back and repulsing the attack. The enemy has suffered serious losses. They hoped to surprise the citizens of Israel. . . . But we were not surprised. . . . Our forces were deployed as necessary to meet the danger. We have no doubt about our victory. . . ."

Later that evening Moshe Dayan faced the television cameras and offered another reassuring assessment: "In the Golan Heights, perhaps a number of Syrian tanks penetrated across our line and perhaps they have achieved here and there some occupation, but no significant occupation. . . . The situation in the Golan Heights is relatively satisfactory. . . . In Sinai, on the Canal, there were many more Egyptian forces and the problem there is different altogether. . . ."

But surging with emotion, the minister of defense promised: "We should know that this is war and we are prepared for the transition period, which is relatively short and then to rely on our forces . . . so that the Egyptian action of crossing the Canal will end as a very, very dangerous adventure for them. . . ."

And in a ten o'clock formal meeting in the Kirya's long conference room, the windows blackened in case of an air attack, the chief of staff revealed to the cabinet the plans for the days ahead. The Syrian assaults, he said, had already been halted. And by tomorrow morning another Israeli armored brigade would reach the Golan. There would be a total of 450 tanks in the north, and they would push the enemy out of Israel. As for the Sinai, the IDF would go on the offensive in two days. Within the week, he predicted, the Egyptians would be driven back across the Suez Canal.

But oblivious to the hard words and wishful strategies, the enemy went ahead with its own plans. The long day's fighting was not over on either front.

TWENTY-THREE

Booster Ridge, Golan/ 6 October 1973/ 2245

Waiting in the darkness, Kahalani heard the Syrian tanks coming. The enemy was rumbling toward him, driving closer and closer. But the night was impenetrable and he could not see them. Heavy, pregnant sounds filled each new tense moment: the hum of motors, the grinding of treads against the volcanic rock. The wait was excruciating.

Worst of all, he knew the Syrians could see him. Their T-55s were equipped with infrared targeting systems. Unlike the Centurions, they could maneuver in the dark. They'd be on top on him, and he wouldn't know it until an enemy shell struck his tank like a lightning bolt.

All he had was a pair of night vision binoculars. Nearly useless, they revealed only a vague, ghostly glow from the enemy's infrared devices. Looking through them was like looking at an object submerged in a pool of murky water. At best, they'd suggest the general direction a T-55 was heading. His gunners required more precise information.

He got on the net to Yanosh: "Enemy tanks facing and moving toward us. Can't estimate the number. They're using I.A. [infrared] and I don't have to tell you our limitations. I must have illumination."

"There are no phosphorus shells at the moment. I hope there will be in half an hour. Meanwhile, use your searchlights."

Searchlights? That would be death. The twin beams of light would be a beacon to the enemy. Hiding in the darkness, they'd target his tanks and fire at will.

There was no choice, but to fight blind. He tried to anticipate what he would do if he were the enemy. He swung his gun in the direction he expected the Syrians to approach. And waited.

In time, a white moon rose in the night sky, full and gorgeous. Its glow gave him some comfort. He looked downrange, and in the moonlight he saw houses that had been abandoned after the last war. Beyond them stood a broad, dome-shaped clump of bushes. He saw a sudden movement in the bushes, and his hands tensed on the machine gun. Infantry? A tank? The wind? He kept watching, but there was nothing more.

His radio broke the silence. Yanosh to all stations: "The Syrians have breeched the antitank ditch. They're working their way to the battalion's positions."

Far off in the night, the deep, distinctive blasts of T-55 cannons interrupted the report. Then Kahalani saw the flames. Bold streaks of color rose up in the darkness. He tried to determine where on the ridge they were coming from, but it was impossible. The darkness was too thick. His force had been spread out for miles around the sector, and there were large gaps between the positions. He could not tell who had been hit, or how badly.

News arrived quickly. Three men were wounded and were now being evacuated. But Amir Bashari was dead. The enemy had snuck up on his tank. Without warning, a T-55 shell had hit the command cupola and killed him instantly. He was the first battalion casualty. Kahalani remembered how days ago Amir had asked when they would stop shooting at barrels.

Blinded and helpless in the dark, Amir and his men had now become the barrels. Who would be next?

Kahalani ordered his tanks to shut down their engines. If they had to redeploy or even retreat, they'd lose crucial minutes. But the enemy's T-55 diesel engines gave off a distinctive low, sputtering moan. Perhaps his men would hear them coming before they heard the report of the enemy's cannons. It was a small strategy, a gesture as much as a plan, but there was little else he could do. On his command, the engines went dead. A fresh, new quiet spread across the ridge. Alert in the moonlit darkness, Kahalani listened to every night sound, sifting through them, waiting.

There was no night or day in Center Ten, only the constant, artificial high noon of electric light. So when the news arrived that the first bridge was open, Shazly found himself looking immediately at the clock: 2230. And then he knew: *We won the first round.*

Shazly mentally congratulated the teams of exhausted engineers. The initial triumph, he knew, was largely theirs. For four steady hours they had attacked the sand barriers with their water cannons. At the start, a disturbing report had come in from the southern part of the Suez Canal. The high-pressured jets of water had unexpectedly turned the sand in that sector to an oozing, belligerent mud that was impossible to clear. When he heard that, Shazly despaired. What if it was that way all along the Canal? But he kept his fears to himself and, instead, gave the order to stop the work in the south. They'd carve sixty passages rather than the seventy he had originally planned. Fortunately, when the engineers went back to work, there were no further problems.

Two hours after the breeches had been opened, the engineering teams assembled the bridges and squads of frogmen guided them across the water. The first bridge had been jockeyed into place. The invasion, *his* great plan, a restoration of Arab honor, was moving ahead of even the most optimistic schedule. It was still early in the war, but his heart was beating quickly and he felt an immense satisfaction.

Already Shazly was receiving reports that tanks were moving down to the water's edge. The pontoons would soon be reverberating with the heavy clatter of the first wave of armor—200 of the formidable T-62 tanks—crossing the Canal and into the Sinai. In two hours all the bridges would be operational; the eight heavy-duty Russian PMPs, and four lighter ones. And by early Sunday morning 800 tanks and 3,000 pieces of equipment—APCs, artillery, SAM-6s—would have reached his bridgeheads.

Then his troops would attack. Just when the beleaguered enemy least expected it. In the last hours of darkness, before the new dawn, they'd drive back what was left of the Zionist armored formations until the Egyptian bridgeheads were entrenched five miles deep in the Sinai. The enemy would never get them out.

"Fire!" Shmuli ordered his gunner. The encirclement had begun. The Syrian tanks were coming at him from all directions. If they flanked him, he was finished. He tried to keep moving even as he shot off another round.

His Centurion bucked as the cannon roared. A tank fifty meters away burst into flames. He was close enough to feel the heat. And in the light of the burning tank, he saw another tank charging at him from the right. It was thirty meters off and closing in. At that range, he could sense the barrel of its big gun pointed directly in his face.

He swung the turret toward the enemy, and yelled to his gunner, "Now! Now!" The two tanks fired simultaneously.

The force of the explosion blew Shmuli out of the turret, launching him high into the air. He landed on the ground far from his flaming tank and lay there without moving.

He was still unconscious when the Israeli soldiers from the bunker reached him. His face and chest were covered in blood. After six hours of fighting, Shmuli's seven tanks were destroyed. The Syrians moved on.

*   *   *

Kahalani searched the ridge with his night vision binoculars and he saw the shining eyes of a beast of prey. A pair of infrared lights stared back at him.

He ordered his gunner to load a HEAT shell.

"Direction? What range?"

Kahalani made his best guess. The gunner fired and Kahalani hoped that the explosion would at least chase the Syrian away. But when he looked again through his binoculars, he saw that the tank had held its position. And that was when he realized its infrared beams were targeting him. The enemy tank was locked on his silhouette, about to fire.

"Back up! Quickly! Move!"

The engine roared to life, and the tank reversed, just as the T-55 fired. When the shell landed, Kahalani's Centurion was at the bottom of a hill.

He had escaped, but now he knew the enemy had infiltrated his position. If one was on top of him, how many others were out there? He looked around, and in the darkness saw only a red lamp glowing on one of his tanks.

"Yair and Emmy, there's a rear or brake light burning on one of your tanks. Douse it immediately."

The tank commanders insisted their lights were extinguished. But Kahalani still saw the red glow.

It could be someone from his battalion. Or it could be a Syrian tank targeting them this very moment. And they would not even know it.

He had his gunner load a shell, then instructed one of his tank commanders to fire a machine gun burst in the air above the red lamp. As the tracers burned a small, bright comma in the night sky, he saw a T-55. It was nearly close enough to touch.

"Fire!"

The shell flashed out of the cannon, and then the Syrian tank burst into flames. The raging fire was as effective as a barrage of phosphorus shells. For the first time in hours, Kahalani could see around him: Intruders were everywhere. The hulking machines had crept in undetected like a pack of evil night animals. But now the ridge was illuminated and in the unnatural glow they were revealed. The enemy had spread across the terrain, interspersed among his tanks.

"Rapid fire," he screamed. "At the discretion of each tank commander."

Cannons fired. Two more Syrians T-55s burned. Others reversed, eager to escape. Shells and machine gun rounds chased them. Kahalani heard a thud as one of his tanks was hit. "We're okay. We're okay," the commander reported on the net. "No real damage." In the fierce light of the burning tanks, Kahalani saw the commander standing tall in his turret, blasting away with his machine gun. My brave men, Kahalani thought with pride.

Finally, Kahalani told his tanks to hold their fire. There was no point in wasting ammunition. The ambush had failed. The enemy had fled.

Through the flames that lit up the flat night sky, he saw the Syrians regrouped down in the valley below Booster Ridge. It looked like an entire armored division. In the morning, they would try again. One hundred tanks against his ten. But tonight, the line had held. They had kept the enemy out of Kuneitra, and off the bridges that spanned the Jordan, and led into the cities.

Amnon Reshef had fought all afternoon and through the night. Exhausted, he lay in his tank, the turret open to the Sinai stars, and tried to sleep. He wanted to retreat into a dreamless void, a numbness, and find a way to escape everything that raged inside him.

At 2 A.M., Gonen's Sinai Command had sent word that the Egyptian advance had been blocked. HQ can say whatever it wants, Amnon wanted to scream back over the radio, but you have no idea what's going on at the front. The Egyptians fought with passion and courage. It did not matter how many we killed. They kept coming and coming. Command's strategy was one misjudgment after another: Rushing armor to the waterline was a fiasco—Sagger ambushes annihilated our tanks; the decision not to evacuate the strongholds when the invasion first occurred was reckless, and now the rescue of the men seemed an impossibility—and yet it had to be tried; and counting on the air force to disrupt the canal crossing had been a colossal arrogance—the Egyptians had expertly replaced the damaged pontoons when a bridge had been hit.

But more than all the anger and frustration, the visions of the dead pressed hard against his mind. He had seen two groups of staff officers killed before his eyes. Friends—he knew their pretty wives, their giggling children—had been blown from their turrets as they stood tall leading the attacks. He had seen entire companies reduced to only two tanks. Three times in the course of fierce, desperate engagements, he had run out of fuel and ammunition and had been forced to retreat to camp and rearm. Then he'd lead his men back into hopeless combat. Yet they had fought on. In his weary mind the day and night had become one unceasing battle filled with the thunder of explosions, the pounding of treads on sand, and the awful, plaintive cries of dying men. Hours later he still could not close his fingers into a fist; he had gripped his rattling machine gun with all his might for too many hours. There had been 290 tanks in the division, and only 110 remained. Somehow he had survived.

He just wanted to sleep. To escape temporarily from all the death. From the generals' foolishness. And from the monstrousness of Israel's defeat. In the new morning, joined by the reserves, he and his men would find a way to continue the fight.

Just before 5 A.M., as he was finally dozing off, the radio blared. The Egyptians were pushing forward. Amnon's orders were to halt their advance.

In the last shadows of the night, his tanks returned to the Suez Canal. Amnon knew he could not stop the enemy. And that there was little chance he would return.

* * *

Shmuli woke up before dawn in a Safed hospital. He had lost a great deal of blood. He could barely speak; his vocal cords had been damaged. As he was being prepared for the operating room, he tried to ask the wounded tanker who lay nearby a question. For a moment no sound would come. Then in a hoarse, burning whisper he said, "The war?"

The soldier, an officer, started to respond, then had to stop. Tears rolled down his cheeks. "There's no more 188th," he said finally. "It's been wiped out."

The Syrians had broken through in the southern Golan. Only fifteen tanks remained in the entire Barak Brigade. Four hundred fifty Syrian tanks advanced parallel to the Rafid-El Al Road, and reinforcements were pouring in.

TWENTY-FOUR

Unit 848, Tel Aviv/ 7 October 1973/0345

His unit on war footing, a busy, sleepless Shabtai Brill sat hunched over his desk at about 3 A.M. when a lieutenant approached. With uncharacteristic formality, the young man stood at attention as he offered Brill the text of an intercept. They had just picked it up off a Syrian field radio, an officer on the Golan reporting to his commander.

"I think you should see this, too, sir." The lieutenant handed the scrap of paper to Brill, then walked somberly away like a man who had just informed the next of kin.

Brill read the short message. Ben Porat had not returned to the unit, and for the time being Brill was in charge. It was his decision to pass the Syrian message on with the daily package of enemy intercepts, or to send it immediately to the Pit, flash priority.

He read the Syrian radio transmission again, and he thought, not for the first time in this incredible night, "Damn them all! Why wouldn't they listen?" The war was only thirteen hours old, and already he feared it was nearly over. He picked up the phone, and told a clerk in the Pit to stand by the telex. In a moment he'd be transmitting. "Distribute immediately," Brill ordered.

An aide awoke Dayan at 4 A.M., and handed him the intercept without explanation. For a moment, the defense minister stared at the page uncomprehendingly. He had gone to sleep two hours ago after a heated argument with the chief of staff over the planning of the aerial attacks on the southern front. Dayan thought the predawn mission should concentrate on the Egyptian tanks entering the Sinai. Dado, with support from the head of the air force, insisted the first priority should be to take out the SAM batteries. Dayan believed such a mission had little likelihood of success. The Phantoms would fail, and the opportunity to stop the flow of armor across the Suez Canal would also be squandered. But he understood the limits of his authority. This was an operational decision; his mandate was political. Having lost the argument, he went to bed, ordering his aide to wake him as soon as the jets were in the air. And so when roused from a fitful sleep in his makeshift bedroom in the Pit, he assumed they had news of the Sinai mission. Instead, he read a dispatch sent an hour earlier by a commander of the 132nd Syrian Armored Brigade:

"I see the whole Galilee in front of me. Request permission to proceed."

Could this be possible? Syrian tanks about to cross the Jordan? His instinct was to believe it was an artful trick, disinformation sent by the enemy to cause panic. He glanced up and saw Dado had entered his room, a calm blanketing his face. From bitter experience, Dayan recognized the look: the composure of a soldier determined not to betray his emotions. And at once Dayan understood the message was not a ploy. Stunned, unable for once even to interrupt, Dayan listened as the chief of staff filled in the details. The Syrians had broken through. A large force had penetrated near Hushniya and continued on in two columns. One had turned north toward Kuneitra, hoping to strike the flank of the Seventh Armored Brigade. The other had demolished the Barak Brigade and was advancing toward the Sea of Galilee. Reserves were on the way, but the enemy had thrown their entire army into the push to capture the Heights. The Northern Command didn't know how much longer it could hold out.

Dayan sat motionless, the full dimensions of the catastrophe taking shape in his mind. At last, Dayan rose to his feet and told his aide to prepare a helicopter right away. He was going to the Northern Command.

As Dayan's helicopter flew northward in the rising sun, Shazly's day—the second day of his war—was just beginning. He took his seat on the Command dais in the Operations Room and surveyed what his troops had accomplished. On the huge wall map opposite him, bright colored divisional flags dotted the entire length of the Canal's east bank: Egypt's Second Army in the north, the Third Army in the south. In eighteen hours, Egypt had sent 90,000 men, 850 tanks, and 11,000 vehicles across to the Sinai. Armor and troops continued to surge over the bridges. The Zionists were still reeling. The Bar-Lev Line forts were overwhelmed, and the three armored brigades and one infantry brigade defending the waterline had been smashed. Only a few dozen tanks remained operational of the 270 in the original Sinai force, and the number of dead and wounded were more than 1,000. The Egyptians had lost 20 tanks and 280 men.

The battle of the crossing had been won.

Shazly anticipated that as soon as Israel's reserves arrived in the Sinai, the humiliated Zionists would be eager to counterattack. But today, with the enemy forces still thin, would bring a lull to the fighting.

He had not been home since October 1. It would be nice to return to Cairo for a few hours, long enough to see his wife, take a hot bath, and change his uniform. But no sooner had he reached for a phone to call his driver than an announcement blared across the Operations Room: Israeli Phantoms were approaching the missile zone.

He hung up, and trained his eyes on the map. If the the enemy had figured out a way to defeat the SAMs, his men would be in the desert without cover. And by the afternoon, Phantoms would be bombing his defenseless bridgeheads to hell. All he could do was watch the attack's progress as it was played out on the map. For now, the war was in Allah's hands.

Dayan stared out the windscreen of the small helicopter, locked in silent thought. The Sharon Plain spread below him. Normally, the sight of orange groves stretching in orderly rows for miles and green, bountiful farms caused his heart to leap with a self-congratulatory joy. After two thousand years of struggle, a once improbable biblical prophecy had been fulfilled. From the arid deserts, a prosperous Jewish state had been created. But today the terrible sounds of bombs and shells exploding in the Golan could be heard, and this was the prism that bent and colored all his thoughts. Now the rich Sharon Plain became in his mind the symbol of all that was about to be lost. When he reviewed the events that had brought him to this point he saw another continuum of Jewish history: a woeful march from Masada, to the Holocaust, to October 7, 1973—the destruction of the Jewish state. All his life he had fought seemingly hopeless battles, but never before had he felt so defeated. Or so responsible for the looming loss. The scope of his miscalculations, the scale of the consequences, left him shattered.

The landing of the helicopter brought Dayan some relief. He hoped to step away from his guilt and lose himself in a soldier's world where there was the possibility that courage and valor could prevail against impossible odds. But the mood in the Northern Forward Command Post extinguished any lingering sparks of optimism. The generals were pessimistic and mournful.

Hofi, steady, reliable Hofi, reported that the Syrians had broken the southern part of the Golan completely open. Gen. Iska Shadmi, an old war horse, moaned in Dayan's ear, "Critical, the situation is critical." He repeated the words so often that they took on the lugubrious rhythm of a graveside prayer. Even Gen. Dan Laner, who had been alongside Dayan from the improvised campaigns of the War of Independence to the heady triumphs of the Six Day War, who had done it all in the IDF, serving as chief of staff of the Northern Command, then commanding the armor on the Sinai front, was ready to give up. Laner approached his old friend and said quietly, "The fighting in the southern part of the Golan Heights is finished, and we have lost. We have no more force to stop them. Additional armor forces, from the reserves, will not be ready to move against the Syrians before noon."

Dayan listened to their words, and also heard what had not been said. At the core of the generals' reports, he believed, was a tacit plea: Help us, Moshe. We're counting on you, Zion's great warrior, to lead us out of this disaster.

Dayan, already low when he arrived and then pushed deeper by all he had learned, quickly issued a series of commands. "Dan," he said, "prepare the Jordan bridges for demolition!" The troops must abandon the Golan, and try to hold off the enemy from the other side of the Jordan River. Hofi looked at him incredulously, but Dayan ignored the general. Time was precious. He told an aide to get him Benny Peled. He needed to speak to the head of the air force right away.

Only the air force could stop the Syrians' advance. Jets must attack the fast-moving columns of enemy armor before it was too late. It did not matter that Israeli tanks were in close combat with the enemy; they could either close their hatches or leave their machines. The Syrian missile batteries would also, contrary to standard doctrine, have to be ignored. There was no time to launch the missions to destroy them. The pilots would fly into the thick barrage of SAMs and antiaircraft fire—and some would get through. All that mattered was the tanks. They had to be stopped before they reached the settlements.

It was 6:30 in the morning when Dayan, calling from the Northern headquarters, reached Peled in the underground air command post in Tel Aviv. The first wave of Operation Tagar had just been launched. Eighty Skyhawk jets were on their way to destroy the Egyptian antiaircraft guns. Several squadrons of Phantoms were also in the air, off to pound the eight airfields near the Suez Canal. But these were only preparatory missions; they were designed to weaken the enemy and make Tagar's main thrust possible. In three hours, a massive air attack would be launched to destroy the SAM missile sites on both sides of the Canal.

Dayan told Peled to bring back all the planes. All further missions along the Canal were to be canceled. Every jet, every bomber, must fly north as soon as possible. The Israeli Air Force needed to begin immediate continuous action against the Syrian armor. "I want them to swoop down without stop so the Syrian tank crews won't be able to lift their heads."

Dayan knew he could not give an order to Peled. Operational commands had to come from the chief of staff. He spoke from the heart, with both affection and despair, one old friend, one sabra, to another. But given his mood, given the circumstances, perhaps that was the only way he could have managed any words at all. "Benny," he said, "unless we stop their tanks, this is the destruction of the Third Temple."

At first light, Kahalani looked beyond the still smoldering tanks. He could finally see where the night's battle had brought his battalion. To the north were the Hermonit Mountains rising like one long frown. To the south was the craggy volcanic rock of Booster Ridge. And in front of him was a wide, rust-brown valley.

He identified his location on his map, and discovered the valley did not have a name. That bothered him. It did not seem right to give your life fighting over a piece of land that wasn't significant enough to have been named. Green camouflaged Syrian T-62s, their cupolas locked and their crews sleeping in the belly of the machines, spread across the wide valley. When the enemy awoke, the grazing beasts with 115-mm smoothbore guns would turn murderous.

"All 'policeman' stations. Battalion commander here. Start engines and activate all systems. Be ready for battle at dawn."

Then he ordered the battalion to move forward and mount the earthen ramps.

The Syrians attacked an hour later with about 150 tanks from both the Seventy-eighth and Eighty-first Independent Armored Brigades. Kahalani had fourteen tanks strung out across the sector defending the road into Kuneitra.

"'Policeman' stations, on our front. Ranges from five hundred to fifteen hundred yards. Many enemy tanks. Into position. Open fire!"

For the first time, Shazly did not like the way things were going. A long dark cloud of Skyhawks had passed above the Suez Canal and yet his gunners had hit only two planes. The enemy rockets had given the Egyptian antiaircraft a beating and many of the batteries were now out of commission. The IAF's big Phantoms had been no less effective. They had demolished four airfields, and six of the MiGs that gave chase were shot out of the sky.

And this was only the first wave. Shazly had been a pretty fair welterweight at the military academy and the strategy his coach had whispered into his ear before he climbed into the ring echoed ominously in his mind: Work the body until they are woozy, then go in for the knockout. The Zionist jets would return. And when they did, they would go after the SAMs.

If their jets succeeded, if they stripped the cover away from his armor and infantry on the east bank, it would quickly become a very different war. And one he doubted he could win.

He paced anxiously, waiting to see what would happen. And with every step his eyes were fixed on the giant wall map. As soon as the Canal radar stations sighted the intruders, the enemy task force's progress would be charted. But the radars found nothing. The jets did not return.

It made no sense. Unless, Shazly told himself, Allah had heard his prayers and answered them. That must be it, he wanted to believe.

The entire Israeli air force rushed north. Formations of Skyhawks, one after another, zoomed over the Jordan Valley. The black smoke of countless Phantoms trailed across the sky. In radio silence, through the thick air traffic, flying at great speed, they made their way up the coast.

For the pilots, there was a shared puzzlement. The Sinai missions abruptly scrapped. Then the sudden unprepared scramble toward Syria. Had Headquarters completely lost its mind?

Only as the planes crossed into the black, featureless terrain of the Golan was a terse explanation broadcast over their radios: Not a single Israeli tank was left to challenge the columns of armor rolling down the El Al route to the Galilee. The mission was to stop the enemy. The only battle plan was to follow their instincts.

In the chaotic first hours, the planes flew 129 ground-support sorties. The improvised strategy was as simple as it was brutal. Flying low and fast, they came in wave after wave and pounded the Syrian tank concentrations. Finally the Syrians ran for cover, deciding to regroup rather than push on immediately into the settlements.

Encouraged by the success of this makeshift operation, Peled risked another bold assault. At 11:30 that morning he launched Operation Dugman-5—the IAF's full-scale attack against the Syrian SAM systems.

But in his haste, many of the long-standing battle plan's carefully designed support missions were abandoned. The air commanders scrubbed a preparatory attack against the antiaircraft batteries similar to the effective dawn mission across the Suez Canal. There was no time for artillery support. Or for reconnaissance flights to identify the precise locations of the mobile SAM-6 batteries. Or to reload the Phantoms flying up from the Sinai with chaff and reconfigure their electronic countermeasure pods against the Syrian heat-seeking missiles. The bewildered pilots came in from their dawn

Tagar missions only to be told they were to fly north to execute Dugman. Grab new maps, rush to your planes, and launch.

The operation was a colossal failure. The jets attacked thirty-one Syrian batteries, but only one was destroyed. And the air force bought this small achievement at great cost. The missiles brought down six F-4 Phantoms and three Skyhawk A-4 planes.

The war was not even twenty-four hours old and already Israel had lost thirty-five planes, nearly 10 percent of its combat air force. If the loses continued at this rate, Peled informed the chief of staff, the IAF would soon reach its "Red Line" and would not have sufficient airpower to defend the country.

Dado summoned up all his self-control. Wasn't it only a day ago that Peled had confidently told him an aerial first strike would deter their enemies? Now amid the strains and turmoil of war, a war they were losing, he had to face a new, astounding reality: The air force was in danger of being destroyed. It took him a moment to absorb the news. Resigned, he issued an immediate directive: The air force must cease all attacks against SAM sites, in the north and in the south.

Kahalani's tanks were fighting a free-for-all. A huge incessant roar of shells and explosions and flames enveloped their entire position. It had come down to this: Either they killed the enemy, or they would be killed.

As he fired the machine gun at an APC, Kahalani surveyed the surrounding terrain. To his left, he saw an abandoned house. Somehow it had survived all the fury. And rising above its front wall was an aerial.

Quickly, he ordered his gunner to fire. The wall crashed down, revealing the turret of a T-62, its long gun turned toward him, ready to fire.

"Give it to him!" Kahalani yelled to his gunner. But as he shouted the order, he knew there was no time. The Syrian would fire first.

Suddenly, the T-62 exploded. Yair Swet, hull down and firing from behind a small clump of boulders, had nailed him. Kahalani poured a machine gun burst into the ruins just to make sure, as Yair moved on.

Kahalani promised himself he would thank Yair later. If there was a later. The Syrians were still coming. Smoke and flames swirled high into the sky. Burning T-62s exploded in a series of thunder claps. Shards of scorched steel fell in a lethal rain over the dark ground. A turret took off like a rocket and landed upside down. And still the enemy kept coming. Could they be that brave? Not even the smoldering hulks of their abandoned tanks, the lost crews, slowed them down. If he were leading the attack, he'd have the tanks approach cautiously, darting up the valley from one bit of cover to the next. But the Syrians' strategy was direct, and suicidal: They charged no matter the cost. And they would continue until nothing was left to stop them.

As he moved and fired, his radio barked with anxious reports: "There are a lot coming at me, but we'll manage." "There are hordes of them coming down the valley." "Getting low on ammunition." "My number one platoon leader has had it." "My deputy. He's gone. The crew has disappeared."

And then Kahalani heard: "Battalion commander, this is Yair's deputy. Yair's gone."

So many had died, but this news reached out across the smoke and din of battle and shook him. Minutes before Yair had saved his life. And now he was gone? Yair had been leaning out of his cupola pulling the wounded from a flaming Centurion when a shell smashed him back into the turret. An image of boyish Yair, his sweet, sweet smile, rose up in Kahalani's mind. But with steely discipline, he forced it away. He would live to keep his promise. Only now he would thank Yair's widow.

"Georgi," He radioed back, "this is the battalion commander. Take over Yair's company."

And so they kept fighting. Ammunition dwindled. The men were exhausted, drained near to collapse. But they hit enemy tank after tank. And soon Kahalani saw that the enemy fire was slowing. Syrian crews were climbing out of their tanks and running back toward the border. By noon, the Syrian advance had come to a halt.

He got on the radio to Yanosh. "We've stopped them. It's quite a sight. The valley is full of burning and abandoned hardware."

"Can you estimate numbers?"

"I guess we hit—eighty or ninety."

Kahalani's men had not left their hot, cramped tanks for twenty-four hours. Now he allowed them out in turns. The air was heavy with death. Yet as the crews walked slowly through the destruction, the twisted metal and the flames, the weight of all they had endured, all they had done, began to lift off them. They had held the road to Kuneitra. And despite their utter weariness, even as they mourned their friends, there was a soldier's pride.

Later, Kahalani picked up the map and looked again at the valley that did not have a name. Well, he thought, it earned a name today: Valley of Tears.

Dayan returned to the Pit that morning to learn Dado had overruled his decision to blow up the bridges over the Jordan. The generals in GHQ thought it had not come to that. After all, the Seventh Armored Brigade, they told him, had kept the enemy out of Kuneitra.

Dayan felt they were not being realistic. They had not been to the north. They did not know how bad things were. But when he tried to explain this to them, he realized what they were thinking: *Dayan has lost his nerve.*

So he kept his grim thoughts to himself. But then at one o'clock the news came that the camp at Nafekh, only six miles from the main bridge across the Jordan, had fallen.

Dayan again despaired: We have lost the Golan. We have lost our best men. The enemy is at the gate. The Day of Judgment is here. This is the destruction of the Third Temple.

TWENTY-FIVE

Delhi, India/7 October 1973/1045

Last night, stranded in far-off Nepal, had been nearly impossible to endure. From the moment Nati had rushed into their hotel room with the first thin news about the invasions, Yossi had felt imprisoned. He had traveled to Katmandu because it was the ends of the earth, or close enough. But in an instant his perspective changed. His absence from home was no longer an adventure, but a betrayal. Israel was at war, and he had to get back.

Both Yossi and Nati worked the phones in the hotel, but without success. He called the local airline, then the airport, only to hear a steady, infuriating ring. After an eternity of waiting, Nati got an international operator and was promptly informed that all circuits to Israel were engaged. "There's a war going on," the operator explained unnecessarily.

Yossi commandeered the radio behind the front desk and twirled the dial relentlessly hoping to find some news, but there was nothing. Static filled the airwaves, and the discordant whine rubbed his already frayed mood. He snapped it off in a rage, and paced up and down the cramped lobby. He had to do *something*. He could not bear to spend another idle moment.

Yossi instructed Nati to pack. They would check out of the hotel, and go to the tiny Katmandu airport. He had no illusion there'd be anything flying tonight, but at least they'd have moved on from the suffocating hotel. In the morning, they'd be ready to catch the first plane. It didn't matter where it was going as long as it carried them out of the Himalayas, and closer to a connecting flight to Israel.

When they arrived, the airport was dark and empty as if abandoned. But a door opened when Yossi pushed it, and they walked hand in hand across the eerily silent terminal. They found a bench where Nati spread out, her head resting on Yossi's lap, hoping to sleep. For Yossi the sheer anxiety of not knowing what was happening, to his country, to his brigade, made sleep impossible. It was a long, uneasy night, and his mind raced with thoughts.

In this contemplative state he decided that his life up to this point had been divided into two distinct journeys. One had led him to be a soldier. The other had taken him to this exotic escape. Nati, he realized, was the link between these two disparate itineraries. And with the decision to return home, a new journey would begin: their shared future.

He tried to think about the war in that way, as providential, the catalyst for the next stage of his life. He tried not to imagine what it might be like tonight on the rocky Golan terrain. Or in the sands of the Sinai. He tried not to think about his friends. Or that he was not with them when they needed him most. He tried not to dwell on how he had been trained to defend the state, and yet when its enemies attacked, he was unable to do his duty. He held Nati's hand as she slept, and that helped hold his world together.

The next morning after his sleepless night, a determined Yossi sprung into action. There was a flight to Delhi and he managed, with an outrageous bribe to the coy ticket agent, to secure the last two seats on the "full" flight. Once he was in the air, his guilt eased. At last things were moving forward.

When they landed in Delhi, he jogged from the plane, and then pushed to the head of a long line at the ticket counter. A man grabbed his arm in protest, but Yossi ripped free. When the ruddy-faced Brit stammered out an indignant complaint, Yossi cut him off with a narrow look and a single word of warning: "Don't." The man wisely retreated.

At the counter, Yossi found a daily TWA flight leaving Bombay for Athens. If they could get to Bombay, there was room on the flight.

"When's the plane to Bombay leaving?" he asked.

"It's boarding now."

He grabbed Nati's hand and they started running across the long, crowded terminal. The gate was at the other end of the building, but it might as well have been in another time zone. They would never make it. Without losing a step, he struggled out of his bulky backpack and let it fall to the ground. He told Nati, "Leave your suitcase. Just drop it." Nati obeyed, but she kept a tight hold on the stuffed monkey. They dashed through the sea of people, careening into annoyed travelers, but never stopping. They arrived at a closed gate.

"Please," Yossi pleaded with the flight attendant. "We have to get on board. Please." And he made sure to give her one of his very best smiles.

She picked up the phone. They waited, catching their breath, hoping.

"It's still at the gate. Do you prefer window or aisle?" she asked, returning Yossi's smile with a glorious one of her own.

In Bombay, they boarded the TWA flight to Athens. They would arrive at about two o'clock on Sunday afternoon, October 7. All flights to Israel had been canceled; they were scheduled to resume late Monday night. In two days, then, he would be home.

It was not until they went through passport control in Athens that a problem arose. The official stamped their passports and asked to see their immunization documents. All arrivals from India had to prove they had the required vaccinations.

"Show the man," Yossi told Nati.

Nati searched in her pocket, and then she stopped. The health booklets were in her suitcase. The one she had left on the floor of the Delhi terminal.

"I'm afraid you can't leave the airport until we have proof you've had your shots," the official told them. "You'll need to remain in quarantine."

"For how long?" demanded Yossi.

"Six months."

As Yossi and Nati hurried across the globe, a restless, compelling urgency pushed Dayan on, too. Within an hour of returning from his sobering trip to the Golan, he dashed off again. He was unwilling to chain himself to a desk and let the war unfold from a distance. He needed to feel the tempo of what was happening firsthand, to see it all with his own astute eyes. He craved activity, not the stale air and inertia of the Pit. That Sunday morning, as the squadrons of Phantoms lumbered toward the Syrian missile defenses on their hastily prepared mission, he boarded a Cessna at the military airport outside Tel Aviv on his way to the Southern Command Headquarters at Um Hashiba.

Upon his arrival, he dragged a drained Gonen from the crowded War Room bunker and led him into the general's smaller private office. As Gonen briefed him, Dayan drank cup after cup of black duty coffee, but the taste was not as bitter as the news. After a day's fighting, the situation in the Sinai was bad and growing worse. The Egyptian infantry held the waterline along the Suez canal. The strongholds were completely cut off, and the men inside, many of them wounded, were pleading desperately to be rescued. The Israeli forces had been repeatedly driven back; they were presently deployed in a thin, weak line about ten to fifteen kilometers east of the Canal. If the Egyptians advanced, they might very well be able to take control of the strategic Mitla and Gidi passes. And if they succeeded, only two depleted divisions would stand between the enemy and Tel Aviv.

On the flight back to Tel Aviv, Dayan mulled over everything he had learned this morning. In a lifetime of tenuous situations, he never had never known such despair. Israel was in grave danger.

Dayan returned to Tel Aviv at about 1:30. A dutiful soldier, he went to the Kirya to pass on to the prime minister all he had learned. But first, as much a compulsive need as a dress rehearsal of what he would say to Golda Meir, he headed down to the Pit to speak with Dado.

His arrival attracted a crowd. Generals and staff officers, the senior command who had not left the subterranean Headquarters since the first shots were fired, huddled in the chief of staff's office to listen to the defense minister's report. The invasions remained a disorienting surprise, and the scramble to throw together a defense had produced a confusing stream of often contradictory dispatches. But now the legendary Dayan had come back from the fronts to clear away the fog of war. To a man, his authority, his position in the nation's hagiography, was unimpeachable. Therefore, his words—and, no less affecting, the transformation of the familiar charismatic warrior into the baleful, fatalistic figure slumped before them—shocked them all.

Another Jeremiah, Dayan preached a chilling message: All was nearly lost. The "Day of Judgment" had arrived. Tanks, planes, and men were being depleted at a punishing pace. Israel, he warned, might soon be unable to protect itself from the Arab invaders. "The destruction of the Third Temple" was at hand, he repeated.

To defend the state, it was tactically necessary to pull back and shorten the lines. In the Sinai, the forces should evacuate from the Suez Canal area and move far north, establishing a last-stand defense at Sharm el-Sheikh. In the Golan, a new line, too, had to be drawn. And then like Masada, held to the last man. After one day of war, he was convinced that a retreat to new borders offered the state its only hope for survival.

Then having delivered his dire predictions, Dayan, as abruptly as a gloomy seer in a Greek tragedy, exited. He hurried upstairs to repeat his performance for the prime minister.

Dayan's sudden departure left a vacuum in the room. A few of the shaken generals turned their attention to the chief of staff who had been remarkably quiet through most of Dayan's presentation. To their surprise, they discovered that Dado not only seemed calm and untroubled, but, many were convinced, he even appeared confident.

Even after a night of horrific fighting, "like a madman from hell," he would say, Amnon Reshef, while not confident, was certainly hopeful for the first time since the war began. He had retreated to Artillery Road, so far back into the Sinai that he could no longer see the gulls circling the Canal water, but he had an inkling that things might soon change. The convoys of reserves had begun to arrive, and they were coming faster than anyone had expected. By evening there would be more than 600 tanks in the south.

Further boosting Amnon's hopes, two veteran reserve commanders were already in the Sinai. At 7:30 that morning Gen. Avraham "Bren" Adan, who had recently retired after five years as head of the Armored Corps, had assumed control of the northern part of the Canal front. Gen. Ariel "Arik" Sharon, who had been head of the Southern Command until three months earlier when he had gone off in a huff to enter politics, had taken charge of the central sector.

Amnon had little doubt their presence would make for a volatile mix at Headquarters. After all, it was not that long ago that both Bren and Arik had commanded Gonen, and now they had been summoned from retirement to take orders from the younger, inexperienced general. Even in the best of times, Bren and Gonen found it difficult to be in the same room. Bren, soft-spoken and thoughtful, was put off by Gordish's growling, preemptory treatment of subordinates; and an insecure Gonen believed the older man's persistent questioning of his judgment was a technique of purposeful humiliation. While Sharon, bustling with self-confidence, inflated with his own perceived authority, did not get on with anybody, and saw no reason to try.

Yet at this low point, Amnon thought it was time to shake things up. Gordish and Mandler had totally mishandled the war; because of their mistakes, the tanks had not been at the waterline to block the invasion and the strongholds had not been evacuated. Napoleon had said he wanted lucky generals. Well, Amnon would settle for a commander with chutzpah, the nerve and audacity to take the fight to the enemy. So when at half past three that afternoon Amnon heard over the net that his brigade, or at least the handful of tanks that remained, had been transferred to Sharon's command, the news cheered him. And Amnon was not surprised when after reporting to the Tasa base in the desert, he heard Arik shouting that if they'd only let him, he'd move out that night. In a few hours, he'd have the Egyptian's bridgehead at Deversoir along the canal wiped out.

Far from the front, in the prime minister's office that afternoon, a somber Dayan recommended another strategy. If the Arabs would consent to a cease-fire, Israel should accept. "Golda," he said, "I was wrong in everything. We are heading to catastrophe. We shall have to withdraw on the Golan Heights to the edge of the escarpment overlooking the valley. In the Sinai, to the passes. And hold to the last bullet."

Golda Meir listened with horror. Her head slumped into her hands, and she covered her dark eyes as if to keep out the world. There had been times over the years when the pain she experienced as the leader of her people had been so unbearable that she had cried openly and without embarrassment, like Rachel weeping for her children. But this extraordinary moment left her beyond tears. Her world threatened to collapse.

Dayan felt culpable. "Golda," he offered, "in all sincerity and friendship, if you think there is somebody more capable of handling the duties of defense minister, then give it to him. It would be a mistake on your part if you don't do what you think right."

"God forbid," the prime minister responded.

So Dayan continued with his presentation. Yet even as Yisrael Galili, the minister without portfolio, listened he refused to accept that after only one day the situation was so dire. He scribbled a note and passed it to Golda Meir's military secretary with orders to take it to the Pit. The note instructed the chief of staff to come to the prime minister's office at once.

Dado did not attempt to disguise what had happened on the battlefields. In contrast to Dayan, he did not hurl thunderbolts or predict catastrophes of biblical proportions. His calm, reasonable manner suggested that although there had been setbacks and the situation was grave, Israel had not lost the war.

He had just spoken with the Southern Command, he told them. Tanks and men were still arriving, and by morning everything would be in place. This evening he intended to fly down to the headquarters at Um Hashiba and meet with Gonen, Bren, and Sharon. And tomorrow Israel would counterattack in the Sinai.

"Today," he said, "we hit bottom. Tomorrow I predict that we'll be able to get our chins above water."

The war council at Gonen's headquarters began that evening at 7:30 without Sharon. None of the generals knew if he had been delayed by a new outburst of fighting in his sector, or if Arik, being Arik, was simply making a point.

Gonen spoke first. His men had suffered the most since the war began, and his wounded pride left him eager for revenge. He wanted to move out that night and grab the Egyptian bridges. Bren's division would attack the Second Army, while Sharon would handle the Third Army at the southern end of the Suez Canal. In the morning, they'd cross over and take on the Egyptian forces massed on the west side.

Dado could hardly believe what he was hearing. One moment

Dayan was calling for surrender. The next Gonen was ready to march into Cairo. Between desperation and rashness, the IDF had to carve out an alternative strategy, one that, as he put it, had "two feet on the ground."

With deliberate tact, Dado dismissed Gonen's strategy as "too pretentious." The counterattack must be modest.

In the morning, Bren's division would hit the Second Army from the north, and in a flanking movement drive southward toward the Great Bitter Lake. Sharon would act as a reserve, ready to assist if Bren's force met with resistance. If Bren succeeded, only then would Sharon attack the Third Army later that afternoon, coming in from the north and gradually moving toward the Gulf of Suez.

To make sure his eager, gung-ho generals understood the tactical limitations of this opening assault, Dado said, "I would like to emphasize that in these attacks we will stay away from the Canal zone, from that area swarming with infantry equipped with RPGs, and from the area where the enemy is employing tanks and antitank weapons from his ramparts. Obviously we will *not* link up to the strongholds, and we will *not* initiate a crossing operation."

Dado had left the bunker and was heading to his helicopter when he, literally, bumped into the late-arriving Sharon. Arik explained that he had been delayed because he had been formulating a plan to rescue the men from two strongholds. In fact, he informed Dado, being here at all was a waste of his time. He should be moving boldly against the enemy while it was still dark, not flying across the desert for meetings. He wanted to take 100 tanks and bring the stranded soldiers back.

"Suppose I let you carry out this attack tonight," Dado said evenly. "Will you be able to mount an assault in the morning as well?"

"No," Sharon conceded.

"Then permission denied." Dado told the general to speak with Gonen who would give him the battle plan that had just been set. Sharon marched off to the bunker without another word.

By ten o'clock, Dado was in his helicopter flying back to the Pit. It had been a trying day. Yet after all the hysterical predictions, all the lamenting about the destruction of the Third Temple, the outlook had improved. In the Golan, the situation appeared to have stabilized. The Seventh Armored Brigade had held the approach into Kuneitra. After the pounding by the air force, Syria had not pushed over the Jordan River bridges. And tomorrow morning in the Sinai, Israel would launch the first major counterstrike. He knew the phased, flanking attack he had designed was a restrained, even cautious approach. But its scale was also its virtue: It was a plan that would work. Its small success would be the catalyst that would begin to turn the tide on the southern front.

Arriving in the disconcerting total darkness of a wartime Tel Aviv, Dado returned at once to the Pit. Meanwhile, in the Sinai, Gonen worked well into the morning. And as the hours passed, a new battle plan took shape.

TWENTY-SIX

Safed Hospital/ 8 October 1973/0700

Lying in his hospital bed, staring intently at the blank wall as if he expected it to reveal what was happening up on the Golan, Shmuli Askarov planned his escape. Yesterday a doctor old enough to be his grandfather assured him the operation had been a success. "We removed a bucketful of shrapnel. Metal all over the place—chest, forehead, even your vocal cords," he explained matter-of-factly, as if those were the sort of injuries he saw every day. With a bedside manner that clearly owed more to the kibbutz than to Hippocrates, he went on to promise that although Shmuli looked terrible, by the time he was released from the hospital in three months, maybe two months if he was lucky, his voice would have returned and his headache would be gone.

This morning Shmuli decided, screw the ancient doctor. And screw the three months, maybe two if he was lucky. He was leaving today.

Yesterday reports had come into the hospital, bulletins passed breathlessly from bed to bed, each more calamitous than the next. The Syrians had broken into Nafekh. The 188th Brigade had been virtually wiped out. Its entire command—Ben-Shoham, his deputy, and the operational officer—were dead. Then, as if the pain of the three deaths wasn't shattering enough, Shmuli learned their bodies were still lying on the battlefield. All night that had eaten away at him. They had died defending Israel with courage and faith, and they deserved to be buried. Their families needed to stand over the graves and recite kaddish. Tradition required it. And the Soldier's Law was no less binding: Comrades were not left behind, dead or alive. He was determined to find his commander's corpse as well as the others, and to make sure they rested forever in peace.

He also knew it was his duty to take their place. He was a battalion commander, a major, and if there was no one else to lead the remnants of the 188th back into battle, he would do it. With the enemy marching across his country, the thumping in his head, the raw pain in his throat whenever he tried to speak, became nothing more than inconveniences. He had to fight, and to lead. Israel needed him now.

As long as he could climb into a tank, he was going back to the front. Yesterday he had begun planning out his escape. Fortunately, he got some help. His brother, a high school senior, had rushed up to the hospital from Tel Aviv as soon as the family had been informed of Shmuli's condition. Despite his rasping, barely audible voice, Shmuli made the youth understand that he needed a new uniform. And after a wily Baruch had accomplished that mission, he had him search the wards for another patched-up tanker eager to head back to the front. Just before midnight, Baruch led Yos Eldar, a battalion commander from the Seventh Armored Brigade, to Shmuli's bed. Sunday night into Monday morning the two soldiers finalized the details.

Now in the gray-blue light of dawn, Shmuli forced himself out of his comfortable bed, and dressed in his new uniform. A look in the mirror confirmed the doctor's diagnosis: He *did* look like hell. He had buttoned his uniform shirt up to the neck, and the mile of gauze circling his throat still remained visible. He felt as trussed as a mummy, but given the raw pain, he didn't dare unravel it. With a single sudden movement, though, he ripped the cumbersome bandage off his forehead. It stung sharply, and the reflection he saw in the mirror reminded him of photos he had once seen of a crater-dotted lunar terrain. But blood didn't flow from the wounds and that was reason enough for thanks. Even better, after a few tours up and down the ward, the world stopped spinning and his head no longer felt as though it might roll off his shoulders and fall to the floor. Without even a wave good-bye, he boldly walked past the nurses' station and out the front door.

Yos was waiting in his jeep and Shmuli, trying to affect a jaunty air, jumped in. That was a mistake. Gravity somehow failed, and he fell over in his seat. Yos helped prop him back up, and after Shmuli uttered some earnest assurances that he wasn't feeling as badly as he looked, they headed east. He had escaped.

Yos would rejoin Yanosh's Seventh Armored Brigade, which was making its stand outside Kuneitra. Shmuli, however, could not return to his brigade. It no longer existed.

He had Yos leave him at the sprawling tank depot outside Rosh Pina. In the scheme Shmuli had worked out yesterday, he imagined himself finding tanks and crews waiting for orders. He would gather them up at the depot, and lead them into battle.

Clusters of idle men crowded the base. Some were newly arrived reserves, but many had been fighting in the Golan and had fled after their tanks had been shot out from under them. He walked up to a burly, competent-looking sergeant and ordered him to bring all the crews to the center of the camp. Major Askarov wanted to address them.

Shmuli was never very good at speeches. He had always believed soldiers followed their officers' example, not their sermons. But this morning, as he stood in the center of a circle of about 150 men, the gravity of what he was about to do affected him. Battalion after battalion of Syrian tanks had swarmed into the Golan in the past two days. The odds were impossible. He would be asking men to die.

He could still only manage a hoarse whisper, but that worked to his advantage. The men listened with attention. Every word shot a fresh bolt of pain through his throat. He simply told them what he believed: If the enemy crossed the Jordan, the Jewish state would be overrun. The farms and cities built by their parents and grandparents would be destroyed. There was no nobler mission, no more honorable duty, than to stop them. He was going back to the Golan and he wanted all of them to join him.

When he finished, they looked at him with blank faces. He was convinced they would follow him. He could not imagine Israelis, regardless of the danger, refusing to defend their homes and families.

An officer walked forward from the circle, and approached him. His voice was loud and impassioned. "I'm a major, too," he said. "And I ran away. You can put me in prison, but I'm not going back to that hell."

Shmuli was too stunned to respond. Besides, he had already said everything there was to say. When the major turned and walked briskly away, the crowd of men followed quietly behind him.

Shmuli found a jeep. Accompanied by a single volunteer, he left the camp ten minutes later, driving toward the noise of war up on the Golan.

Shazly, too, was up with the dawn that Monday morning. After experiencing the war through reports and watching its battles replayed with markers and arrows on the wall map in the Operations Room, he was on his way to the front.

He drove first to the Second Army HQ, and as he rode by the men in his open jeep he experienced an incredible elation. The look of satisfaction on their faces, the unembarrassed grins of the young soldiers who with their bravery had restored the country's honor, left him overwhelmed. As he passed by, the troops whooped, "We did it! We did it!" At that moment, Shazly wanted to stop and tell them that the crossing of the Suez Canal would forever be part of Egypt's history. Like the pyramids and the pharaohs, their accomplishment would be recalled with pride by generations to come. But swept along by their shouts and cheers, as they surged forward to greet him, all he could do was nod, or touch his cap in mute recognition of their praise and in testimony to their sacrifices. If he said a word, he feared he might break down and shed tears of unrestrained joy.

Afterward, Shazly rode south to keep a promise. Last Friday—a mere seventy hours ago, but it just as well have been seventy years—Shazly had crouched behind a sand rampart at Ismailia and looked across the Suez Canal into enemy territory. With Gen. Saad Mamoun, the commander of the Second Army Division by his side, he had stared at the Israeli stronghold rising above the east bank and furtively searched for any sign that the enemy expected their attack. Then and there he had vowed one day soon to stand as a conqueror inside its walls.

This morning hope became deed. As soon as he crossed over the Suez Canal, the fury and destruction of the war—four blackened tanks, an abandoned armored personel carrier lying on its side, huge gaping shell craters—became real in ways that had been impossible to appreciate from his desk in Center Ten. As a consequence, the sight of the Egyptian flag flying above the fort affected him more than he had anticipated. He saluted the banner, paying silent tribute to the men who had raised it; and then he walked tall and erect, as though leading a column, through a narrow corridor lined with sandbags, and entered the heart of the fort. He looked around and thought: All this arrogance! All the foolish plans and squandered money! The Zionists' "impregnable" fortress is now ours. He offered up a small prayer. "*Alhamdu Lillah, Allahu-Akbar.*" Thanks be to God, God is the Greatest.

Shazly completed his inspection, and then went outside. He wandered along the waterline until he found a rock, and sat. He needed to be alone with his thoughts, to put into perspective all his army had done, and to consider the challenges that lay ahead. In another day, Israel's reserves will have arrived. Then the enemy would counterattack. He tried to put himself in their chief of staff's place; and when he did he saw the attack his men would face tomorrow as clearly as if it were drawn on paper. Israel would make a solid charge. Employing a massed, concentrated armored force they'd try to smash through one of his bridgeheads. That's what he would do if he was giving the orders in Tel Aviv. It would be bloody, but his men would be dug in and ready.

He was still sitting alone in the warm sun, deep in thought, when General Mamoun approached and announced gravely, "The enemy's counterattack has begun."

Shazly felt a sudden uneasiness. This was a full day sooner than he had anticipated. Did the Zionists have a strategy, perhaps even a weapon he had not considered? He hurried back to Center Ten so he could monitor the battles.

He arrived at his desk only to find another surprise waiting for him. The Jews were not attacking as he had imagined. Their tactics were so astonishing that he repeatedly asked for confirmations of each report that came in. It was hard to believe they were accurate. But when they were reconfirmed, his spirits stirred. Shazly had always wanted the enemy to fight on his terms, but until now he had never thought they would cooperate.

Later, when it was too late, Dado would insist that if the Southern Command had executed his limited, phased attack, the army at the day's end would have been "sitting in Suez." However, Gonen, after huddling in his command post into the morning with Sharon, had revised the operation to include the specific elements that Dado had summarily rejected: the rescue of the strongholds; an approach to the waterline; and the possibility, if the tempting situation presented itself, of a crossing. In the aftermath, when accusations flew about the Pit as fast and as lethally as Sagger missiles, Dado maintained he had never been informed of these last-minute alterations to his plan. Gonen, for his part, produced a brief, vaguely phrased battle order that he had sent at 3 A.M. to Tel Aviv that *could* have been read as an official notification—if the chief of staff had seen it. An exasperated Bren said, "I went through the whole war never knowing that he had changed the plan." And as for Sharon, he argued that he had never heard Dado's plan that night, and certainly no one had ever mentioned anything to him about a "phased attack." Besides, to his unwavering mind, Dado's plan *and* Gonen's were flawed. They should have listened to him: Attack the northern bridgehead with both divisions, and then proceed as a unified force to the south.

So, with all the simmering conflicts, intrigue, and confusion, perhaps it was inevitable that the attack would fail.

From the crest of a hilltop south of the Suez Canal, Amnon saw it all begin. He was part of Sharon's force, ordered to stand in reserves as Bren's battalions launched the initial attack. He was disappointed that his men, for the time being at least, were only spectators. Yet he could not help but feel an overpowering surge of excitement, a familiar battle readiness, as he watched Bren's three battalions move toward the enemy. It was just 8:15 in the morning, but he felt confident that before the day was over, Israel would reverse the course of the war.

Amnon heard the Egyptian artillery suddenly coming to life. But when he looked through his binoculars, Bren's tanks were moving steadily through the barrage. Two brigades headed south, concentrating on the wedge of territory between Artillery Road and the Canal front. The third brigade moved east along the Artillery Road. Transmissions on the radio net confirmed what he was able to see through the dust of battle: The tanks had the Egyptian infantry on the run. Masses of gray uniforms were retreating back to the waterline positions. When he heard a report that a force of Egyptian T-62s had been beaten back, four kills without the loss of a single

Israeli tank, Amnon cheered. After the ferocious pounding his men had taken over the past two days, they were finally punishing the enemy.

Gonen smelled victory, too. And at 10:05, he activated the second part of his revised plan. His deputy contacted Bren on the radio with an "important, very important" message. "There are some slight indications that the enemy has begun to collapse," he said. Therefore, Bren's brigades were now to move west to the Canal. They would rescue the men in the strongholds, and then prepare to cross the Canal on the Egyptian bridges. "Rush at maximum speed with all your forces," he instructed Bren.

Bren listened, surprised. Instead of his forces attacking the Egyptians from the flank as they'd agreed last night, they would be charging into the heart of the enemy's fortified positions. The morning's fighting had spread his brigades far apart; the gaps between them were as much as twenty kilometers wide. They would approach the waterline deployed in thin, separate formations, not a concentrated mass of tanks.

Bren considered challenging these orders, then decided Command must be better informed of what was happening at the front than he was. Besides, he asked himself, *What am I, anyway. A coward? Do I want them to think I lack the courage to advance?*

"Roger. Understood," he replied.

In Tel Aviv that morning, Dado was briefing the cabinet on how he expected the counterattack to develop, when he was summoned to the Pit. As Dado hurried away, an aide whispered that there was news from the Southern Command.

Ten minutes later Dado returned to the Cabinet Room and he could not restrain himself from sharing what he had just learned. The attack, though only two hours old, was "surpassing all expectations." Bren's forces had already reached one of the strongholds and rescued the trapped men.

After the past two harrowing days, the cabinet's mood had been dark and despairing, but now it shifted. Optimism began to rise up: The war was not over! We are fighting back!

Dado resumed his presentation, but moments later an aide interrupted again, this time handing him a note. "The way they're nagging at me," he joked to the ministers, "we could already have a bridgehead on the other side." The report he read was nearly as good: A point force from Bren's division was about to cross the Suez Canal. In fact, it may have already done so.

Yet none of this was true.

In the confusion of war, opportunities for misinterpretation abounded. And somehow, as battle reports traveled between Southern Command and Tel Aviv, orders were transformed into accomplishments. What Bren had been ordered to do became, instead, what he had done.

It was a pernicious alchemy; and a flurry of misguided decisions quickly followed. As Dado returned to the Pit he received word that Gonen wanted permission to move Sharon's division south without delay. Since Bren had the enemy on the run, it was no longer necessary to hold forces in reserve, he argued. Besides, if Sharon started south now, he could engage the Third Army that afternoon. This was a powerful Egyptian force; intelligence estimated that between 500 to 600 tanks backed them up. But Arik was confident. He would demolish their bridgehead, and his men would be crossing into Egypt before sunset.

"It's a risky business," Dado told Gonen. "Perhaps we should stick to the original plan." But the head of the Southern Command insisted. And Dado had to concede that Bren's force did not need any assistance; they were already crossing into Egypt. A moment later, Dado gave his permission: Sharon could move south at once.

This is wrong. Very wrong, Amnon thought. Haven't we learned anything?

Amnon watched with mounting apprehension as Bren's tanks

raced toward the waterline at 40 kilometers an hour, right into the center of the Egyptian positions. Without infantry support. Deployed in small groups. These were the same disasterous tactics they had used the afternoon the war broke out. Somebody had to stop them!

But it was too late. Amnon watched the ambush unfold with a sickening familiarity. A sea of gray uniforms swarmed from behind sand dunes and camouflaged infantry pits. He heard the whine of Sagger missiles. The pounding of RPGs. Tanks exploded into soaring flames. Chunks of metal cascaded through the air. Bursts of machine gun fire rattled across the desert. Everywhere was confusion. A frenzy of huge, rushing machines as commanders tried to regroup, or escape.

A harried battalion commander screamed for help on the net. Amnon told his men to get ready. At any moment they'd receive orders to rush down and help. After all, that was why they had been deployed on this hilltop. They were reserve support, armored cavalry ready to run to the rescue.

But the order Amnon received from Sharon's field command was to stand put. The plan had changed. And they radioed Bren's brigade, "We are about to move south, and we will need this battalion."

"Meanwhile, my men are being killed," the astonished officer in Bren's force yelled back.

As the battles continued by the Suez Canal, as Bren's divisions stumbled into ambushes, Amnon ordered his men to move south, away from the fighting. His conscience raged, but he obeyed his orders. Still, on the long trip across the desert, he kept asking himself over and over: Why didn't we help? Why didn't we help?

In the Pit, optimism soared. Dayan once again was the confident warrior, the effusive politician. When the news circulated about the room that Sharon had asked for permission to cross over into Suez, Dayan predicted that Arik wouldn't stop until he reached Cairo. "At any rate," he joked, playing shamelessly to the room of political power brokers, "what's certain is that he'll go to the Likud."

In all the hearty laughter, no one mentioned that before Sharon executed a crossing, he would need to battle through the Third Army and its 500 tanks. Or, for that matter, at the moment, his division had only just started to trudge through the sand on its journey to the south.

Finally, a devastating barrage of truths fell on the Southern Command Headquarters. At one o'clock Gonen learned that Bren had not reached the strongholds. In fact, he was hours away, and his men were fighting for their lives. At the same time, he also found out that Sharon's main force was bogged down in the desert, nowhere near the Third Army. Then, the final blow, he received word that the Egyptians had launched a powerful counterattack. The enemy was advancing with armor and troops all along the front. He listened on the radio net with shock and horror as the Egyptians overwhelmed what remained of Bren's forces.

Four hours after he sent Sharon to the south, Gonen ordered him to return. It was too late in the day to launch an attack against the Third Army. And Bren needed his help. But as Sharon retraced his path back north, he discovered that the Egyptians had taken control of the territory he had abandoned. For the second time that day, Sharon would not mount a counterattack to rescue Bren. "I can't see it," he radioed back to Gonen.

Under heavy fire, reeling from their losses, Bren's brigades had no choice but to retreat.

"What happened?" Bren asked over the net. "Why are you withdrawing?"

"If you continue to ask me questions, there will be nobody left to answer in a few minutes," a battalion commander replied.

Bren gave the order to fall back.

As night fell over the desert, the burning carcasses of Israeli tanks lay strewn about the sand. Bren had led a force of 170 tanks into battle. He returned with an even hundred.

There were many casualties. Three battalions, one in each of Bren's brigade, had been virtually destroyed. Of the battalion commanders, one had been killed, another wounded, and a third captured. The doctors in the field hospitals worked all through the night, immersed in blood and the odor of death.

Sharon's division returned as the sun was setting. They had spent the day traveling, moving to the south, then returning north. There were no casualties, but then they had hardly fired a shot.

The Egyptian troops had pushed forward. Their line was several kilometers deeper into the Sinai than it had been in the morning.

Yesterday, Israel had been in grave danger. It was the lowest point in the nation's history.

Today the situation was even worse.

TWENTY-SEVEN

Purkan Fort/ 8 October 1973/2030

Amnon was furious. An entire day had been squandered. They had been ready, a fresh division of tanks and men, and they had spent the day wandering about the Sinai Desert like the Twelve Tribes. Only at the end of their journey they never reached the Promised Land. They never engaged the Third Army. They never crossed the Suez Canal. They simply returned to camp.

Anger and frustration boiled inside him, but he also felt shame. All his life he had taken orders. He understood the necessity of command. Yet he could not come to terms with Sharon's refusal to help Bren's battalions. Arik was a fearless, swashbuckling commander. Yet—and this deeply troubled Amnon—Sharon seemed intent on waging his own personal war against the enemy. Sharon had *his* strategy, *his* priorities. It was disloyal, even the thought made Amnon feel like a traitor. Nevertheless, Amnon suspected that Israel's sparring generals had caused nearly as much harm today as the enemy. But above all this, Amnon felt the weight of his own guilt. Good men had died, and he had done nothing to help them.

With all this burdening his mind, Amnon entered the Tasa Command Post. The room, to his surprise, bustled with activity. A rescue operation was being hastily organized. The thirty-three soldiers trapped in the Purkan stronghold had decided to make a run for it.

Last night Egyptian tanks with mounted flamethrowers had attacked an adjacent fort. The Purkan soldiers had listened over the loudspeaker-telephone that linked the Bar-Lev Line to the cries of men being burned alive. Tonight, they feared the tanks would come for them. Their only hope was to flee. In the dark, they hoped to scramble past the thousands of Egyptian troops surrounding the Canal front, and make their way fifteen miles through the desert to the Israeli positions.

Sharon had immediately gotten on the line and tried to dissuade them. "You haven't got much of a chance," he warned. But he was arguing with men whose friends had been incinerated, and who believed they faced an identical fate. "We're leaving anyway," Sharon was told. "Well," he agreed at last, "if you think it will work, do it."

The rescue task force would go behind enemy lines and try to meet up with the soldiers from the fort. The officer Sharon had designated to lead the operation stood by a map, improvising his plan to a cluster of soldiers even as he spoke.

Amnon listened for a moment, then impulsively ran up to Sharon. "Arik," he said, "I want to be the one to rescue them."

"You're a brigade commander," Sharon said. "You have other responsibilities." The general turned and walked off.

"No way!" Amnon shouted. The words had erupted from him, and now there was no taking them back. The entire room fell silent, and focused on what would happen next. "Those men are *my* responsibility," Amnon went on. "Purkan is in *my* sector. They are *my* soldiers."

Sharon fixed him with a stony gaze. His temper was famous. But when he spoke his voice was level. "It's your job," he decided. "Bring them home."

* * *

Shmuli lay on his own cot in the Barak Brigade's forward camp, and tried to sleep. He was exhausted, and he knew tomorrow he would need all his strength. Yet the throbbing in his head had returned, an aching, steady torment. So he just lay there, resting uncomfortably, open-eyed in the dark, and as he did his long day came back to him.

Despite his failure to recruit a force at the Rosh Pina tank depot, Shmuli drove straight to Nafekh. Prepared to find the post swarming with Syrian troops, he approached with his Uzi in hand, finger curled on the trigger. But Israeli soldiers had retaken the base. With a renewed sense of hope, he parked the jeep and went off on foot to search for his friends' bodies.

He walked down from the camp, and made his slow way through a graveyard of charred and ravaged tanks. It was a sorrowful journey, and whatever hope had buoyed him was quickly lost. In his mind he reconstructed the fury of the battle, and the futility of the defense. The Barak Brigade had been outnumbered and overwhelmed. He headed reluctantly toward a tank that had been upended, tossed as if it were a child's toy. It was the commander's tank. Shmuli struggled to pull himself up to the turret and, after resting a moment from his exertions, crawled into the open canopy. Fire had blackened the crew space, and the smell of burning was still raw and strong. He entered a cave of darkness, and Shmuli cursed his own stupidity for not having thought to bring a flashlight. But in time he found the body. Ben Shoham lay on a bed of metal shards, his arms extended like a bather floating serenely in a pool. With great care, Shmuli brushed a film of dirt and debris from the face and looked at his friend. Ben Shoham had died a soldier's death, and Shmuli found solace in that. He managed to carry the body from the tank and lay it out on the flat, dark ground.

The deputy and the operations officer were about 100 meters away. Their tank had run out of shells, and armed with machine guns, they had made a last stand behind a clump of rocks. Bullet holes riddled their bodies.

When all three bodies were finally together, arranged head to head in a row, Shmuli pulled himself to attention and executed a farewell salute. He promised himself that one day he would visit their graves to recite kaddish. But now he walked up the slope into the camp and arranged for the bodies to be retrieved. Then he returned to his jeep and drove off.

Less than half an hour later, he entered the forward Golan base of what had once been the Barak Brigade's mighty Fifty-third Battalion. He could barely believe what his battalion had been reduced to. As a boy he had heard his grandfather's stories about the survivors of the Nazi camps, how even in life they were so dispirited it was as if they had not escaped death. Until this moment he had not fully comprehended what his grandfather had described. Now he understood. The listless men wandering about had battled nearly nonstop through two ferocious days of combat. They had survived while friends had died. And now in their shock and exhaustion, they had retreated to some remote place in the depths of their souls to take shelter. They had had enough.

Shmuli saw the strange, distant look on their faces and his instinct was to leave them alone. But he knew he could not do this. The enemy was on the march.

For the second time that day, he gathered men around him. He did not make a speech. These were professional soldiers, all that remained of the proud Barak Brigade, not *jobniks* called from their families. Calmly, methodically, in his rasping voice he told the soldiers what had to be done. He acted as if it were an ordinary day.

And they set to work. Mechanics poured over the battered tanks, repairing what could be fixed, and, when necessary, salvaging parts from abandoned or inoperable machines. Shmuli divided the men into new four-man crews. Loaders found shells for the cannons. The turret machine guns were primed. Treads cleaned. By nightfall, eleven Centurions were ready. The Barak Brigade, or at least a determined remnant, had been re-created.

General Hofi's deputy, Col. Uri Bar-On, visited the camp that evening to meet with Shmuli and discuss what Command wanted them to do. But he took one look at the major and ended the discussion.

"I am ordering you to go back to the hospital," he said.

"I refuse," said Shmuli.

"What?" stammered the staff officer.

"I'm commanding this brigade now," Shmuli explained. "And in this camp I give the orders."

Bar-On considered the situation. "Okay," he decided. "I am ordering you to go back to the hospital as soon as the war is over."

Then he gave Shmuli his assignment. At dawn the eleven tanks would proceed north to support Yanosh's Seventh Armored Brigade. After three days of intense fighting, they had kept the Syrians out of Kuneitra. But they were worn down. If the enemy made a concerted push, the Seventh would need all the help it could get. Eleven tanks would have to do the job.

And now lying in his cot, pain crashing through his head, Shmuli decided it really didn't matter if he slept. He had survived to fight again, and that in itself was a miracle. He had no right to expect another. After tomorrow, there would be plenty of time to sleep. A world of sleep. He lay awake with his thoughts, wondering what it was like when you died.

In the north that night, there was a lull.

Kahalani had battled all day and into the night, and finally the Syrians had again pulled back to the Valley of Tears. He wanted to believe that this time they'd had enough, and in the morning they would not attack again. He sat on the tank deck in the white moonlight and looked out toward the valley, keeping watch on the enemy until the cold drove him inside his tank. Once in the compartment, he became drowsy. He slept, until the explosions woke him up.

He climbed quickly to the open canopy, and saw the night sky burning with a bright orange glow. The Syrian artillery was laying a savage barrage on Kuneitra. As he stood in the turret, the bombardments seemed to intensify until they surged into a single solid, evil noise. The earth beneath his tank shuddered, as if it, too, was cold and helpless.

And he knew there was only one reason shells were falling on Kuneitra. With the dawn, the Syrians would attack again. And this time Kahalani doubted his weary men could summon the strength or the will to hold them back.

"Fire a flare. We need to know where you are," Amnon screamed into the radio, hoping he would be heard over the tremendous noise of the battle.

His rescue force had taken cover just below the crest of a tall sand dune. Beyond the dune, spread out across remarkably flat, featureless terrain, a brigade of Egyptian tanks attacked three Israeli Centurions. Egyptian infantry supported the tanks, hundreds of men moving in the night shadows across the cool, dark sand. From behind another crest that ran parallel to Amnon's position, Egyptian howitzers fired over the heads of their men, each volley getting closer to the Israeli tanks. And somewhere in the no-man's-land of battle, amid the raging tanks, the falling artillery shells, and the swarming infantry, were the thirty-three men from Purkan.

It was 4 A.M., and after walking across the desert for hours with only the stars to guide them, they had stumbled into a fortified Egyptian position. Now they were as trapped as if they had stayed behind the fortress's concrete walls.

Stealth was no longer possible. But Amnon refused to abandon the men. After the day's failures and frustrations, he was determined not to let these men down.

Suddenly a green flare rose up high in the night sky. It had been fired about 500 yards to the west of his position. "Move out," he ordered his men.

Two tanks and four armored half-tracks filled with infantry climbed over the dune, and headed into the battlefield. Amnon instructed a tank and the half-tracks to proceed toward the flare. His tank would swing left to provide cover.

As Amnon crossed the flat, gray sand, he saw a group of men in the distance. He radioed to the other tank, "I think I've found them."

Excited, he drove ahead at full speed. It was only as he got closer that he realized the men were Egyptians. They began to shoot, and now he was right on top of them. His cannon was useless. He clutched the turret machine gun and began spraying bullets, his entire body shaking from the exertion. He yelled to his driver, "Charge! Run them over." His tank lurched into the mass of bodies, crushing and grinding. He continued to fire as the tank smashed through the wall of men. Then the Centurion turned in a semicircle, and charged back. Straight into the enemy. Amnon was killing with pleasure, looking for vengeance, and he knew it was not normal. But he swung his gun back and forth, spraying bullets in a wide arc, until the line broke and the Egyptians ran off into the night.

With his private battle over, he raced toward his task force. All four of the half-tracks had been hit by Sagger missiles. One was in flames, and sat abandoned in the desert. The other vehicles, filled with the dead and wounded, limped back behind the sand dune to the Israeli lines. But where was the other tank? And the men from Purkan?

Then he saw something moving through the battlefield. Artillery blasted, tank cannons boomed. But this *thing* kept coming, weaving through the thunderous intensity of the fighting. Amnon stared into the distance at what looked like a horrific many-headed beast. A thing crawling with bodies. It got closer, and now he realized that thirty-three men had climbed up onto a tank. They were holding on to the turret, gun barrels, each other, whatever they could grab, as they rode to safety.

With the dawn, Amnon returned to the base. They had rescued all the soldiers from Purkan, but it had been costly. Five men killed, twenty-one wounded. Nothing in this war, he had begun to realize, would be easy.

* * *

Was there anyone Yossi didn't know? Any Israeli who wasn't his best friend? Who wasn't eager to help out the smiling hero in the famous photograph? As Yossi followed the pretty El Al stewardess up the aisle to the cockpit, Nati remained in her seat alone with her thoughts.

Yesterday, Nati had also sat back and watched her husband work his unique magic. No sooner had they been shuffled off to a dreary holding room at the Athens airport with the promise that the next six months would be spent in quarantine than Yossi was on the phone. An hour later the Israeli ambassador to Greece accompanied by two important-looking police officials as well as a Greek colonel led them out of the airport. They were driven in a limousine to the ambassador's residence. The ambassador would be delighted to have Yossi and Mrs. Ben Hanan as his guests for however long it took before planes were once again flying to Israel.

But Monday, an entire day spent waiting impatiently for the El Al night flight, had been a curse. Yossi had been on the phone to Israel a half dozen times. He called the army trying to get details about what was happening, if his brigade was in combat, if there were casualties, but he received only vague answers. He couldn't tell if they were reluctant to say too much over an open international line, or if they simply didn't know. He spoke with his parents and told them what to bring to the airport: his gun, his tanker overalls, a heavy jacket for the Golan cold. Then he called back again to remind them, "Don't forget the overalls." He knew they wouldn't, but it made him feel better to be in touch with people back home. He felt ashamed: Israel was at war and he was sitting on the sofa in the ambassador's comfortable living room.

But Monday night, when the first plane left Athens, they were on board. At last they were on their way home. They hadn't been in the air long before a stewardess walked by, glanced his way, and squealed, "Yossi!"

"Tzipi," he answered back with no less cheerful recognition, and, compounding Nati's surge of annoyance, gave her one of his most charming smiles. A moment later Tzipi was leading Yossi to the cockpit so he could speak to the pilots and find out the latest war news.

He returned ten minutes later and shared what he had learned. "Yossi," the pilot had told him, "this time the war has ended without you. You've already missed it. We already have forces near Damascus and one of our divisions has already crossed the Suez Canal."

Still, Yossi made sure he was the first person off the plane when it landed in Tel Aviv just before dawn. He didn't wait for the bus to take him to the arrival hall. He ran across the tarmac as Nati, still carrying her stuffed monkey, tried to keep up.

This time they breezed through passport control, and hurried to where their parents were waiting. Yossi immediately asked, "Are we still fighting?"

They looked at him incredulously. Then Michael Ben Hanan spoke. "What are you talking about? Do you know what's going on at the front? It's horrendous."

TWENTY-EIGHT

The Pit/9 October 1973/0400

It had come to this.

At 4 A.M. Dado and Dayan, their spirits broken, had returned to Tel Aviv from the Sinai. For two hours they had sat through an acrimonious postmortem listening to the Southern Command generals trade accusations about why the counterattack had failed. At its conclusion there was only one certainty: The Egyptian bridgehead was still firmly in place.

Once back in the Pit, Zeira gave them more disheartening news. Syria's elite Republican Guard Brigade, a formidable force of T-62 tanks, had moved into the Golan. Commanded by Rifaat al-Assad, brother of the Syrian president, the brigade was usually deployed to protect Damascus. But in the morning, they would lead the charge through Kuneitra.

On both fronts all reason for hope had vanished. Dayan summoned the general staff into a predawn meeting in the chief of staff's room.

The time had come, Dayan announced gravely, for Israel to prepare to make a final stand. On the Golan there must be "no retreat.

Not even a single centimeter." The army must fight "to the last bullet." At the same time, "the whole country" must be armed with antitank weapons. Old men, boys, whoever can hold a rifle, should be mobilized at once. The enemy would soon be in the streets of Haifa and Tel Aviv, but there could be no surrender.

And with the looming destruction of his lifelong dreams, with events accelerating so rapidly, Dayan decided one other last step had to be taken. He dismissed the other men and sat with the chief of staff. He told him what was on his mind, and Dado nodded in mute consent. It was as if he could not bear to speak the words.

They had fought a losing war for seventy-two hours and now the end game had begun. They would ask the prime minister to authorize a series of actions that until this moment both men had believed were impossibilities.

The code name for the weapons was "Temple." The name had been deliberately chosen. It was meant to reinforce the conviction that these were weapons of last resort: a force to be used only when the existence of the state—the Third Temple—was threatened. Now that time had come. At 7:20 that morning in the prime minister's office, as the fourth day of the war began, Dayan asked permission to arm missiles and jets with nuclear weapons.

When Dayan finished, Dr. Shalheveth Freier came into the room. Freier was the nuclear physicist who ran Dimona, the top secret Negev factory that manufactured Israel's nuclear arsenal. He explained how many bombs were available, how long it would take for the weapons to become operational, and led a discussion of possible targets. "If they push us into the sea, they will find out they have nothing to return to. Cairo, Damascus—poof! *Gone!*"

Everyone in the room looked at Golda Meir. Only she could make this decision.

The night before, her personal secretary, Lou Kadar, had given her a bottle of pills. Two were all she would need. She put the bottle in her bag. When the time came, she would rather die than witness the destruction of the Jewish state. Death would be the only honor left to her. And if it came to that, if Israel went up in flames, why not bring the rest of the Middle East down with it?

Yes, she told the chief of staff. Begin the preparations to launch the Temple weapons.

As nuclear bombs were loaded on to eight specially marked F-4s at Tel Nof air base, and as Jericho missiles armed with nuclear warheads were raised onto the launch pads at Hibrat Zachariah in the foothills of the Judean Mountains west of Jerusalem, Maj. Shmuli Askarov prepared to lead his eleven tanks north. They would join up with what was left of the Seventh Armored Brigade and fight to the last man to keep the Syrians from crossing the Jordan.

He was about to climb up to the turret of the lead Centurion, when a hand grabbed his shoulder. He turned in anger; there was nothing more to discuss.

Only now he said, "I thought you were in Nepal. On your honeymoon."

"The honeymoon is over," Lt. Col. Yossi Ben Hanan answered. "Now we fight and win."

PART IV

"REPEL THE ENEMY AT THE GATE"

Sinai/Golan Heights
October 9–18, 1973

Who shall be brought to a low state . . .

TWENTY-NINE

Unit 848/9 October 1973/0900

Colonel Ben Porat returned one morning to his desk as if nothing had happened. He offered no explanation for his intemperate behavior and the apparent seizure that followed. Nor, for that matter, did he seem to have an opinion about why Aman, after having collected so much evidence, had continued to insist that the probability for war was "low, even lower than low."

Instead, the preferred topic for earnest stocktaking was the beating Israel's forces were taking on both fronts. This war was not the Six Day War, the unit's commanding officer lectured, as Brill listened with silent, building fury. The Arabs' numerical superiority in men and weapons was about three times what it had been in '67. Back then they had been able to put 300,000 men into battle; now they had 1 million troops. Same with tanks: 1,700 compared to more than 5,000 today. And planes: 350 to more than 1,000. And field artillery: 1,350 against 4,800.

But even more significant, according to what Brill realized was fast becoming Military Intelligence's institutionalized excuse for the bleak situations on the battlefields, was the wizardry of the enemy's weapons. The dense SAM missile systems had effectively reduced the role of the previously invincible air force. The SAM-6s, particularly, had done a lethal job on the attack squadrons. The SAM-6's tracking radar with its rapidly changing frequencies could not be jammed or blinded. Flares or chaff did not easily fool its homing device. And the pilots did not have a "black box" capable of alerting them that the radar had locked on. Without warning, tree-trunk-sized SAM-6 missiles zooming at Mach 2.8 slammed into the planes. The SAM-7s, mounted on armored vehicles, traveled to the front lines in eight-barrel launchers. Then they'd be fired in salvos of four or eight; a pilot might find the skill or the luck to evade one missile, possibly even another, only to be hit by the next. And if a jet swooped in low hoping to avoid the intricate web of complementary surface-to-air missile systems, then the guns went to work. The Russians possessed the world's most technological advanced antiaircraft weapons, and they had provided the Arabs with their best: a self-propelled quadruple 23-mm AA cannon, the ZPU-23-4. While the threat of the missiles intimidated the pilots, antiaircraft fire destroyed more planes.

The long-range Saggers and the shoulder-mounted RPGs were not new weapons. However, the quantity was extraordinary. The Sinai desert crawled with several thousand well-armed Egyptian tank-killer teams. It was a strategy Israeli tank doctrine had not foreseen. Battle after battle, wedges of Israeli armor surged ahead into devastating ambushes. An advance barrage of artillery fire, even ordinary mortars, followed by mechanized infantry troops going into combat along with the tanks—these mixed tactics would have had the "creepy crawlies," as the antitanks teams became known, on the run. But the Israeli armored corps in the Sinai stubbornly refused to abandon its all-tank, cavalry charge doctrine.

And, there was a good deal of grudging admiration for the "new Arab soldiers." Not only were they proving brave, guiding in Saggers as hulking Centurions bore down or making charge after suicidal charge despite heavy casualties on the Golan, but they were also undaunted by the complex technology of their new Soviet weapons. Dado talked tough; at a press conference on the evening of October 8, he had growled, "We'll break their bones." But the bitter joke being whispered around the unit was a better assessment of the painful differences between this war and the last: The Arabs had learned from the Israelis how to fight, while the Israelis had learned from the Arabs how to lie.

Yet in all the aggrieved discussions in the unit, in all the search for blame, Brill was astonished by what had gone unmentioned. It was as if there had been no surprise. It was as if the lack of sufficient warning of the attacks had not been a large reason for the present disaster. How can you rewrite the past? he wanted to scream. If the reserves had been brought up to the Golan. If the armored brigades had been deployed according to the Dovecote plan along the Suez Canal waterline. If the strongholds had been fully manned with professional infantrymen from the regular army. If the air force had been prepared to launch a coordinated strike against the missiles. If Ben Porat, Zeira, *anyone*, had listened to him. Then the nation would have been ready. Israel would not be in such straits.

Brill, however, did not say a word. What could be gained by reminding the hierarchy of his efforts to sound the alarm? It was too late to remake the unchangeable past. Men had died, and more deaths loomed.

Still, Brill had not expected the twist their conversation would take when Ben Porat, after studiously avoiding as much as eye contact during his first few days back in command, finally confronted him. "Is it true you went to General Lidor?" Ben Porat demanded.

"Yes."

"You should not have done that," Ben Porat said with slow, rigid resolve. Then there was the flash of a derisive smile, as he taunted, "Now you can say it, 'I'm right.' "

Ben Porat walked away without another word. But the impact of his commander's smoldering anger left Brill stunned. Prescient as always, he understood. The messenger would be blamed for the news. He would be made to pay.

Zeira remained unruffled. He had spent nearly the entire war in the Pit with the general staff, and no one had yet dared—or for that matter had the time—to point an accusatory finger at him. But let someone try. His conscience was clear.

From his unyielding perspective, Military Intelligence had done its job. Aman had provided real-time information detailing the unprecedented buildups on both fronts. It had clearly documented Egypt's and Syria's increased capabilities. The chief of staff, however, had decided not to act. Supported by the minister of defense, Dado had gambled on his ability to read the enemy's intentions. *That* was the disastrous mistake. Mobilization of reserves must be based on the enemy's capabilities. Not on an assessment, however well reasoned, of what the enemy might do. Any attempt to make Aman responsible for the failures on the battlefields was nothing more than nasty politics, a crude move to cover up military blunders and a lack of realistic operational planning. The army had only itself to blame.

Yet as he reviewed all the history that had led Israel to this precipice, one aspect of the tragic journey began to trouble him. The first step had been the Concept. After the general staff and the politicians had latched on to its certainties, nothing would budge them. They were convinced that Egypt and Syria would never go to war. And who, he soon found himself asking, had planted this poisonous seed?

The In-Law.

And in the next jarring moment he wondered: Could the spy have passed on this flawed intelligence deliberately?

Once this first question was posed, others followed in a cynical flurry. Why had the spy delivered a false war warning last May? Or waited until nearly the last minute to summon Zamir to London? Was it plausible he didn't know about the invasions until only the day before they were launched? Could he have not known the correct time of the attacks? As Zeira began to consider the answers, a startling adjustment to his way of looking at all that had previously been fixed in his mind began to take form.

Dado, however, was not concerned with blame or with intrigue. He had a war to fight. And today, the fourth day, began without illusions. The unforgivable fiasco of yesterday's counterattack in the desert was now fully known. There were no more reserves to summon. And the Syrians were preparing to push into Kuneitra. The nation was fighting for its survival.

Dado entered this critical stage of the war with, he felt, only a single reliable weapon in his arsenal: the Israeli soldier. The courage, cunning, and resilience of the Israeli fighting man, though outnumbered, though facing superior weapons, and caught unprepared, would have to lead the way out of the ruins. In the ordeal ahead, he was all Israel had.

THIRTY

Kuneitra Salient/ 9 October 1973/0800

With the first light of the gray mountain dawn, the Syrian guns began to fire. Volleys of Katyusha rockets tore into the ground, spitting up chunks of dirt and black rock. Formations of MiG-17s came in low and fast, dropping bombs. The battle-weary men of the Seventh Armored Brigade closed their tank turrets, took cover, and hoped the barrage would soon stop.

By eight o'clock that morning, as the fury intensified, with a hellish downpour of bursting shells and screaming rockets, Col. Yanosh Ben Gal knew with certainty that the Syrians would be coming.

The long-barreled cannons of the Republican Guard Brigade's T-62s would climb up from the valley. There were 100 tanks in each attack group, accompanied by armored infantry. He had 17 tanks—crewed by exhausted men, low on ammunition, all that remained of the 110 Centurions that he had led north four days ago. And he had to stop them.

At nine o'clock the Syrians began their slow, relentless advance.

From the high ground of the ramps, the Seventh Armored Brigade Centurions began firing. Israeli tank commanders stood in their open turrets directing their gunners as artillery shells rained down around them. In the valley, T-62s burst into flames. But it did not matter. The great force kept grinding its way up the slope, heading inexorably toward the ramps. The battle had not been fought, but its end was set and fated.

Command came on the net for Yanosh. Withdraw from the Golan, they ordered. *Now!* Or else your men will be stranded. The bridges across the Jordan were about to be blown. It was the only way to slow the enemy advance into the heartland.

"I hear you," Yanosh shouted into the mike over the roar of battle. "But don't worry me with new details. I'm too busy." He instructed his communications officer to switch to a different radio channel. He didn't want to be bothered by Command. He would not leave the Golan.

Then he spoke over the brigade net to his men. "Pull back from the ramps. We need to get out of this artillery fire." They were to withdraw four hundred yards and form a new defensive line along a wide, jet-black gully.

Yanosh was ready to die. After four days of constant combat he was no longer afraid. In fact, he discovered, he liked war. The excitement of fighting alongside men he loved for the country that had taken him in as an orphan charged his being with a gleeful, energizing passion. He cherished his opportunity, even the threat of impending death, as if it were a gift and not a perversion of life itself.

"They will not pass through," he vowed to his men. "The fate of Israel rests on your shoulders. "They will not pass."

Coming down from the ramp, Kahalani sped toward the gully. He knew it well. On Sunday Syrian tanks had snuck through in single file, before emerging to charge his position on the high ground from the rear. With the brigade ordered to stretch out in a new line along its lip, Kahalani wanted to make sure the gully was empty.

His tank approached using a wall of basalt stone as cover. Then it turned the corner. Around the bend were four T-62s. Two were already in firing position, the others were climbing like monstrous beasts out of the gully.

"Stop!" he screamed to the driver. The driver braked so sharply that Kahalani nearly fell to his knees. But he recovered quickly. He grabbed the cannon swivel-stick and the turret swung toward the nearest tank. It was twenty yards away.

"Fire, fire!" he ordered the gunner, as he ducked down to avoid the shrapnel.

"What range?" the gunner asked.

"It doesn't matter," Kahalani yelled in frustration. Didn't he see the enemy was right on top of them? You could throw a rock and hit it. "Fire already!" In rage and impatience, he kicked the gunner.

The tank lurched as the shell exited. It pounded into the T-62, but there was no flame. Kahalani, though, saw the commander leap from the immobilized machine. At the same time, he hurried to train the big gun on a tank to the right.

"You see this one?"

"Yes. Just don't kick."

"Fire fast!"

The round punched a hole through the turret of the Syrian tank. A bull's-eye.

But only yards to its left, another T-62 had stopped, lowering its hull as it prepared to fire. Behind it, the fourth enemy tank drove forward, its black cannon muzzle pointed toward them.

"Fire! Fire!"

Kahalani expected to feel the tank rock as the shell sped to its target. Instead he heard the gunner shout, "Misfire." The casing of the last shell clogged the breech. The loader had both hands deep into the muzzle, frantically trying to pull it out. But it would not budge.

Thirty yards off, the T-62 stood with its cannon aimed directly at them. For Kahalani time slowed. He gripped the handles in the command cupola, ready to jump to the ground. He had been trapped in a burning tank in the last war, and he would not allow that to happen again. It was as if he could feel the moment of impact approaching, suspended in an eternity of waiting.

Then the jolt. The tremendous boom of the cannon. To his astonishment, he saw the Syrian tank ignite. It was our gun, he realized. The gunner had cleared the muzzle. "Fire again!" he yelled.

Another direct hit. As the tank burned, Kahalani noticed for the first time that the sun had broken through. And more important, the artillery had stopped. If they could retake the ridge, they would once again be able to maneuver freely. Could they reclaim the firing positions on the high ground?

More tanks emerged from the gully, predators crawling up the slope. While in front of him, another wave of T-62s rose up from the valley, mounting the crest of the hill, heading up to the ramps.

The enemy's strategy was clear: Surround the Jews. Come at them from all sides. Close in. Then crush them.

The brigade's position was hopeless. Unless, Kahalani decided, we can beat them to the top of the hill. If we can retake the ramps, then we can fight. The Seventh Armored Brigade could make a last stand on the high ground.

He got on the net to tell Yanosh his plan.

Yossi felt ashamed. He looked at Shmuli, at the bandage wrapped over his friend's throat, the raw wounds on his forehead, at the pallor of a sick, spent man. He saw the others, bleary-eyed, unshaven, faces fixed with blank, defeated stares. He thought of Ben Shoham, all his dead comrades, all his friends had endured, all the sacrifices they had offered up, while he had been off pursuing a child's vision of adventure. He had let them down. His clean uniform, his unfired gun, were rebukes to his courage. He was determined to redeem himself.

With great speed and only small ceremony, Shmuli handed over command of all that remained of the 188th, the Barak Brigade, to Lt. Col. Yossi Ben Hanan. Yet Yossi was moved. An image of Ben Shoham smiling merrily, a glass in hand, at his wedding came to mind. Only two months ago. Now Ben Shoham was dead. And Yossi was taking his place. Yossi promised himself that Ben Shoham's death, all the extinguished lives, would not be in vain.

The eleven tanks were arranged in a linear formation, with Yossi's Centurion in the lead. Command ordered them to proceed north, toward Kuneitra. Yanosh and the Seventh Armored Brigade were in trouble. They could not hold out much longer.

Yossi heard the mission and, despite the urgency and desperation, he could not help but feel a rush of anticipation. Yanosh, his closest friend, his cohort in so many escapades, was in danger. And now from halfway around the world, Yossi had come back to save him. The stories they would tell about this reunion. If, he acknowledged, they lived to tell them.

An officious voice in Command interrupted Yossi's musings. Brigade commander, we need a call name for the radio net. How do you want to be known?

"Call me Morning Exercises," he answered quickly. Yanosh would be able to figure that out. So many dawns they had returned from long nights in time to hear Yossi's father on the radio urging the entire nation to wake up and do jumping jacks. Yossi grinned at the prospect. As soon as he heard the call name, Yanosh would know who had come to his rescue.

Moments later, the engines of the eleven tanks came alive. But before they moved out, Yossi got on the net and spoke to his force. "Do your best. Israel is counting on you. We have to succeed. We have to keep the flag of the 188th flying."

Shmuli stood in the cupola of the tank behind Yossi's and listened to his friend. He recalled his own failed, hoarse-voiced attempt at rallying the men. But Yossi was a leader. He spoke easily, with assurance and conviction. They were all tired, but he was fresh and clean: like a soldier in a movie. And for the first time since the war began Shmuli felt a sense of confidence. With Yossi Ben Hanan back, anything was possible.

Counterattack, Yanosh decided. It's the only way. Let them know that we will fight to the last man. Maybe that will scare them off.

He had worked it all out with Kahalani on the radio. Your men take the ramps, he had said. Block them coming up from the valley. "Don't worry, sir, I'm a Black Panther," Kahalani had promised, resurrecting their old joke about his Yemenite blood. Yanosh laughed and thought, What an honor to serve with men like this. Even in defeat we can be proud.

When Kahalani rushed to the crest of the hill with about half a dozen tanks, Yanosh would lead what remained of the force in a charge against the Syrians coming in from the rear. After he had bloodied them, shown the enemy they still had some fight left in them, he'd pull back to the hill and regroup with Kahalani's tanks. Kahalani's cannons would face the Valley of Tears; his would be aimed toward the gully. It would be like an American western movie, the wagons circled on the high ground, fighting to the last.

Yanosh got on the radio and told Menahem Ratess, a lieutenant colonel who had about five tanks left in his battalion, to join him in the charge.

"Yanosh, you are crazy," Ratess said. "We are all going to die. All of us. Look at their spearhead. Fifty tanks."

"What choice do we have?" Yanosh asked. They were old friends, and he felt like he was saying good-bye.

A moment passed, and then Ratess was back on the radio. "Yanosh, I love you, so we do it. Someone else, I say, 'Go to hell.' "

Yanosh explained the battle plan. They would drive north to south and seal up the gully. But as they moved up out, Yanosh remembered that the day before Yom Kippur Ratess had asked for permission to leave for a night to see his girlfriend. Yanosh, who never had any difficulty bending rules, agreed. Now charging into the line of Syrian tanks, cannons firing, the smell of cordite and burning metal high in the air, he asked, "You never told me. How was your fuck?"

"I think it will be my last fuck," Ratess answered forlornly.

Yanosh let loose with one of his deep, sly laughs. Then suddenly his face felt on fire. An intense heat spread over him. Instinctively, his hands rushed about, checking to see if he was burning. But he had not been hit. He quickly turned to his right and saw that it was Ratess's tank that was in flames. No one had escaped.

Yanosh sighed. Ratess had been right: We will all die today. He charged ahead, into the enemy.

As Kahalani moved up to take the hill, he looked behind him and discovered that the other tanks were not following. He yelled into the radio, urging them to join him, but it was useless. The men were spent; after all the battles, all the dying, the will to fight had finally drained away. In its place, a profound despair had settled in. He moved forward alone, a single tank mounting the hill.

As he climbed higher, he looked ahead and let out a curse: The Syrians were racing up from the other side. A T-62 fired a shot at him, but it was wide. He knew that if the enemy got to the ramps first, everything would be lost. If they gained the high ground, the Golan would fall.

He grabbed the radio microphone. "Look at the enemy's guts! He takes his positions and looks us in the eye. What about us? What the hell is happening to us? Who's stronger, us or these Arabs? Now move forward and straighten the line with me. Move!"

Kahalani waited. The tanks stood still, heavy and immobile. They would not move.

He urged them forward in his mind. But he knew the choice was theirs.

Then one tank lurched forward. And another. And suddenly as if pushed by some unseen force, they all began to advance.

"Don't stop, don't stop," he shouted, filled with an almost giddy exhilaration. The tanks pressed on, coming into line on his right and on his left. In formation, they began the climb to the top of the hill.

"Don't stop. Keep moving," he coaxed. "Be ready to fire." He was scared. His men were scared. But they needed the high ground. From the ramps they could shoot into the valley at will. Just fifty yards to go.

"We're better than them. We're better than them," he urged. Twenty yards more.

Then they were at the ramps. Below them was the valley, clear in the sunshine, and swarming with the enemy. Hundreds of tanks threaded their way through charred hulks that had accumulated over the days of fighting. The enemy surged in a dense green mass up the slope, coming at them.

"Shoot only at the moving ones," Kahalani ordered. The Centurions cannons began to blast. A hail of shells poured down into the valley. The crews were crazed with battle, out of breath, out of energy, and were fighting for their lives. The loaders jammed round after round into the breeches. The gunners pulled the heavy triggers without pause. A Centurion was hit, and the men scrambled out. The others barely noticed. They were determined to destroy everything in the valley before it climbed up into their midst and destroyed them.

THIRTY-ONE

Valley of Tears/ 9 October 1973/1130

Yanosh did not see how they could last. His Seventh Armored Brigade had been reduced to seven tanks. They had been killing tanks for hours, but the Syrians were coming closer. With resignation, he got on the net to Command and described the situation. There was no choice but to pull back.

"For God's sake, Yanosh," Gen. Raful Eitan pleaded. "Hang on just a few minutes more. You will soon be receiving reinforcements. Try, please. Hold on!"

"I will try," Yanosh agreed without conviction before signing off.

An instant later "Tiger," who had been defending Kahalani's southern flank near Booster Ridge, called him. "I can't hold on. We're down to two shells."

"You must. Use small arms, grenades if you have to," Yanosh ordered. "Help is on the way."

But even as he said the words, Yanosh wondered, Who's left to help us?

Then he heard a crisp, assured voice on the net.

"Brigade Commander, this is Morning Exercises coming to save you."

Yanosh was confused. There was no one in the brigade with that call sign. Unless. But that was impossible. Yet—

"You should be in Nepal," he shouted with disbelief as his spirits soared. "You're crazy. This is hell."

"I've come to avenge the 188th," Yossi announced. "It's my present to you. I didn't have time to bring you anything back from my trip. Saving your ass will have to do."

Yanosh broke into a laugh. Yossi, my brother, he thought happily, impossibly.

But there was no time for reveries. He told Yossi to flank Kahalani on Booster Ridge. Tiger's crews would pull back to rearm, and Yossi would take their place.

"Roger. How should we proceed once we deploy?"

"If you are my savior, Yossi, you'll know what to do," Yanosh said before signing off.

With his tank in the lead, Yossi's force drove up toward Booster Ridge. He knew the terrain well, and was already working out in his mind how he'd arrange his tanks. But as he got higher, he saw Syrian tanks approaching from the other direction. There was no time for strategy. Tiger had abandoned the ridge. It was now open territory. And whoever got there first would control the battleground.

"Let's go! Let's go!" he rallied on his men.

Over the rise, a T-55 appeared. He swung the turret in its direction and yelled, "Fire!"

The blast smashed the Syrian tank backward. Yossi's force sped on.

"Keep going," he urged. "Faster!"

They got there, and the ridge was theirs. Yossi ordered the tanks into a battle line. As the Syrians approached, they opened fire.

It was a shooting gallery. From the ridge, Yossi's gunners destroyed everything that approached. The orange flames from the enemy tanks rose into the sky. Battered machines, gaping holes punched into the metal, stood abandoned, turned in all directions, a chaos of sustained violence. In less than half an hour, they had destroyed thirty tanks.

Then suddenly an explosion rocked Yossi's Centurion. He fell from the cupola, landing in the belly of the machine. He touched his face, and his hands dripped with blood. He was scared, but he was also astonished. In all his service, he had never been wounded. Now just half an hour into this war, he was injured.

He radioed Shmuli. "I've been hit. You take over until I can resume command."

His loader wiped away the blood and began inspecting the wounds. Shrapnel was embedded in Yossi's cheeks and his nose. But his glasses had protected his eyes. It looks worse than it really is, the loader told him as he bandaged the wounds.

"Yanosh," Yossi announced with mock formality over the radio. "I'm wounded. But I will still keep my promise to save your ass."

"You do that and I'll get you a medal. But only if you stay alive." Then Yanosh added, "Be careful, my brother."

With a mask of white bandages crisscrossing his face, Yossi returned to the turret and assumed command of his force.

All the while, the battle raged on. His force kept firing shells. A seemingly impenetrable fusillade of noise and smoke rose up between them and the Syrian tanks moving up the hill.

Yossi's tanks spread out to look for better firing positions. As the line thinned, a group of Syrian tanks broke through into the gaps. The enemy was right on top of them.

Shmuli saw a T-62 just yards away. "Fire!" he ordered.

Nearby, standing in the cupola of his tank, Yossi heard the loud blast of Shmuli's cannon and looked over to see the enemy tank burning. Crewmen leaped from the T-62, but Shmuli paid no attention. His eyes focused downrange, searching for the next target.

And, therefore, he had no knowledge of the scene Yossi watched unfold with a helpless horror.

A Syrian crewman stood outside the blazing tank, his assault rifle aimed at Shmuli.

"Watch out!" Yossi yelled into the radio. In the same moment, he swiveled his machine gun at the Syrian. Yossi released a burst, and bullets riddled the soldier.

But the Syrian had already fired. A single report and Shmuli's head turned blood red. He fell over like a tree cut by an invisible ax.

Frantic, Yossi called for medics, and he watched them carry Shmuli's body away. But he knew.

"Yanosh," he reported in a grave whisper, "Shmuli's dead."

The battle went on into the afternoon. As it did, the men's hopes began to grow. In the valley, Kahalani saw that the Syrian advance had slowed. "They'll break eventually," he dared to tell Yanosh.

And then they did. The Syrians tanks began to withdraw from the Valley of Tears. At first it was orderly. But then tanks started turning in a frenzy, reversing in sharp, awkward lurches. In the confusion, crews abandoned their tanks with the motors running, making their way on foot through the jungle of flames and smoke and smoldering metal. They ran back across the border.

Yanosh rushed to the crest of hill and looked down into the Valley of Tears. It was a graveyard of destruction. Hundreds of Syrian tanks, hundreds of armored personnel carriers, the enemy's mighty force, covered the smoking black earth. "They shall not pass," he had vowed. And he had kept this promise. On the net, General Eitan announced to the Seventh Armored Brigade in a voice filled with awe: "You have saved the people of Israel."

In the Pit, Dado listened to the reports from General Hofi, and he shared the incredible news with the general staff. "Yanosh has come through an attack of T-62s with Yossi Ben Hanan." The general estimated that Syria had lost 700 of the 1,300 tanks they had at the front. Against all odds, the Seventh Armored Brigade had held Kuneitra.

And there was more good news. "There are no missiles. There are just no missiles," Dado told the assembled officers. The Syrians had run out of SAMs. And now Israeli Phantoms were on their way to Damascus. The air force would bomb strategic targets in the Syrian heartland, the chief of staff promised, until someone yelled "*Gevalt!* Stop! Stop shooting!"

In the north, for the first time it seemed the war might be beginning to turn.

Shmuli's body had been dumped onto the pile outside the field hospital with the other corpses. They were all heroes, but only the living received attention. This grim mound was ignored. It was a stack of lifeless uniforms smeared with dark stains. The permanent, official silence of death.

A medic went by carrying a fresh bag of blood for a transfusion. His eyes were fixed on some distant point, and he was in a hurry, but as he passed the corpses, he stopped and looked again. Then he yelled as much in fright as astonishment, "That man's arm is moving."

A doctor rushed over. With the medic's help, he lifted Shmuli's body. They carried him into the hospital, and placed him back among the living.

THIRTY-TWO

Tasa Command Post, Sinai/ 9 October 1973/1000

Amnon awoke quickly. He had returned an hour earlier, the desert sun already large and beaming, with the hard-hit task force and the thirty-three men from Purkan. As soon as he was back in camp, all he could think about was finding a place to lie down. He fell asleep with his boots on. But now a soldier stood above his cot announcing that General Gonen himself was demanding to speak with him. He yanked himself from the comfortable oblivion he had settled into and hurried to the Tasa Command Post.

Amnon picked up the receiver expecting to be quizzed about the rescue. Perhaps, his mind started to run in fanciful anticipation, there might even be a word of praise.

Amnon was wrong. Gonen never mentioned last night's operation. Instead, hard, direct, and curt, the general wanted to make sure Colonel Reshef understood today's orders: He was not to attack.

He was not to approach the Suez Canal. He was not to take

any aggressive actions unless he was certain there would be no casualties.

"Yes, sir," Amnon said. "Understood."

"Any questions?" Gonen challenged.

"No, sir," he said, and the general broke the connection.

Amnon's stomach tightened as he reflected on what he had just heard. The general running the Sinai war did not trust Arik Sharon, one of his division leaders, to relay orders down to the brigade level. He had to do it himself. Not only that, the relationship between Gonen and Sharon was so acrimonious, so out of control, that Gonen made no attempt to hide it. This was insane, Amnon decided with a flash of irritation. The generals were squabbling like vindictive schoolboys. How can we win a war when the men leading us are colliding against one another? He tried to keep a steady mind, but instead he found himself grasping uncomfortably at a heresy: The generals were not worthy of the men they were leading.

Nevertheless, Amnon would have to tell Sharon. Arik was his immediate superior officer and Amnon had been a soldier too long to violate the chain of command. When he reported the conversation with Gordish, Sharon listened without interruption. Then speaking very slowly, giving each word a theatrical emphasis, he said, "You do exactly as told." He repeated the instructions two more times. It was important, he reiterated, that Amnon understood General Sharon had not authorized him to disobey the orders of the day.

Amnon returned to his men. Yet the deliberate, pedantic quality to Sharon's words left him speculating. It was almost as if Arik was coaching him for some future military tribunal. What precisely was going on?

It did not take very long to get the answer. That afternoon a staff officer at the Tasa Command Post ordered Amnon's brigade to assist another brigade from the division. They were to retake two strongholds, Machsir and Televizia, near the Suez Canal.

"What about my previous orders?" Amnon asked.

"You were authorized to take whatever actions necessary as long as there were no casualties. Make sure no one is hurt."

In the Pit, all attention focused on the Seventh Armored Brigade's desperate stand at Kuneitra. No one knew Sharon's division was once again moving into action.

Earlier that morning, when Dado had learned that one of Sharon's brigades had been arrayed on the Artillery Road and was preparing to head out, the chief of staff contacted Gonen. His voice a key higher than usual, Dado ordered, "Let him pull back. Improve his positions. Exploit the advantage of a tank shooting from an emplacement at the armor moving toward him."

He emphasized that Arik was not to approach the Canal. "Don't go there. . . . We're sticking to the principle of a defensive battle. . . . *They're* the ones who are supposed to get worn out while advancing." After the folly of yesterday's counterattack, Dado's strategy in the south was to form a defensive line along the Artillery Road and regroup. Hundreds of tanks fortified the Egyptian bridgeheads and Sagger-toting infantry crawled through the sands. This was not the moment "to move forward again and fritter away more tanks." The Sinai policy, at least for the time being, was containment. "If we play our cards right," he told the staff officers, "the Egyptian armor will simply run out of steam."

That settled, Dado once more turned to the latest reports from the crucial battles in the Golan.

It was another brutal firefight.

Sharon's two brigades had moved west from the Artillery Road and then split into two attack prongs. One sloped down from the north toward the Machsir fortification. Amnon hooked around from the south, his approach roughly parallel to the Great Bitter Lake. At first it had gone well. But as the Egyptians withdrew, the northern column of tanks gave chase. And when the brigade moved near the Canal, they were caught in a cross fire of Saggers and pounded by enemy tanks firing from entrenched positions.

Amnon led his men up through flat desert about fifteen miles from the northeastern shore of the lake. But then he received a report that an immobilized Israeli tank was trapped under heavy fire in the high dunes near Televizia. With the memory of the brigade's failure to support Bren's battalions still raw, Amnon rushed to help. His force made quick work of the enemy. Three crewmen were saved. But in the battle, the battalion commander whose tank earlier that morning had carried the thirty-three reservists from Purkan to safety was killed. Over the past four days Amnon had experienced the death of many friends. But Shaul Shalev's death nearly broke him. On the same day that Shaul, against all odds and even credulity, had maneuvered a tank draped in a swarm of bodies through a ferocious battle to emerge without a scratch, he was cut down by a single infantryman's bullet. In an operation that, quite arguably, was in violation of the orders Amnon had received from the head of the Southern Command.

Amnon reported Shaul's death to Division and asked for further clarification of his mission. His brigade was on a route that might take them to the Great Bitter Lake. But he could not guarantee there would no further casualties. Should he return to camp?

No, he was told. Proceed.

In Center Ten, Shazly followed the progress of the new Zionist attacks. With each fresh report, he became more convinced that today was developing like yesterday. The enemy was continuing to throw away the lives of its tank crews. The cavalry charge, brave but foolish, was their only tactic.

When Shazly had conceived his original plan, he had predicted that if his tanks and infantry dug into positions on the east bank and remained sheltered beneath a canopy of surface-to-air missiles, the impatient Jews, goaded by the conceit of their invincibility, would come rushing to them. Now they were doing just that. Day after bloody, futile day.

* * *

When Gonen learned that Sharon's brigades had moved out, he immediately boarded a helicopter and flew to the Tasa Command Post. What he had to say was so important, he wanted to make sure Arik received the message. But given Gonen's bellowing rage, he could have stayed in Um Hashiba and Sharon still would have heard him.

Do not launch a new attack, he'd ordered and Sharon had agreed. Or at least Gonen, who returned to Southern Command, thought he had. Later Arik, with a born politician's instinct for ambiguity, would explain that while his men had engaged the Egyptians, they had not attacked. They had simply "tailed" the enemy. And in the chase, unfortunately, his division had lost another fifty tanks.

Standing in the cupola of his Centurion, Amnon looked in all directions and saw nothing but tall, gray sand dunes. He heard the thumping engines of his column, but little else. He had entered into a stark, isolating landscape. The arcing walls of hard sand might just as well have been purposefully constructed to keep out the war.

Cautiously, he treaded a zigzagging course between the dunes, heading west toward the sunset, and the waterline.

His attention was keen as he scanned the horizon for a telltale movement. His great fear was that without warning the calm desert would all at once be transformed into a slithering mass of soldiers. At any instant, Saggers could come screaming in. But there were no signs of enemy patrols. The farther he went, the more the reassuring sense grew that the enemy would never find him. Once he had slipped among the dunes, it was as if a gate had been locked behind him.

Yet when he found his location on his map, he saw how close to danger he was. He was behind enemy lines, just kilometers south of the paved Akavish Road. As he studied the map, an idea began to form: If he continued for about fifteen miles, he'd intersect with another main road, Lexicon. From there it would be a quick dash to the northeastern corner of the Great Bitter Lake. Farther north was the eight-kilometer-deep Egyptian Second Army bridgehead fortified with thousands of infantry and hundreds of tanks. But this route among the dunes just might allow a force to slip between the Second Army to the north and the Third Army to the south. It could be a way to reach the Suez Canal through enemy lines undetected.

The inchoate plan grew in his mind as he continued to study the military map. But one landmark on the way to the canal gave him concern: the Chinese Farm. The curious name had started as a soldier's joke. The Egyptian government with UN assistance had developed an expanse of arid desert in the 1960s as an agricultural settlement for veterans and Bedouins. When Israeli forces overran this farm on their way to the Canal's east bank in the Six Day War, they maneuvered across a vast network of irrigation ditches filled with equipment with Oriental markings. The soldiers assumed the letters were Chinese and in tribute dubbed the exotic settlement "the Chinese Farm." When it was later discovered the writing was actually Japanese, the military officials simply shrugged. The name stuck.

Amnon's quick look at the map revealed the strategic importance of the settlement's location. The Chinese Farm lay on the axis of two Sinai roads, Lexicon and Tirtur. A force emerging from the dunes would have to pass the farm on the way to a crossing point. But there were no intelligence reports of a significant Second Army presence in the farm. And even if there were a few troops bivouacked in the old farm buildings, how hard would it be to push them out?

Amnon smiled at his own impetuosity. He still had not made his way out of the dunes. Tank attack teams could be hiding in any wadi. He sent a reconnaissance unit to scout ahead. Then he got on the radio and informed Divisional Headquarters that he was traveling a newly discovered route toward the Great Bitter Lake. So far there was no sign of the enemy.

* * *

Amnon's news excited Sharon. He had lost fifty tanks today, but he sensed a great opportunity to redeem himself. If only the weak-willed Gonen would allow a daring commander to grab it. But he knew that would never happen. He would have to go over Gonen's head and appeal directly to the general staff.

"I have my feet dipping in the waters of the Great Bitter Lake," Sharon announced with some exaggeration in a call late that afternoon to Gen. Dov Sion in the Pit. He begged Sion, who was Dayan's son-in-law, to persuade Dado and the others to countermand Gonen's orders. He had a new bold plan: He wanted to take the Chinese Farm and cross into Egypt *tonight.*

By six o'clock that evening, with the Phantoms back from their successful bombing of the Syrian Defense Ministry in downtown Damascus and the Seventh Armored Brigade's miracle at the Valley of Tears, Dado surged with a new confidence. Suddenly the possibility that tomorrow they could push the Syrians back beyond the Purple Line seemed real. Then he picked up the phone to answer Gonen's call, and his newfound hopefulness shattered in an explosion of pure, unfettered rage.

Gonen asked that Sharon be relieved of his command. And as he recounted Sharon's insubordinate behavior, as he cited the number of tanks lost in the field on a day explicitly designated for defensive actions, as he reported Sharon's new scheme, each bit of news ratcheted up the chief of staff's anger. Dado hung up the phone, and bellowed across the Pit, "Sharon took his division and attacked. . . . And now he wants to cross over to the other side. He was told that we have no intentions of crossing, and nonetheless moved the whole division there!" A moment later Dado was on the phone again and now he was screaming at Gonen: "Get him out! *I am not going to cross!*"

Dado slammed down the phone. Sharon had to go. And something also needed to be done about Gonen. He was too young, too inexperienced to control senior commanders like Arik and Bren. He wasn't up to commanding an entire front.

Resigned, Dado went to see Dayan.

"What does Arik want?" Dayan asked incredulously after the chief of staff had already explained Sharon's latest plan.

"What does he want? He wants to cross!" Dado shot back.

"Cross how? How is he going to cross?"

"He even wants to go and take the Chinese Farm at night. . . . I'm being sucked into a reckless adventure, a gamble I can't afford to risk," Dado worried.

Dayan, however, would not agree to Arik's dismissal. All too often, Dayan conceded with merry philosophy, he had wanted to murder Sharon. Yet at least Arik was someone *worth* murdering. He saw him as resourceful rather than insubordinate. Besides, Dayan pointed out, Arik was too popular with the men, too politically powerful, and too cozy with the press, to be dismissed in the middle of the war. The repercussions would open a third front. As for Gonen, that was another matter. Dayan, too, was convinced that Gordish did not have the capabilities to run the Sinai campaign.

But Dado's anger was spent. Calmer now, he proposed a compromise, a way to control Sharon and in effect replace Gonen without either humiliating or dismissing him. A high-ranking officer could be brought in to serve "alongside" Gonen. Chaim Bar-Lev, the former chief of staff and present minister of commerce, was his choice. Dayan agreed.

"Get down there and make decisions," Dayan told Bar-Lev.

Gonen was livid when Dado called to explain the new arrangement. His only alternative was to resign. "In this war I have a private chief of staff of my own," he acquiesced with thin, uneasy humor.

With the stunning news of Bar-Lev's appointment, neither the general staff nor the Southern Command paid much attention to another event that occurred at nearly the same time. Late that night, Amnon's patrol reached the edge of the moonlit Great Bitter Lake. They had found a passageway—a "seam" in military parlance—that took them undetected between both the Egyptian Second and Third armies.

THIRTY-THREE

Rambam Medical Center, Haifa/ 10 October 1973/0830

The bullet had smashed into Shmuli's forehead just above his left eye, continued on through his skull, and then exited. In its journey, it had ripped his brain apart.

Four neurosurgeons examined Shmuli after a medical helicopter had raced him south from the field station to Rambam Medical Center in Haifa. He was unconscious. He did not respond to the light shined in his eyes or the probes stabbing his arms and legs. The X rays of his skull revealed cataclysmic trauma.

Three of the doctors said any attempt to repair Shmuli's brain would be hopeless. He would not survive an extensive operation. Their time would be better spent treating other soldiers with head wounds.

The fourth, Dr. Yitzhak Shechter, told the nurses to prep the major and wheel him to the operating theater.

"What do you see that we don't?" one of the neurosurgeons challenged.

"Nothing." But Shechter had heard how Shmuli had gathered up the remains of the Barak Brigade and arrived up north just in time to rally the exhausted Seventh Armored Brigade and hold off the Syrian advance. "Still, it's my duty to try. After what he did for Israel, I owe him that."

Dr. Shechter excused himself, and went off to scrub for the operation.

Nati woke up in the bed she had slept in as a child. She lay on her back, looking about the bright familiar room, and for a moment it was as if nothing in her life had changed. Then her eyes strayed to the window with its panorama of trimmed green lawn and the memory of her wedding came back to her. Just two months ago, and already it belonged to a time that, like her childhood, was irretrievably gone. She remembered the young tank officers in their white dress uniforms standing about, drinks in hand, and the delight they took in each other's company. How many of them were now dead? On both fronts, the papers reported, the armored corps was experiencing the roughest combat. Her father had told her last night over dinner in a stunned, breathless whisper that the 188th had been destroyed.

And now Yossi was off fighting, too. He would know the names of their friends who had been killed and she found herself asking him. She liked to talk to Yossi when she was alone. It made him seem closer. And not dead.

"Where are you, Yossi?" Nati wondered without expecting an answer. But being able to ask helped to persuade her that she was not, like so many others, a widow. "Promise me you won't die," she begged her husband. "Promise me."

But even as she mouthed her urgent appeal, she knew it was a pledge no soldier could make in good faith. Nati turned over in her bed and began to cry.

If only he had managed to get off the machine gun burst an instant sooner, before the Syrian had pulled the trigger, Yossi thought.

Shmuli shouldn't even have been on Booster Ridge. The man could barely talk; he shouldn't have been allowed to leave the hospital. Shmuli was dead and it was all his fault, Yossi agonized. He could have ordered Shmuli to return to his hospital bed. Yet he had done nothing, and now the image of Shmuli's lifeless body laying across the turret of his tank was the filter through which everything passed. Yesterday, chasing after the retreating enemy, leading his force to the edge of the minefield bordering the Purple Line, there had been no time to mourn. But today grief rocked him. He would need to tell Nati, and the prospect of her sorrow, only deepened his distress; she had loved Shmuli, too.

He arrived at Yanosh's 9 A.M. briefing full of this sadness, yet ready to go back to war. He anticipated launching a counterattack to drive the enemy out of the Golan. This was his only comfort. In Katmandu, the prospect of going to war had raised in his mind ideals like honor and service. After a single day at the front, his thoughts had turned to vengeance. He had moved into the milling crowd of officers awaiting Yanosh's arrival, when a voice from another war called out to him, "Yossi, old friend. Welcome home." Capt. Yoni Netanyahu pumped Yossi's hand. "I hear you had to cut your honeymoon short. No doubt you'll make up for it," he said with a mischievous grin. "And I'm sorry I missed your wedding." Yoni had been in the United States studying mathematics at Harvard and receiving the latest round of treatment on an elbow that had been smashed by a bullet in the Six Day War. He had returned to his elite commando unit, the Sayeret Matkal, only weeks before the war had broken out. The first two days, he told Yossi, sharing his exasperation over the makeshift way his men had been used, they had fought in the Sinai. Then they were rushed up north to stalk Syrian commando teams that had infiltrated the lines. Today? Tomorrow? Who knows what they'll have us doing.

"Well," said Yossi, as he saw Yanosh enter the tent, "it's good knowing you're around. Never can tell when you 'special guys' will come in handy." He held out a hand again, and, as was the way in wartime, there was a heaviness in even this small farewell. Then Yossi found a seat with the other tankers.

Quiet descended as Yanosh began. The orders of the day, he announced, were "sleep, rest, grease, repair the machinery, take a breather." The men were worn out, literally falling asleep on their feet and in their tanks. More reserves, more tanks, will arrive today. After that we shall see what Tel Aviv wants. "But," he said speaking from the heart, a soldier to other soldiers who had shared a time when death had seemed inevitable, "whatever else happens, what you men did yesterday—no one can ever take that away from you."

After the briefing ended Yossi approached Yanosh hoping to talk.

"I've been looking all over for you," Yanosh interrupted. "Shmuli—he's alive. I found out just before I got here. They're operating on him at Rambam."

"Thank God. Thank God," Yossi managed, struggling to hold back his tears.

While at both fronts the day passed as an interlude of relative calm, in the Pit the generals and ministers went at one another without pause. A crucial decision had to be made and it was as if its weight lay tangibly on their shoulders, pushing each constituency to dig in deeper.

After being caught by surprise, unprepared, and then nearly overwhelmed, Israel had fought back. In the south, Egypt still held the east bank of the Suez Canal, but their troops had not advanced deeper into the Sinai. While in the north, the armored corps had driven Syria back over the Purple Line. On the fifth day, the time had come to move into the next stage of the war.

But what should its aim be? Should a battered Israel, with so many of its soldiers dead and wounded, urge the United States to push for a cease-fire along the present lines, with Syria holding the Mount Hermon outpost and Egypt the east bank? Or should it go on the offensive, launch massive assaults and possibly gain new territory? And if they were to press on, should it be on both fronts?

All day the general staff had reviewed the facts and considered the possible strategies. The nation had extricated itself from a fight for its survival, but this endgame decision would shape *how* it survived. It was that momentous. Finally at 9:30 that evening, the generals and ministers led by Dado and Dayan, marched into the prime minister's office.

They gave her three alternatives.

Dayan had sunk once again into another of his low moods, and he saw little hope for success in any attempt to drive back the enemy. In the Golan, Israel should organize for defense along the 1967 Purple Line border. At the same time, one of the northern armored divisions could be transferred to the Sinai. In perhaps two weeks, after the Egyptian forces tired, a "limited" crossing of the Suez Canal might be attempted.

Gen. Yisrael Tal, the chief of staff's deputy, wanted to lay a trap in the south. The army should pull back from its present line and move deeper into the desert. Let the Egyptians come to us, he urged. Once they charged beyond their missile umbrella, Israel's planes and tanks would hammer them.

Dado conceded that Dayan's and Tal's plans had tactical merit; they were reasonable, even clever. However, if the war was not won decisively before the United States and the Soviet Union manipulated a cease-fire, then not only would territory be lost, but also the triumphant Arabs would soon find reason to launch a new war. Retreat, therefore, was not an alternative. Nor could they fall into defensive positions. The only way to win the war was to fight. The Seventh Armored Brigade had demonstrated that Israel's soldiers, despite facing impossible odds, would battle on with courage. It was this, faith in his troops, in their refusal to back down when honor and duty required that they charge ahead to defend the Jewish state, that fixed his course.

He wanted to attack. In the morning, they should move out in full strength and drive through Kuneitra straight to Damascus. Get close enough for artillery to target the capital, and the Syrians would be the ones begging for a cease-fire. After Israel had brought Syria to its knees, then the IDF would begin its offensive in the Sinai.

Golda Meir listened. Like the chief of staff, she feared the superpowers might at any hour implement a diplomatic settlement along the present troop lines. Israel could not wait. It had to win the war, and do it quickly. And while she was not a soldier, she, like Dado, believed in her troops.

At midnight, she made her decision: Tomorrow they would push on to Damascus.

Two days earlier, Yanosh had only 20 tanks in his brigade. By Thursday morning with the arrival of the reserves, the Seventh Armored Brigade was back to a full complement of 110 tanks.

Yanosh divided the men into two forces; Kahalani would lead one, Yossi the other. Their mission was to cross the border in the mountainous north and take the Syrian village of Mazrat Breit Jan and Tel Shams, a strategic hill. Then, on to Damascus.

Kahalani assembled his battalion commanders. Many were new faces; most of the men he had fought with were dead.

"First, for all those of you who just joined us and still don't know where you are," he said formally, "this is the Seventy-seventh Battalion of the Seventh Armored Brigade. Battalion commander Kahalani stands by chance before you."

He wanted them to know they had joined a battalion whose valor was famous. And it was his way of telling them what was expected of them.

"Before I explain to you our mission," he continued, "I want to know who you are and what your tasks are."

One after another, the new men told him about their homes, their wives and children, their civilian jobs.

He wanted them to hold these images in their minds as they went into combat. It was his way of telling them that although many of them would not return, these were the reasons their sacrifices were necessary.

When his speech was done, they ran to their tanks.

Yossi led what remained of the 188th Barak Brigade. Not a single company commander had survived the first days of the war. Only one of the previous deputy commanders and two platoon commanders were still in their tanks. Yet at eleven o'clock that morning a brigade that had been destroyed crossed the Purple Line and headed into enemy territory.

As they advanced, Yanosh reached Yossi on the net. He had received word from Rambam Medical Center. Shmuli's operation had lasted eight hours.

"And?" Yossi interrupted.

"He's unconscious."

"But still alive?"

"Yes. *Alive!*"

THIRTY-FOUR
Tel Shams/12 October 1973/0630

Yossi did not want to think about the attack. He would close his mind down, and lead his men. He would not think of Nati. But as soon as he told himself that, she was there. He could feel her arms locked tight around his waist, holding on, long black hair billowing from her helmet, as the Honda barreled down the road toward the snowcapped Himalayas. And that sparkling memory, the majesty of those peaks, had the perverse effect of bringing him full circle. The comparison to the gloomy landscape where he now found himself was unavoidable. He stared with great attention at the craggy pile of volcanic rock he was about to storm.

Since they had crossed the border yesterday morning it had been a nearly constant battle against a Syrian infantry brigade backed by armor. The enemy had been tenacious. At short range, Yossi's force had grappled for every new piece of terrain. Yet last night under heavy enemy fire his column of tanks had captured the Druze village of Horfa. He charged in as the villagers fled, their braying donkeys loaded down with pots, pans, and bedding. And in the fighting, a spear of shrapnel had sliced Yossi's hand. Now another heavy bandage complemented the gauze mask crisscrossing his face. Two days and two wounds. It was easy to be superstitious in wartime, and he hoped that if bad luck indeed came in threes, then his next injury would be as superficial as the others. But today after they had moved out at daybreak into the translucent haze of the mountain dawn and easily taken a small ridge along the Damascus Road, he found himself mocking his own anxiety. Then he received the order to capture Tel Shams.

Southwest of the Damascus Road, Tel Shams was a dreary, abandoned settlement perched atop a steep volcanic hill. The war, however, had given it new significance. From this summit, Syrian artillery batteries could open up on any force moving down the highway to the village of Sasa, a gateway to Damascus. Tel Shams had to be taken.

A narrow road climbing straight up was the only way to the top. The jet-black volcanic plains laying on either side were unpassable. A maze of giant boulders blocked the way and, regardless, tank treads could gain little traction on the basalt. The attack had to be straight up the road. And into whatever the Syrians had waiting.

Yossi's tank led the assault, the column moving in an orderly line up toward the first crest. He stood in the cupola, his bandaged hand easing the machine gun first to one side of the road, then the other. Each moment seemed ready to burst, but there was only quiet. They climbed higher.

Then from behind a clump of boulders, Yossi saw a slew of antitank teams emerge. At the same moment, on the other side of the road, infantry stepped out from behind the rocks. He heard the high, chilling whine of missile fire. Saggers flew in fast, traversing his line from both sides. There was no protection; the road was straight and bare. Advancing through this barrage was suicide. "Fall back! Fall back!" he screamed into the radio mike.

A gully near the base of the hill provided the column some shelter. But in order to fit into this narrow trench, the tanks had formed a line, and now there was no room to maneuver. This was a reckless deployment, Yossi knew, but he had no other choice. Now at least they were out of range of the missiles.

He hoped the antitank teams would come after him. The enemy soldiers would be forced to step out from behind the boulders, and advance toward the lip of the gully. And when they did, his gunners would put shell after shell into them. "Come to me, you bastards," he silently coaxed.

They sent planes instead, and he heard the MiGs before he saw them. By then it was already too late. Their rockets found the tanks and explosions rumbled through the ravine.

"Button up!" he yelled into the radio mike, as he scrambled down the ladder. Closing the heavy turret lid behind him with his injured hand was a struggle. But at last, after one sustained burst of effort, he slammed it shut. And at that moment a rocket pounded against the turret like the fist of God Almighty. The force of the explosion threw him to the belly of the compartment and his head shuddered with pain as blood poured from his ruptured eardrum. The crew hurried over.

For the third time in as many days, he had bandages wrapped around him. Still, Yossi sustained himself with the realization that despite his three injuries he was still alive.

They needed to leave this gully before the planes returned. On the net he asked Yanosh to send an armored force to cover his retreat down the hill. Then he and his men waited for their arrival, as they watched the sky for MiGs.

The Turkish coffee was as delicious as it was unexpected. A Druze villager served Yanosh and Yossi as they sat in the sun and looked out toward Tel Shams from the balcony of the man's stone house in the village of Hales. It was such a pleasant moment, so much like their old freewheeling times, that Yossi could almost pretend they weren't plotting an operation that might very well get him killed.

Yanosh summoned him as soon as Yossi was out of the gully and back on the highway. He had something he wanted Yossi to see. So

Yossi took a jeep to the Seventh Armored Brigade's field headquarters in the village of Hales. He drove past pastel-colored houses pierced with shell holes, a burnt-out Syrian tank that stood in a front yard like a piece of sculpture, and a flock of birds busily picking at a dead dog and too bold to scatter when he honked the horn. He found the brigade commander seated in a straw chair on the balcony, his long legs jutting straight out, and his eyes peering into the distance through a pair of binoculars at the unobstructed vista of Tel Shams.

Yanosh put down the binoculars and fixed Yossi with a deep look. Then, laughing, he rose to hug him. "You look like a mummy." Gesturing at the assortment of bandages covering Yossi, he asked, "What will your girlfriends say?"

"You forget I'm a married man."

"And I'm betting as soon as we get out of this damn war, it won't take you long to forget, too."

Rather than argue, especially with someone who knew him so well, Yossi changed the subject. "What'd want me to see?"

Yanosh handed him a stack of photographs, aerial recon shots of Tel Shams. "Look at the north approach. Do you see what I see?"

Yossi studied the photographs, then picked up Yanosh's binoculars and pointed them at the hill. He looked intently for a while. Then said, "Maybe. Just maybe."

And so as the Druze, with an instinctive hospitality, brought his guests Turkish coffee, Yossi and Yanosh sat on the balcony and planned the attack. The photographs revealed, and the binoculars confirmed, a twisting natural path through the boulders on the north face of the hill. A small force of tanks could sneak up to the summit through this back route. If their treads could maneuver on the basalt. If the Syrians didn't spot them and turn their field guns on them, or unleash their jets. And if there weren't any troops with Saggers already hidden on this far slope waiting to ambush them.

After they had worked it over from all angles, Yanosh said with sudden gravity that he imagined there was a fifty-fifty chance of success. He could not issue an order to attack based on those odds.

"Fifty-fifty," Yossi repeated thoughtfully. "That means one of us would succeed. Okay, I volunteer."

An army of boulders was scattered about the north face, rising high and mighty like stony sentinels, but the gaps between them were as wide as they appeared on the photographs. The Centurions had no trouble weaving between them. In first gear the tanks found traction on the basalt and were able to climb the volcanic plain. There was no need to consult a compass. There was only one way to go: up.

Yossi had eight tanks, and once they were underway the force advanced with ease. It was one of those missions, he told himself, where if they made it, people would say "of course." But if they didn't, people would say they'd thrown their lives away. All the way up he kept waiting for a volley of Saggers to streak across the expressionless sky.

They reached the top of the hill unnoticed. In front of them, arrayed in a semicircle in the fading afternoon light, stood ten tanks. Their cannons were pointed in the opposite direction. His force could hit the enemy from behind, without warning.

With great deliberateness, Yossi gave his men instructions. Each had a single target; he had two. He looked at his watch—four o'clock—and then, after the moment had been recorded in his own mental log, he yelled into the mike, "Fire at will!"

The heavy shells boomed out of the big cannons. At this range, it might as well have been target practice. The gunners tried for the turrets, hoping a shell would ignite the fuel line. The ten enemy tanks exploded almost in unison, and a tremendous noise echoed off the hilltop. A bonfire of flames, magnificent in its fury, climbed into the sky. Yossi was 500 yards away, but waves of heat lapped against his face.

Through his binoculars he had a perfect view of the Syrian outpost that lay at the summit, beyond the cordon of flaming tanks.

The enemy field artillery was aimed toward the Damascus Road below. There were no signs of additional tanks or infantry.

He had to make a decision, and he had to do it quickly. He could try to go back down the way he had come up. But it was getting late in the day. Descending a basalt slope in first gear and zigzagging between boulders in the evening shadows would be treacherous. As long as the Syrians controlled the hill, the road he had tried so unsuccessfully earlier in the day remained an impossibility. Which left a final option: He could storm the stronghold. If he charged before the infantry marched up from the road, he could take it. Maybe.

He radioed Yanosh. He had mentally sorted through the alternatives, but this was only pretense. He had known what he was going to do from the start. He would do what soldiers do. "Yanosh," he announced, "we're going to take the hill."

Yossi divided his force for the assault. Two tanks would give cover fire, and the other six would charge ahead in an arrow formation. Yossi's tank was at the tip. "Forward! Attack!" he screamed as they advanced.

He stood in the cupola, and as his tanks got closer to the stronghold, he felt a surge of elation, a building sense of victory. He looked ahead and there was nothing to stop him.

Then he heard the first missile. The Sagger streaked over his head, and its tail of electrical guidance wires tangled about his helmet and shoulders. He clawed at the fine strands, desperately trying to extricate himself as the tank lurched forward. He might as well have been a struggling insect caught in a malicious spider's intractable web. Then the next rocket hit. There was an explosion, a profound, resonating boom. And all at once he was lifted out of the tank, and hurled through the air.

Yanosh had been following the attack over the radio. He had heard Yossi urging his men forward. Now he listened to an empty, crackling static. Then the radio went dead.

* * *

The heat rising from his burning tank brought Yossi back to consciousness. He screamed with pain. He lay on the ground not far from the flaming machine with his left leg twisted at a cruel, unnatural angle. Jagged white bone jutted through his trousers just below his thigh. Blood spurted from his calf. The pain was excruciating.

But his mind was clear. He looked up at his ruined tank and thought: I am like a horseman without his horse. On my own and lost. He felt his life begin to drain out of him. Yet he struggled against death. It seemed astonishing to him that everything would end on a bleak volcanic hilltop after just twenty-nine years. The colossal unfairness of such an undistinguished ending to his life goaded him on to resist.

"Help," he managed to call out weakly. "Help."

THIRTY-FIVE

Center Ten/12 October 1973/1800

At the same time as Yossi struggled for his life on a Syrian hilltop, General Shazly was locked in his own desperate fight. He, too, had been taken by surprise, ambushed not by the enemy, but, as he had always feared, by President Sadat and Minister of War Ismail.

He found it hard to believe that only yesterday Egypt's prospects had left him so full of confidence. That morning he had made his second visit to the front. Sitting in the subterranean Operations Room, as reports arrived detailing new assaults by Sharon's and Bren's armor, he had begun to worry that the Zionists had discovered a weak spot in the Second Army bridgehead and were trying to exploit it. But after traveling down to the Suez Canal, meeting with Second Army Commander Mamoun, walking among the troops, receiving their respectful cheers, he knew his fears had been groundless. He was so proud of these brave men, and what they had accomplished.

The army was entrenched on the east bank and he was certain the squeamish Zionists would never pay the bloody price needed to push them back across the Canal. Already intelligence had reported that Dayan and some of the other ministers had had enough and were willing—even eager!—to make peace. Two years ago he had conceived High Minarets, a plan for Egypt to win a limited war and restore honor, and now it was unfolding just as he had predicted. He felt an immense pride.

No sooner had he returned to the Operations Room from his brief tour of the front than Shazly received word that General Ismail wanted to see him. Unsuspecting, he entered Ismail's small, windowless office. It was like entering a cave: tight, dark, and, in retrospect he realized, ominously quiet.

Without preamble or apology, Ismail asked, "Could we build on our success to develop our attack to the passes?"

Ever since the invasion had succeeded, it was the one question Shazly feared he might very well soon hear.

Shazly responded with rage. Years ago in a similar mood he had knocked Ismail to the ground with a single punch. Now he was prepared to do that and more. Duty demanded his zeal. He argued vehemently to preserve Egypt's strategic advantage on the battlefield. He fought, too, for the soldiers, *his* troops. Their courage had taken the nation so very close to an historic victory, and now Ismail's foolishness would put their lives in jeopardy.

"No," he insisted. "The enemy air force is still too strong to be challenged by our own. And we do not have sufficient mobile SAM units to provide air cover." It was the identical rationale for a limited assault he had presented when the unsuitable Ismail, over Shazly's protests to the president, had first been appointed minister of war. Last April Shazly had warned that it would be a disaster to move from beneath the protection of the missiles. The enemy jets would rain death and destruction on their men and armor.

If Ismail did not understand, if he didn't listen, his actions would cost them the war.

Shazly made his case and then, hoping to end the discussion, stormed off. Ismail was a vain and silly man, and like most bullies what he feared most was an opponent who would fight back. Shazly hoped his forceful argument would convince the minister of war once and for all that he was venturing into military issues that were far beyond his expertise.

But the next morning Ismail reiterated that it was time to advance the troops deeper into the Sinai. Syria needed immediate help, he explained. Egypt's counterattack would reduce the pressure on the northern front. Rather than rolling farther down the road to Damascus, the Zionists would divert tanks from the Golan to the desert.

"Look," Shazly began, hoping that a quiet logic would succeed where his temper had failed, "despite their loses the enemy still has eight armored brigades out there in front of us. The enemy air forces can still cripple our ground forces as soon as they poke their noses beyond our SAM umbrella. Advance and we destroy our troops without offering any significant relief to our brothers, the Syrians."

This time Ismail listened without protest, and Shazly was convinced that at last the minister of war understood. Perhaps, Shazly chided himself, it was his own fault. With as insecure a character as Ismail, he should have appreciated from the start that a cool, well-reasoned approach would be more effective than a challenge.

But then at midday, Ismail reappeared at Shazly's desk. "It is a political decision," he said.

A sickening despair enveloped Shazly as he understood for the first time who had been pressing for the assault into the Sinai. It was not Ismail; the minister of war was simply the messenger. President Sadat wanted it.

"We must develop our attack by tomorrow morning," Ismail continued.

And with those words, Shazly realized that the war had slipped beyond his control.

What would Egypt do?

In the Pit and in field headquarters across the Sinai, the generals mulled over the possibilities and tried like soothsayers to read the enemy's mind. Egypt could keep its five infantry divisions dug in along the east bank, and defend their narrow strip of regained territory against an Israeli attack. Or they could transfer the 900 fresh tanks of the Fourth and Twenty-first armored divisions from the west bank and go on the offensive, charging across the Sinai to the strategic Mitla and Gidi passes.

Back and forth the generals went. What would Egypt do? It was the crucial question.

Today on the war's seventh day—just a week, but then again that was all it had taken, Dayan pointed out, to create the world—Israel had begun to consider its own bold possibilities. No longer was there talk of the "destruction of the Third Temple," or the arming of old men and boys with antitank weapons and sending them out into the streets and alleyways. The nuclear rockets had come down from their launchers. The reserves had arrived and on both fronts men and tanks were once again at fighting strength. In the north, the battle for the Golan had been won; and Damascus loomed like a new, ripe prize. And in the south, the time had come to attack across the Suez Canal.

But in war, as in any well-reasoned contest, each new move depended to a significant degree on the opponent. And the timing of Israel's invasion into Egypt became in the minds of most of the generals a function of Egypt's intentions. Israel could wait, hoping the enemy's two armored divisions would be brought to the east bank and sent out in a desert offensive. Or, the IDF could start its crossing as soon as tomorrow, October 13. The 900 tanks would be waiting for them and it would be a dangerous, high-risk battle. However, a victory would give Israel a foothold in enemy territory before the superpowers instituted a cease-fire.

The chief of staff scheduled a meeting with the prime minister for 2:30 that afternoon. Once again, Golda Meir would have the final say.

* * *

Meanwhile, Amnon sat in the Tasa Command Post listening to a booming Sharon. Not for the first time in this war, Amnon did not like what he was hearing. Sharon saw no point in waiting, or even in trying to anticipate what Egypt would do. He wanted to strike now. Hit the Third Army positions by the coast of the Great Bitter Lake and then cross into Egypt.

He outlined his plan to Amnon, as though success was simply a matter of will. He was unconcerned that the Third Army had an entrenched position fortified by tens of thousands of infantry and 500 tanks. Amnon was beginning to grasp that for Sharon typical military considerations, such as the enemy's deployment and balance of forces, were of little significance. Sharon's battle plan seemed to be guided by an almost mystical sense of destiny. He could not imagine Israel, the modern realization of the ancient prophecy of a Jewish state, being defeated by Egypt. And as a consequence, his hard-charging path was set.

Nevertheless, when Sharon finished he asked Amnon what he thought of the plan. Amnon answered with directness. After all he had witnessed in the past week's fighting, to do otherwise would have been impossible. A charge into an entrenched Egyptian position, even with the Sinai Command back to full strength, would end in a catastrophe.

Sharon heard him out. Then, instead of the flash of dismissive temper that Amnon had expected, he said, "Come, let's see what Gordish says."

Gonen listened to Sharon and summarily rejected the plan. The helicopter flight to his headquarters had lasted longer than the meeting.

To Amnon's discomfort and embarrassment, Sharon immediately demanded to speak with Bar-Lev. When he was informed Bar-Lev was sleeping, Sharon said he would wait.

But as he waited, all his previous calm dissolved. He ranted to Amnon, to anyone who would listen. "They've got no guts," he roared. "They know neither the terrain nor the enemy. They're holding us up all the time. I tell them it is possible to cross. I'm prepared to go and do it, but they just sit there and decide it can't be done.

"I must talk to Moshe," he decided in a sudden flash of irritation.

Dayan's daughter Yael answered the phone. The minister of defense was not at home. "Listen," Sharon bulled on, "if you talk to him, tell him that the whole division here is champing at the bit. My horses are ready for war. You remember the picture—like the eve of the Six Day War. Explain that to him. He must understand that there is enough initiative here to burst up this Egyptian business."

This is madness, Amnon thought. Arik is out of control. Full of indignation, his own sense of mission, Sharon would eagerly lead his division to slaughter. And he would do so in the belief—and this left Amnon shaking—that he was serving a high ideal.

When Bar-Lev awoke, Sharon asked a bewildered Amnon to accompany him. Bar-Lev listened a bit more patiently than Gonen, grimaced visibly as Arik railed against the rest of the Southern Command, and then turned to Amnon. "What does your brigade commander think?"

Amnon told him. And Bar-Lev said he agreed with Colonel Reshef. He decided against Sharon's attack.

On the helicopter flight back to Tasa, Arik made a point of telling Amnon there were no hard feelings. Then he lapsed into a guarded silence for the remainder of the trip. Amnon used the time to reflect once more on his commander's complicated personality. On the one hand, Arik had known he was vehemently against the plan yet the general did not hesitate to take him into the meeting with Bar-Lev. On the other, Sharon's confidence was so overbearing, so unseemly, that he would not hesitate to undermine the general staff or jeopardize his men in pursuit of glory. Amnon had a newfound respect for Sharon. But that didn't stop him from believing that there would always be a danger lurking in Arik's command, a rashness or an unruliness that—again the thought occurred to him—was nothing less than madness.

Bar-Lev must have had similar thoughts. When his meeting ended with Sharon, he called Dado and proposed, just as his predecessor Gonen had, that Sharon be relieved of command. Dayan, again citing the exigencies of politics, overruled the suggestion. The internecine war between the Jewish generals raged on.

In Egypt, the generals battled, too.

Shazly's allegiances were pulled in two directions. An attack to the passes would fail. In protest, he could resign as chief of staff. But that would not stop the offensive. Sadat would simply promote someone to take his place. Or, since less than twenty-hours remained before H-hour, Ismail might assume command. That would only exacerbate the inevitable disaster. Shazly's honor would be assuaged, but only at the cost of betraying the troops. He could not leave the attack in Ismail's hands. He could not do that to them, after the way they had fought. His brave men.

Reluctantly, he reviewed with his staff officers the orders to advance. At 1:30 that afternoon, he signed the battle plans with his customary demonstrative signature and dispatched liaison officers to deliver the documents to the Second and Third armies. The die was cast.

Yet Shazly soon learned that others shared his misgivings. After receiving the attack orders, General Mamoun, commander of the Second Army, called. "I resign," he announced. "I cannot operate under such conditions. It is impossible to fulfill the orders you have just sent." Only minutes later General Mwassil from the Third Army contacted him. The general didn't resign, but he, too, had large doubts the plan would succeed.

Shazly heard their complaints, and with a renewed determination, went off to battle Ismail. Both field commanders, he told the minister of war, were unwilling to leave their fortified positions and attack. To force generals to lead men in an offensive that was contrary to their own assessment of the field situation could only result in defeat.

Ismail considered Shazly's new argument, then ordered the field commanders to report immediately to Center Ten. He would explain the situation to them.

That afternoon, as Egypt's plans for the offensive took shape, Brill was on duty in the windowless electronic battlefield of unit 848. He had become a man alone. Ben Porat shunned him with a deliberateness that was unmistakable, and the men had begun to follow his cue. It bothered Brill, but he knew he had been right. The more he was ostracized, the more he found consolation in his astuteness.

And he had his work. One of his responsibilities was the "special means of collection." Now operational, the receivers and recorders were monitored around the clock by a designated squad of translators and signit technicians. Brill routinely went down the hall to their soundproofed cubicles and glanced at the real-time translated transcripts of what was being said in Center Ten. It was fascinating reading; he was at the enemy's side, sharing his thoughts. But today as he began reviewing the Egyptians' discussions, he realized this new, still-developing intelligence was immediately vital to the nation.

He rushed off to inform Ben Porat, and as he did he couldn't help but wonder if his spiteful superior would speak to him. Let alone act on his recommendation.

As the discussion in Center Ten dragged on through the afternoon and into the evening, it occurred to a weary Shazly that it was all pointless. It did not matter that both field commanders had joined him to press their shared objections. Or, that Ismail couldn't marshal a military argument to refute their concerns. Ismail was afraid. The president had issued an order and if Ismail refused to carry it out, he would be dismissed. Or, quite possibly, a wartime charge of treason would bring something worse.

In the end, it was settled as it had begun. Ismail, however, did offer one small concession. Since the meeting had gone on for so long, an attack tomorrow was no longer feasible. It was postponed until Sunday, the fourteenth, at first light. The rest of the ill-conceived plan stood. The Twenty-first Armored Division and all but a single brigade of 100 tanks from the Fourth Armored Division would cross the Suez Canal and take part in the offensive. As a result, the west bank would be stripped of its armor reserves. This was a grave error, Shazly knew. But while he could see the disaster that loomed, there was nothing he could do to prevent it.

In the prime minister's office, after all the hours of wondering about Egypt's intensions, the time had finally come to make a decision. Since there was no way to know what Egypt would do, the greater danger would be to wait. At any hour, a cease-fire might be announced. Dado and the majority of the generals agreed that Sharon and Bren should move westward through enemy lines tomorrow, cross over the Canal, and then battle the armored divisions on the other side.

The decision was the prime minister's, and the attention in the room focused on her. She had just asked the chief of staff about the timing of the attack when an excited aide summoned General Zeira from the meeting. Moments later, Zeira interrupted the discussion to share the intelligence he had just received: Egypt would transfer its two armored divisions across the Canal and attack toward the passes within days.

Now that the generals and the prime minister knew what Egypt would do, the decision was made for them. The crossing would wait. Instead, the Sinai Command would prepare for the enemy's counterattack.

Even the mercurial Dayan was buoyed by the way things had worked out. A precipitous crossing had been averted. And the opportunity was now at hand to crush Egypt's new offensive.

Then, at about 8:30 that evening Dayan wandered into the War Room, where a briefing on the northern front was taking place. He heard that the attack on Tel Shams had stalled. And that Lt. Col. Yossi Ben Hanan, who had led the assault, was missing in action, and presumed dead.

THIRTY-SIX

Tel Shams/12 October 1973/1845

How long had he laid there? Half an hour? An hour? A lifetime? Yossi felt the hand shaking him back into consciousness and all he knew for certain as he slowly opened his eyes was that it was dark. Dark like death, he thought for one horrible instant. But then he recognized the voice calling his name repeatedly. It was Tzvika, his tank driver.

"Yossi, what's happened to you?"

"My leg. I think it's gone. The others?"

All the tanks had been hit, Tzvika said. Some of the men had fled down the hill. The rest were dead.

"You should go," Yossi told him. "Get out of here while you can. The Syrians will come looking for us. If not tonight, by the morning."

"I'm not leaving you."

Yossi offered a silent prayer of thanks. But he said, "You change your mind, I'll understand."

The tanks burning on the battlefield were the only illumination. All else was dark, lonely, and forbidding. He tried not to despair as the pain rushed through him in steady waves. It would peak, and then the excruciating cycle would begin again. He did not know how much longer he could bear it. He needed to come up with a plan before he sunk back into unconsciousness. He could not allow his life to end here.

"Tzvika," he asked finally. "Think you could try to get the radio?"

Bright orange flames leaped up in a ring around the tank's turret. Feet planted on the hull, Tzvika searched for an opening as he prepared to dash through them. He found none. He would be burned, it could not be avoided. But it was the only way to retrieve the radio.

Yossi watched as his driver flung himself into the fire. Flames crawled over his uniform, and in his panic Tzvika seemed about to lose his footing. But he steadied himself and a moment later stood beyond the fire, in the turret, furiously patting out the glowing embers on his chest and legs. With a small farewell wave to Yossi, he disappeared into the tank.

Yossi waited anxiously. It was easy to imagine that the tank's main compartment was an inferno. Tzvika could be trapped. And if the driver could not get out, Yossi realized he was finished, too.

But when Tzvika emerged and yelled to Yossi from the turret, not only did he have the radio but also a jerican of water. This time he jumped through the fire without hesitation, and landed with a thud and a smile on the hull. "No problem," he called to Yossi.

Minutes later, as Tzvika dribbled a delicious trail of water into Yossi's parched mouth, Yossi noticed that the hand holding the jerican had been burned to a bright, raw pink.

They had to move, Tzvika said. Before Yossi tried the radio, it was imperative that they get away from the tank. When he had been down in the compartment, Tzvika had seen shells scattered about the floor. A single flame, even just a spark, could ignite the ammunition. The tank would be blown and, without a doubt, the two of them along with it.

Tzvika put his arms under Yossi's armpits and locked them across the injured man's chest. Yossi's boots dragged along the ground, and he was in agony. The sharp pain from his twisted and broken leg swept up his spine and made him drift into unconsciousness.

When he came to, he was lying in a ditch about fifteen meters from the burning tank. Tzvika stood above him with the radio. Yossi took the handset, and in a thin, gasping voice began to transmit.

"I hear you, Yossi. I hear you!" Yanosh responded with excitement. "Where are you? Where are you talking from?"

"Outside my tank." His voice was a whisper. "My tank, the others . . . they've been hit. Most of them—dead."

Silence descended, a large and mournful acknowledgment.

"My leg, Yanosh," Yossi said after a pause. "It's gone. I'm going to die here on this hill."

"Yossi Ben Hanan, you will not die," Yanosh said firmly. "Your brother will save you."

Throughout the north, soldiers remained by their radios, eavesdropping on the exchange between these two friends. Yanosh was not simply offering automatic words of encouragement. The commander of the Seventh Armored Brigade had committed to one more epic stand. Only this time he was locked in battle with the Angel of Death, trying to hold Him off, to stop Him from carrying Yossi away.

In the *sayaret* encampment, Yoni Netanyahu followed every word.

"Tell my wife I was thinking of her, Yanosh. Promise me you'll tell Nati."

"Sure, Yosi, sure. But what about your girlfriends? You want me to call them, too? Especially Rachel. You're not around, I bet I'd stand a chance with her. You think so, Yossi? I mean, I'd like her, right?"

"Yanosh, I'm getting tired."

"Close your eyes. Rest if you want. *No!* Don't close your eyes. Talk to me, Yossi. Remember that time on the beach at Caesarea? *Talk to me!* I was with that redhead. You were with—Who were you with again?"

". . . Sara."

"That's right, Yossi. Sara. Tell me, Yossiele, she better than Rachel? I mean, tell me. I want to know. Talk to me, Yossi. Talk to Yanosh. I got to know these things, I'm gonna take over all your girlfriends."

"Yanosh, I'm so thirsty."

"Wait, Yossi. A doctor is here. Give the handset to Tzvika."

In a careful, measured voice the doctor began to tell Tzvika how to put the jutting bone back into place. "Push it, but gently," he said. "Then we'll make a tourniquet to stop the bleeding." His tone suggested it was simple first aid, nothing more complicated than putting a bandage on a cut.

Yanosh, however, paced. And as he crossed the room he saw Capt. Yoni Netanyahu coming toward him. "I am volunteering myself and my unit. We will bring out Yossi Ben Hanan and his driver."

"Get Yossi out of there," the commander of the Seventh Armored Brigade begged. "Bring me my brother."

In the darkness, a dozen *sayaret* commandos drove in two armored personnel carriers behind enemy lines. They approached the hill from the north, as Yossi's force had done. But the armored vehicles could not find traction on the basalt, and the commandos were forced to climb the hill on foot. They approached each boulder with their Uzis set for automatic fire. They were well trained, comfortable in the shadows, and they used the darkness as a cloak. They made steady progress.

As they continued their ascent, Yoni, however, grew concerned. He reached out to Yanosh on the net. "Yossi will never last if we have to carry him down this hill. We'll secure a site. But you need to get a chopper up here to fly him out."

Yossi awoke and realized he must have fainted when Tzvika had pushed the bone back into place. "Was I out long?"

Tzvika shrugged, as if to say it wasn't important. He seemed tense, not nearly as confident as before. But he told Yossi that Yanosh had sent a rescue party.

"Then there's nothing more for you to do here, Tzvika. Save yourself. I have the radio. They'll find me."

Tzvika refused. Still, Yossi could not help noticing how the driver's eyes kept darting about. "Tzvika, what's wrong?"

"I heard voices. Arabs. I think they're out here looking for us."

Yossi listened. The night hung dense and thick around them and his concentration magnified every sound. But he did not hear the enemy. He was reasonably certain.

"If you're not going to escape," he told Tzvika, "take this." With some difficulty he removed the lieutenant colonel's insignia from his tank overalls and offered it to the driver. After a moment's hesitation, Tzvika took it. "Now give me yours," Yossi ordered. Tzvika obeyed. Nothing further was said, but both men knew why they had traded ranks: The Syrians did not execute officers.

"You think our guys will be able to find us out here?" Tzvika worried.

"Yes," Yossi said, not knowing if he himself believed it. All he had for sure were Yanosh's words, and he clung to them in the heavy darkness. They were the credo of his sustaining faith. His brother would save him.

Yanosh drove like a race car driver over the pitch-black, rutted mountain roads to the air force field headquarters south of his camp. The IAF kept a helicopter there to rescue Phantom pilots who bailed out after their jets were hit. If the chopper was on a mission, he didn't know what he'd do.

He was in luck. The helicopter had just landed and the pilot was still in the cockpit, shutting down the craft as Yanosh approached. Without a word, Yanosh took the seat behind him.

The pilot looked at him quizzically. "One of my men is down. Injured," Yanosh explained. "We have to go get him."

"Where is he?"

"Tel Shams."

The pilot paused. When he spoke, his words were curt. "Intel says they got artillery, antiaircraft up there. We're to stay clear. A chopper coming in at night, they'd pick us off before we got close."

"Fly with me," Yanosh said evenly.

"Anyway, I'm here for blue, not green. They give me my orders." The pilot wanted the officer to understand that although he was a colonel, he was not air force.

"Fly with me," Yanosh repeated.

"Sorry. Now I gotta . . ."

"Fly with me," Yanosh said once again in his flat, steady voice. But this time added, "Or I'll shoot you in the head." His Colt pressed against the back of the pilot's skull.

". . . Let me just tell 'em I'm heading out again," the pilot said. He reached for the mike, and Yanosh pulled back the hammer of the gun.

"No calls. We just go."

The pilot began flicking switches and the rotors started turning. A moment later, the helicopter began to rise.

"You can put the gun down," the pilot suggested.

"When we get there," Yanosh told him. He shoved the nozzle with renewed force against the pilot's skull. They both would die if he fired, but Yanosh was prepared to pull the trigger.

"Where exactly are we going?"

"Head to the hilltop. I'll tell you more when we get there."

They flew in silence for a while. But as they continued north, Yanosh became more of his old self. "Don't worry, you'll probably get a medal out of this. Golda will pin it on you herself. You're rescuing a national treasure. All his girlfriends will want to thank you. This is the luckiest night of your life."

But in case the pilot was still unconvinced, Yanosh kept the gun hard against his head.

There it was. Again. Now Yossi was sure. That wasn't a night noise. It sounded like boots scraping against the ground. He looked at Tzvika. Tzvika nodded. Whoever it was, they were trying to move in silently. But the two men's ears were trained on every tiny movement. *Something was out there.*

All at once the rattle of machine guns and the sharp reports of assault rifles ripped across the night. The two men crouched deeper in the ditch. Yossi had his revolver out. During the long hours of waiting, he had reached a decision. He would not surrender. If he had to die, he would die with honor.

He waited for the enemy to come.

Then in the next instant, he understood. "Tzvika, look," he said. "They're not shooting at us. They're shooting at the fort. It has to be our guys. It's a diversion."

"We're here! Over here!" both men shouted.

A moment later, Yoni leaped into the ditch, his Uzi clutched in front of him. He hurried toward Yossi with a broad smile. "You don't look so bad," he lied.

"Yoni," Yossi answered, "be careful. They're shooting. Get down."

"Yossi, shut up. I'm the commander now. Let's get you out of here."

"It's nothing but rocks," the pilot said. "I can't go down there. There's no place to land."

"That's why you're gonna get a medal. Of course you can do it. You're an ace," Yanosh told him. "You don't, you know I'll shoot you."

"The Syrians are *already* shooting at us," the pilot shouted.

"Then you might as well put this thing down on the ground. Let's go. Follow the green smoke in."

Reluctantly, the pilot began to descend. A flare illuminated a small stretch of fairly flat ground. The *sayaret* had formed a cordon around the area, their guns ready. Standing beside a boulder was Yoni, and next to him was a soldier lying on a stretcher. From the air, it was impossible to tell if the man was alive.

"C'mon," Yanosh barked. "Take her in. Now!"

The chopper came down slowly, like a wary bather easing into a steaming-hot tub. As the ground rose up beneath them, Yanosh suddenly feared the pilot was right. There was no room to land. But the pilot continued his careful descent. The craft drifted lower, hovering just a few feet above the ground. No longer able to wait, Yanosh leaped out and raced over to Yossi.

"You look like hell," Yanosh told him as he leaned over and kissed his cheek.

"I feel worse," Yossi managed.

Two *sayaret* commandos rushed Yossi's stretcher to the helicopter. As they carried him, Yanosh unzipped Yossi's overalls and looked at his wounds.

The commandos secured the stretcher to the rear compartment and Yanosh announced with one of his naughtiest grins, "I just checked. Everything important is still there. I guess that means I won't be getting your girlfriends."

Yossi tried to smile. "I'm a married man."

"Yes," Yanosh agreed. "You are. I'll get word to Nati. She'll meet you at the hospital."

A commando medic who would accompany Yossi to the hospital started him on a morphine drip. There was no room for Yanosh, so he jumped off. But Yossi called to him, and he turned. "I knew my brother would save me," Yossi said weakly.

Yanosh watched the helicopter rise into the night sky, and bank south. Then he caught up with Yoni and began the long walk down the hill, and back to his war.

THIRTY-SEVEN

The Pit/14 October 1973/0300

In the small hours of the morning, Dado paced about the Pit awake with worry. He was beginning to have doubts. Zeira had promised the Egyptian armored divisions would cross to the east bank in preparation for the offensive, but there was still no sign of activity. Perhaps it had been a mistake to delay grabbing a foothold in Egypt simply because of one piece of intelligence. After all, the last time he had listened to a spy, he had been told war was an impossibility. Had he once again been deceived by another mistaken Concept?

Then he received word from the Sinai Command. Forces from the Egyptian Fourth Armored Division had crossed over the Suez Canal to the Third Army's southern bridgehead. The Twenty-first Armored Division had moved north, joining the Second Army.

"It's about time!" the chief of staff cheered.

"Keep your fingers crossed," Dado told the general staff. "We need a massive, big beautiful offensive of lots of Egyptian tanks—to wipe them out here, east of the Canal, and then we'll go on to cross. That's today's program."

He was alive with a focused energy. The decisive battle in the south was near.

The plan was Ismail's. There was no subterfuge, no feints in its design. Its inspiration rested on a very simple geometry: The shortest distance between two points was a straight line. He had laid out four independent frontal assaults, but he might just as well have taken a ruler and connected dots on the map.

In the south, an armored brigade would charge twenty miles across the desert to the Mitla Pass; an infantry brigade would move to the Gidi Pass. In the center, two armored brigades would rush the command post at Tasa. And in the north, another armored brigade would head out across the swamps in the direction of Baluza, below the Mediterranean. Ismail envisioned a succession of gallant charges, the rumble of his massive force of tanks driving across the desert sand, and the enemy lines breaking under the sustained pressure.

But while it was the minister of war who drafted the attack, it was Shazly who had to order the men into battle. And he knew it had no chance of success. In armored warfare, firing position determined the course of the battle. A brigade driving into a well-deployed defensive alignment without the element of surprise would be slaughtered. Israeli armor hidden behind the tall dunes or firing down from the desert ridges would get off the first shots. And the second and the third, while the Egyptian tanks would be scrambling to find cover. These foolhardy tactics had cost the enemy in the opening days of the war, and Egypt would blindly, tragically, repeat its mistakes. Worse, after the attacking forces had advanced beyond the mobile SAM-7s, the Israeli jets would deliver the devastating final blow.

Shazly searched the plan for something that gave him hope. The attack would begin with artillery and the 500-gun barrage might do some damage; its ferocity alone was designed to crush the enemy's will. The sheer number of advancing tanks, too, would be an awesome sight. The Jews had taken an unexpected beating in the past week and the prospect of another great battle might be too much. The enemy could panic and run. Perhaps such a victory would be Allah's gift.

But it wasn't Allah sending the men off to fight. Shazly had to give the orders, and he wanted to refuse. But he did not. At 6:15 that morning, 2,000 tanks faced one another along the entire Sinai front, preparing to collide.

Since 5 A.M., veiled by the rising mist of the fresh sultry day, Amnon had been waiting. He was well positioned behind a tall, rolling dune on high ground, with his hull down. Like the knuckle of a clenched fist, only his turret was exposed. An orange sun was at his back, and his long cannon pointed west over the sand, toward the Suez Canal. He had seventy-one tanks under his command, once again a full brigade, and he had spread them out to take advantage of the undulating folds of this ridge in the central sector. Any force that hoped to push them back would need to be very large, and very determined.

Nevertheless, he reminded himself, tanks were nothing more than heavy, slow-moving armored-plated machines with guns. Ultimately, they were only as good as the soldiers that manned them. He wondered about his crews. They were mostly reserves; so many of the regular tankers had fallen in the chaotic first days. In his tank, the entire crew was new, *jobniks* who had never known combat. His loader had long straight blond hair that reached nearly to his shoulders. The prospect of counting on this hippie to get the heavy HEAT shells into the breech in the frenzy of battle filled Amnon with doubts. Still, it was a marvelous thing to see his brigade, destroyed in the ambushes that began the war, brought back to life.

Just after six, the sun burned through the mist and as if that were a signal, the enemy started in with their big guns. Rockets followed. The noise was tremendous and, more frightening, the barrage had range. He was reminded of the first afternoon, Yom Kippur, and his surprise and incomprehension when without warning the earth shook from the artillery blasts. Today at least they were prepared, in position to strike back. But moments later, a howitzer shell grazed his tank and he no longer felt inured to the danger. Suddenly, his decision to stand tall in the turret seemed reckless. "Button up!" he ordered over the net, as he scrambled down the ladder into the belly of the machine. The top closed over him with a firm, reassuring thud.

The interior of the tank was dark and blessedly cool. Shells thundered down, yet Amnon had no idea whether it was the prelude to a full-scale attack. He looked through the periscope, but the steady torrent of exploding shells hurled a whirlwind of sand and obscured his view. He waited five minutes. Then another five. Finally he could no longer bear it. He climbed up the ladder and threw open the turret.

Amnon had lived in the desert long enough to appreciate its vagaries. Often on bright, cloudless days, a sudden cascade of water from the rain-swept mountains would race down the wadis. Now he heard a similar sound: a huge, rolling, streaming flood. But when he looked at the wadis they were dry and empty. A moment later he realized his mistake. Emerging through the whirl of dust and sand, he saw what looked to be two hundred tanks rushing straight at him.

His first thought was, How can I stop this?

But he knew he would have to try. "Fire positions!" he screamed into the radio.

The turrets of seventy-one tanks swung toward the approaching force. Their 105-mm guns adjusted for range. Wait, he told the men. Let the enemy get closer.

His tank fired first. And on his signal, seventy tanks let loose. Without waiting for command, they went into their reload cycles. Amnon no longer had any doubts about the men or about the battle. He wanted revenge for the humiliation, for the ambushes, for the good men who had died. His force continued to fire steadily from the high ground.

The battle lasted only a furious half hour, but for the men in the tanks each moment had been lived with intensity that was its own lifetime. Missiles had struck three of Amnon's tanks, none were hit by tank fire. And when the swirling sand settled, the silhouettes of ninety-nine Egyptian tanks were strewn about the battlefield, immobilized and burning in the scorching sun.

Sharon had good hunting, too. At nine o'clock that morning a reconnaissance report from his operations room at Tasa reached him in the field. "There's a thick hunk of armor west of Hamadia that you can batter away at and have yourself a ball."

His tanks swooped down from the dunes and when the Egyptians continued to advance in a headlong attack, Sharon's force opened up with rapid fire. His men destroyed forty tanks, with only the loss of a single armored personel carrier.

Now his blood was up. He wanted to attack, to push the enemy back from the Suez Canal. He reached Bar-Lev and begged for permission to go on the offensive. "They're all on the run. If we just ride the momentum, we can go all the way and hit them where it hurts."

But Bar-Lev refused to send Sharon into the heart of the Egyptian bridgeheads. The Sagger-armed infantry was still too dangerous a threat.

Sharon, however, sensed the opportunity for a great victory. "I'll be careful," he promised. "I saw the Twenty-first Armored Division today. I saw them, and if I may use a crude expression in a conversation with a minister, it's the same old shit: They came, they were beaten, and they started running away. . . ."

Bar-Lev was adamant. Today's mission was strictly defensive. Their goal was to repulse the enemy's counterattack. Sharon ended the call in a huff.

Bar-Lev worried. Would Arik obey? Or would he pick away at some conversational nuance until, however disingenuously, it became his justification for an attack? He decided to make certain Arik explicitly understood the orders.

For over an hour, he attempted to contact Sharon, but Arik could not be found. Bar-Lev did not know if this was due to a failure in the communications equipment or Sharon's unwillingness to be reached.

Not for the first time, Bar-Lev thought, Sharon is out of control. Something has to be done.

Shazly, too, was trying to reach one of his generals without success. As the grim reports from the battlefields came into an oddly quiet Center Ten, he decided the only course left was an orderly withdrawal to the Suez Canal bridgeheads. He phoned General Mamoun at the Second Army HQ to authorize the retreat. But the general's aide said he was "having a rest."

In the midst of a battle? Shazly wondered. But if the general wanted to sleep, he would not disturb him. There was nothing Mamoun, or anyone for that matter, could do. The counterattack had failed. Shazly told the aide to circulate the order to fall back.

Dado did not want the enemy to retreat. Since the war began nine days ago, he had envisioned a morning like this, and he did not want it to end. His careful, defensive strategy had been vindicated.

Sharon had been the only wrinkle. By the time Arik finally reported in, he had chased down another twenty-five tanks. His ambition somewhat assuaged, he agreed not to press his attack. Bar-Lev, though, boiled. Sharon, he told Dado, was not fighting as a commander of a division but as a politician hoping to see his name in the headlines.

By noon the Israelis had repulsed each of the Egyptian attacks. Not a yard of territory had been gained. Israel lost a total of six tanks. Two hundred sixty-four Egyptian tanks, including a full brigade of the dangerous T-62s, were put out of action in the firefights. As the Egyptians retreated, Israeli jets gave chase and knocked out an additional sixty tanks before they scurried back beneath the protection of the missiles.

Yet Dado hoped the Egyptians would launch a second wave in the afternoon. He wanted to deliver a demolishing, possibly even fatal blow. He contacted Bar-Lev on an unsecured field phone and the two of them moaned loudly about the beating Israel had taken that morning. Our positions are ready to break, they said. But either the Egyptians were unpersuaded by their acting, or simply had had enough for one day. They did not resume their offensive.

At one o'clock that afternoon Sadat entered the Operations Room and approached Shazly. Shazly did not want to see him. He could not forgive him. Men, tanks, even victory itself had been squandered. And for what reason? he wondered. Even if we had taken the passes, would that have persuaded the Zionists to pull back in Syria? It made no sense.

Sadat offered no explanations to Shazly. Instead, the president brusquely ordered him to report to the front. Shazly was to raise the morale of the men.

It was a fool's mission, Shazly decided as he arrived at the Second Army encampment later that afternoon. What is done cannot be undone. He received further proof of how precipitously things had deteriorated when he asked to speak with Mamoun, and learned the general had not been napping. He had suffered a breakdown. The details of each of the failed assaults had rained down upon him until he collapsed under the unbearable weight. Now he lay in bed, a broken man, a commander of a broken army.

Shazly began to believe for the first time that all might very well be lost.

In Tel Aviv, the chief of staff shared the full extent of the day's victory at a midnight meeting with the cabinet. When he finished his report, he asked for permission to begin the final stage of the war.

The prime minister did not hesitate. She approved the orders to cross the Suez Canal tomorrow night.

THIRTY-EIGHT

The Damascus Road/ 15 October 1973/0200

In Syria, Yanosh and his men settled into a defensive line fifteen kilometers beyond the old border. Each day the enemy let loose with artillery fire, and small bands of commandos tried to infiltrate their positions. But there were no more battles. There had been 1,700 Syrian tanks in the combat zone when the war began. Only 500 remained, with just 200 in the first line of defense. The war in the north had been won.

In this lull, the battalion adjutant arrived at their camp and gave Kahalani a roster of the dead and wounded.

"Amir Bashari, Yair Swet, Yisraeli Barzilai, Yoav Bluman . . . What? Yoav dead?"

"Yes."

"Where? When?"

"On the third or fourth day."

"Are you sure he was killed? Where's the information from?"

"It's a hospital list and it's precise."

Kahalani continued down the list. He knew every name.

When the war was over, he would visit the families, but he could not go just yet. He ordered his adjutant to leave in the morning and pay a condolence call at each of the men's homes. Tell them about our battles, he instructed, and why they were important. He wanted the families to know their sons and husbands had not died in vain.

The next morning when he awoke, it was raining, a heavy downpour, and the harbinger of dark winter storms. He thought of his home and the roof he had been tiling when Yanosh had called on Rosh Hashanah. He had never finished; he had not returned home since that afternoon. And now the rains had come.

He hurried to catch the adjutant before he left. Call Dalia, he said, and tell her to get someone to lay the tiles on the unfinished roof. Whatever the cost, it would have to be paid. He did not want his family to be rained on, or to live in dampness.

When the adjutant returned, he told Kahalani that the roof had already been fixed. Volunteers from the community had done the work. It was, they had told Dalia, the least they could do.

"The families?" Kahalani asked. "Did you explain to them why their loved ones' sacrifices were necessary?"

"I did," he answered. "They understood, too."

Yanosh was spent. He had been fighting for nine days and he had had enough. He had not reached Damascus, but he told himself, he wasn't in Kuneitra either. Or, the Sharon Valley, for that matter. The nation had counted on the Seventh Armored Brigade, and, impossibly, they had stopped the enemy. No matter what else happened in his life, that accomplishment, that miracle, would always be his.

But now Yanosh was tired and he needed to rest. What had Dayan told the chief of staff? "This war is being run by Yanosh, and after that by all the rest of the people of Israel." Truth was, he felt that way. If the generals were content to let the war grind to a halt in the north, he had no complaints. He wanted to lie down for a few days. Rest up, then go visit Yossi in the hospital. Oh, the fun they'd have. And if Yossi wasn't ready to join in, he'd carry the load himself. That night he fell asleep imagining all the pretty nurses, and their delightful smiles.

Surgeons had worked for six hours trying to repair Yossi's leg, and now he slept. Nati watched him from her chair across the hospital room. It was two in the morning, and even after sitting with him for hours she was open-eyed and alert, and full of thoughts. Before their wedding day two months ago, she had shared with Yossi her dream of the house they would one day build for their family. It would be big and white and open on a view of the sea. Now the doctors had told her that Yossi would be spending the next year in the hospital. If all the operations went well, if he was lucky, he would walk again. Well, Nati told herself, so much for new homes and families. She felt like crying.

But she had cried for an entire day, weeping over the unfairness of life, and she could not summon the tears.

As she sat in the silent darkness, she filled with a growing resolve. Her husband had survived, and she would survive, too. *They* would survive. In the morning, she would go to her parents' and pack a bag. Then she would return and make this room their new home. She thought of something, and began to laugh. She would bring that silly monkey Yossi had bought in the Himalayan village with her, too. They would be a family, and they would survive. The power of her new certainty transcended all that had come before, and she felt a sensation rising inside her that for the first time suggested the true happiness of married life. She had loved Yossi before she had met him, but only at this moment did her feelings begin to make sense.

In the morning, before she left the hospital to gather her belongings, she visited Shmuli. His operation had been nearly a week ago, but he remained unconscious in his room two floors above.

Nati entered a room muffled in silence, and walked to his bed. She grasped his hand, and stared into his blank eyes and prayed that he was not beyond repair.

Then she bent over and whispered in his ear, "Listen to me, Shmuli. You will get well. You will survive, too."

THIRTY-NINE

Tasa Command Post/ 15 October 1973/1200

For once, the bunker was quiet. Throughout the war, Sharon's desert command post had bustled with the atmosphere of a convivial, sometimes even raucous dinner party. The mess was first-rate, the cheese selection particularly impressive, and there was always a crowd of reporters, both Israeli and foreign correspondents, to keep the conversation lively. Arik played the diligent host, dishing out between the courses streams of good, if unembarrassingly self-serving, copy to his grateful guests.

But on the morning of the tenth day of the war, the reporters and hangers-on were abruptly hustled out and armed soldiers took up posts at the doors. Before noon, the helicopters began to arrive. The High Command—Dado, Dayan, Bar-Lev, Gonen, Bren—and their aides joined Sharon and his staff in the bunker's cavernous War Room. They had come to finalize the bold, complex plan that could decide the outcome of the Yom Kippur War. If all went well, tonight Israel would cross the Suez Canal and take the war into Egypt.

Over the many years of uneasy peace, the Sinai Command had diligently planned and then practiced Operation Stout-Hearted Men, a deep-penetration assault across the Suez waters. Sharon, during his three and a half years as head of the Southern Command, had paved roads so that bridging equipment could be swiftly transported from the deep desert base at Refidim. He had constructed a wide, camouflaged marshaling area—the "yard"—protected by high sand walls near the water's edge so engineers could assemble the pontoons and control the bridge traffic. He had even selected a preferred crossing site by the Matsmed stronghold, where a calm stretch of water opened out into the Great Bitter Lake.

However, in all the years of planning, none of the generals had ever anticipated that the enemy would be entrenched on the Sinai bank. Or, that the battle-proven core of Egypt's Second Army, its Twenty-first Armored Division and the Sixteenth Infantry Division, would control the approaches to the crossing zone. Yet this was the situation. It would be a fight to establish bridgeheads on both sides of the Suez Canal.

Shortly after midday, following a briefing by Gonen that outlined the few minor changes to Operation Stout-Hearted Men at Matsmed, Sharon moved onto center stage. A tight, icy silence fell over the room. Many of the generals had come to believe that Arik had let them down in this war. He had been too reckless, too eager for glory. Yet Sharon, to his utter delight and bursting pride, had been chosen to lead the way across the Suez Canal. The plan for seizing the bridgeheads had been left to him, as well. Dado's hope was that Arik would take this as an opportunity to redeem himself. He would let nothing stop him.

"The problem," said Sharon as he began to reveal his strategy to the generals, "is to reach the water and set up the bridgeheads before dawn—so that the Egyptians will not discover the plan and meet us with massed armor on the west bank."

Timing and surprise, therefore, were essential. And as Sharon had thought long and hard, as he had looked for a way to achieve those crucial elements, he recalled Amnon's accidental discovery on the fourth night of the war of a seam through the two Egyptian armies. The more he mulled it over, the more convinced he became that this passageway through the tall dunes was the key that would unlock his daring plan.

And now he laid it all out to the men in the crowded bunker. The initial attack force would sneak through the nineteen-kilometer-long desert trail. Catching the enemy by surprise, they'd clear the two east-west supply roads, Tirtur and Akavish. Once these routes were under control, they'd push back the Egyptians from the adjacent Chinese Farm so the invasion force would not be menaced by Saggers and artillery. With a safe corridor to the Matsmed crossing point established, the bridges would be brought forward.

Paratroopers in rubber boats would make the first crossing at 8:30 that night, and secure the bridgehead across the Suez Canal. But by 11 P.M., Sharon confidently promised, both bridges would be in place and with the breaking dawn two armored divisions, more than 400 tanks, would be in "Africa." Bren's division would be responsible for moving westward and destroying the SAM sites; then Israel's jets would finally be set loose. While Sharon's primary job after the bridges were in place would be to defend them against counterattacks.

Bar-Lev listened to the plan, and considered all it encompassed: an attack force sneaking through the trackless dunes at night; a battle for the roads and the Chinese Farm; a paratroop brigade rowing across the Suez waters in rubber boats; towing the giant pontoons from deep in the desert over the Tirtur and Akavish roads, then assembling the bridges; and finally, two divisions, thousands of men and 400 tanks, crossing into Egypt. All by dawn. Bar-Lev doubted it was feasible. He scrutinized all the complicated elements, each piece dependent on its own tactical miracle, and when he did, his apprehension grew. Sharon's impetuosity was once again pushing events. He suggested the operation be delayed. Perhaps Arik would like another day to prepare.

Sharon was tempted. He understood the scale, the intricacies of what he was setting out to do. He, too, had his doubts. But he also was aware of the opportunity. They were giving him the chance to lead the invasion, to grab this war's great prize. If he hesitated, the High Command might change its mind. No, he told Bar-Lev. "We'll be in Africa in the morning."

Dado, too, had concerns. The chief of staff thought it overly optimistic that two bridges would be spanning the Canal before midnight. But he also felt—an intuition deep in his commander's heart—that the moment had come to win the war. Yesterday they had smashed Egypt's will. He did not want to let up. There were dangers, of course. But, he decided, "if one bridge is standing by morning, that'll be fine with me."

At five that evening, Operation Stout-Hearted Men would begin.

Amnon knew his men were in for a rough night. Sharon had assigned one tank brigade the cumbersome job of towing a 200-meter bridge and the dozens of pontoons needed for the second bridge along the narrow, crowded Sinai roads. Another brigade headed west from Tasa to distract the enemy from discovering what was really going on that busy night. But Amnon's brigade would have to fight. He had four tank battalions—ninety-seven tanks—and three infantry battalions on half-tracks, and once he emerged from the dunes, his force would be attacking in every direction: west toward the Canal, east to clear the roads, north to the Chinese Farm, and south to secure the "yard."

An entire division, Amnon decided, would be hard-pressed to accomplish all that. Yet he accepted the mission without complaint. In fact, he wanted it. On the opening day of the war, the Egyptians had ambushed his force; only a quarter of his tanks survived. But now the Fourteenth Armored Brigade had been re-formed. Yesterday they had fought a defensive battle. Tonight he would attack. His brigade would surprise the enemy, bursting into their flank, and then hitting them hard. War, he had come to realize too well, was all about killing, but it was also ennobling. This war had been forced on his country. Tonight's battles would be the turning point, and he was honored to have been chosen to spearhead the fight.

Honor, too, prompted a small ceremony as his brigade made its final preparations. In all the days of brutal fighting, Amnon had thought his own life-and-death battles were at the center of the conflict. But today the news of the Seventh Armored Brigade's defiant last stand on the Golan had reached the Sinai, and he belatedly acknowledged with a twinge of guilt that this was a two-front war. There had been many hells.

His initial reaction to the victory was one of shared pride; it was his fellow tankers who had pushed back the Syrians. But soon his elation was mixed with grief. As the names of the dead and wounded were announced, he found he knew nearly all of them. Shmuli's story, particularly, touched him deeply. Discharging himself from the hospital, resurrecting the Barak Brigade, leading them into the thick of an impossible battle—and to what end? To become an inert, unconscious body in a hospital bed, unable to speak, even to move. Such courage deserved recognition, and such sacrifice a nation's gratitude. Amnon was going to fight a battle that would bring the war into the enemy's own land, but this had been made possible by others who had not wavered. He wanted to acknowledge their valor, and he wanted to inspire his brigade so that they, too, would do what had to be done. In tribute, he renamed one of his fiercest units, a fire-breathing mixed force of paratroopers and armor. They would fight tonight as Force Shmulik.

At nightfall, the brigade moved out. The long column followed a trail between the high, peaked dunes. Amnon had ordered a silent march, and the loudest sound was the steady rhythmic undertow of straining engines as the force struggled through the deep sand. There were only nineteen kilometers to cover, yet the route might as well have been taking them to the far ends of the earth. A chalk white moon shone down from a clear night sky and lit the way like a beacon.

* * *

The force emerged from the dunes onto Lexicon Road and headed north. Exposed, they traveled parallel to the Great Bitter Lake, and on this clear night the sea smells were fresh in the crisp air. Amnon was in the middle of the column. He stood upright in the turret of his tank, and he knew that if he were the enemy this would be the time to strike. His force was strung out along the road, the water blocking one escape route, the deep sand another. He searched the desert for gray uniforms. He listened for the screech of Saggers, the first explosive thud of an RPG. He was behind enemy lines, but the night remained still and quiet. He drove on.

As he approached the Tirtur Road intersection, he divided his force. A reconnaissance battalion went west to secure the crossing point and the staging area. Another tank force turned east toward Tasa, hoping to clear the paved Akavish Road for the paratroopers who would be traveling to the water in half-tracks. Amnon continued north, sneaking up into the heart of the Second Army. As he moved forward, he had the growing sense that this was going to work. He'd secure the roads and the Chinese Farm compound before the Egyptians realized he was in their midst.

His column began to cross the Tirtur junction, and as they did, Amnon received heartening news. The Matsmed crossing area and the yard had been taken with no opposition at all. Now he was certain. We'd watch the sun rise while standing on the sands of Egypt.

The column proceeded across the road. Amnon looked back over his shoulder. Nearly all of his tanks had crossed. Up ahead, his lead battalion approached the Chinese Farm. His hand gripped the machine gun in the commander's cupola as he scanned the road. He knew the Egyptians were out there in the darkness, but they continued to ignore his force. Had yesterday's losses knocked the fight out of them? Were they giving up? Or perhaps they hadn't realized this was an unfriendly column moving in their midst. Whatever the reason, he'd take it. His tanks streamed forward.

Then, behind him, a booming volley of tank fire. The explosive pounding of RPGs. He looked back. Bright orange flames climbed into the night. In only a moment, Amnon had lost ten tanks from the rear of his column.

"Forward," he shouted into the radio. "Charge ahead."

The Egyptians closed around them from all sides.

The lead tanks surged north and suddenly found themselves in the heart of the Second Army's vast supply depot. Hundreds of vehicles were positioned in orderly rows. Tanks, trucks, jeeps, armored personnel carriers. SAM launchers. Ammunition dumps. Artillery batteries. The muscular materiel of war surrounded them. The Israeli tank commanders looked about with astonishment. They had stumbled into this enormous stockpile of machines and weapons, and there was no choice but to fight their way out.

They fired their 105-mm cannons and it was impossible to miss. Each shell scored, and the fires spread like raging storms. Explosions rocked the night. When the ammunition dumps went up, one after another, the desert erupted in a vortex of cascading sand. Gravity threatened to fail and they feared they would be sucked deep into the very center of the earth. But the ground shifted quickly back into place, and as it steadied, the Egyptians came after them. Infantry swarmed about them, firing RPGs and Saggers. The tank cannons were useless at this range. The desperate crews hurled grenades and sprayed their Uzis into the night. And still the Egyptians kept coming.

The rear of the brigade was trapped in the Chinese Farm. Soldiers crawled out of the deep irrigation ditches and fired hundreds of Saggers at point-blank range. In their fury to escape, the huge tanks collided with each other, metal smashing into metal, a jumble of confusion. Commanders fired their guns, but it was useless. The only way to survive was to be lucky.

Amnon, positioned in the middle of these two battling wings of his brigade, fought his own relentless fight. Enemy tanks charged at him from out of the night, and it was only when they were on top of him, their long guns staring at him with a vengeance, that he detected their presence. "Crew! Tank! Fire!" he screamed. His men obeyed, shouting again and again and again. He had hit four tanks before they could fire back.

"I've just destroyed four tanks," he broadcast over the radio net. It was not meant as a boast. He wanted the men to know that their brigade commander was in this, too. The whole world was in flames, but they were a brigade and they would not run. "Force Shmulik," he repeated over the net. "Force Shmulik." It was a battle cry, and a call to honor.

Amnon's brigade was spread out for seven kilometers around the junction roads leading to the Suez Canal. They fought through the night.

The paratroopers, meanwhile, were stalled. First there were no half-tracks. Then no rubber boats. And finally when they solved those problems, they drove on to the four-meter-wide Akavish Road and were stuck in a monumental traffic jam. It was as if the entire IDF was on the move to the Suez Canal—hundreds of tanks, ammunition trucks, jeeps, bulldozers, armed personnel carriers. It took them two hours to travel less than three miles to the yard.

But at 1:25 A.M.—nearly five hours behind schedule—a flotilla of black rubber boats slipped into the water. Crouching low in the boats, their paddles dipping deeply into the bleak water, the paratroopers headed to the west bank. As the first boats neared the shore, the men waited for an enemy flare to light up the night, for artillery fire to rain down on them. But all was quiet. The boats pressed up against the bank and the men climbed out onto an empty, sandy shore.

"Acapulco," the paratroop brigade leader radioed Command at 3 A.M., using the prearranged code. Israel had a force in Egypt.

It was the only success in a difficult night, and a small one. The bridges never reached the Suez Canal. The 400-ton roller bridge had broken loose from the tanks, careening off the road and into the desert. It would take at least a day to repair, if the job could be done at all. The pontoons were still stuck in traffic, miles away from the yard.

In desperation, the engineers had improvised amphibious rafts to ferry tanks across the Canal, and at 6:52 A.M. the first Israeli tank reached the west bank. Within three hours, there would be 27 tanks and nearly 2,000 men in Africa. But this was far less than the two divisions and 400 tanks Sharon had guaranteed.

And more cause for concern, after the long night, Egypt still controlled the crossing roads and the Chinese Farm. At the first light of the new day, as the fighting at last ground to a halt, Amnon surveyed the destruction. Fires burned. Charred tanks and vehicles lay scattered about the sand, huge machines gutted and upended. Bodies were everywhere, corpses under the bloodred dawn.

Amnon's casualties filled him with guilt. There were 128 dead and 62 wounded. His brigade had lost 56 of its 97 tanks.

Yet as Amnon completed his grim inventory, he knew he was not done. Today the fight would go on. He still had to secure the roads and the Chinese Farm if the two divisions were going to cross into Egypt. But a day had been lost. And now there would be no surprise. The enemy knew he was coming.

FORTY

Center Ten/16 October 1973/1000

Shazly wanted to believe it was not too late. The enemy was on the west bank, but not in force. Israeli tanks had harassed a few rear SAM units behind the Suez Canal; yet this was the work of a raiding party, not an invading army. The Israelis had fought all night, but in the end they had failed to secure a crossing site. The Second Army had doggedly beaten them back. And these brave troops remained poised to smash the Zionists' next attempt. All was not lost.

Shazly left his desk and walked over to the large wall map and studied the situation. He stared at the cluster of plastic flags and triangular markers dotting the Sinai, and not for the first time appreciated all that had been accomplished. Regardless of the final battles, this war had already been won. History had been rewritten. Egypt's armies had crossed the impregnable canal, caught Israel by surprise, and now held the Sinai shore. Arab honor had been restored.

He chided himself for nearly succumbing to the anxious mood in the Operations Room. Sadat and Ismail had foolishly squandered tanks and men in their ill-conceived drive to the passes. Nevertheless, that debacle was two long days ago. A general needed to look ahead, to plan future moves. He studied the map with renewed concentration. There still was an opportunity to turn things around.

This evening, after Sadat and Ismail returned from the People's Assembly session in Cairo, he would propose his plan. Victory could still be grabbed, Shazly reassured himself. He had found a way to trap the enemy.

Sharon, too, believed he could wring a decisive triumph out of an apparent defeat. He had failed to secure the roads and crossing point. Egyptian tanks and infantry occupied the Chinese Farm. The bridges were not in place. But in the light of a new day he quixotically decided that his previous plan was irrelevant. To hell with the bridgeheads. The important thing was to get behind the Egyptian lines.

He radioed Gonen and, brimming with his usual confidence, offered up his new strategy. At this moment, thirty-seven of his tanks were in Africa attacking SAM sites. He wanted to ferry additional tanks across and rush through the enemy's rear lines. Bren's division, too, should cross on rafts. The bridges were unnecessary. The road to Cairo was open *now*. If Israel delayed, if it fussed over pontoons and threw its troops into skirmishes to control a few muddy irrigation ditches, the moment would be lost.

Gonen disagreed. From his perspective, Sharon's revised plan was not bold; it was irresponsible. Without a supply line, the tanks and troop on the west bank would run out of fuel, food, and ammunition within a day and would be stranded behind enemy lines in Egypt. And the notion of transporting an entire division across on rubber rafts was ludicrous. Once Egypt's artillery was alerted to what was happening, the vulnerable rafts would be sunk to the bottom of the Suez Canal, and Bren's corps along with them. It was imperative to clear the enemy out of the crossing junction and get the bridges across the water. Sharon was not—repeat, not—to transfer any more tanks to the west bank.

"Gonen," Sharon exploded into the handset, "if you had any balls, I'd tell you to cut them off and eat them."

Then Arik broke the connection and, slipping back into civility, moved up the ladder of command to Bar-Lev. But Bar-Lev's patience with Sharon had worn perilously thin. "It may be less glamorous to fight for the holding of a bridgehead than to drive your tanks into Africa," Bar-Lev lectured. "Nevertheless, the holding of a bridgehead may be the crucial move in a battle."

Sharon, he reiterated, was not to float any more tanks across the Canal. Bren's division would assume the fight for the blocked road axis and the transport of the pontoon bridge. Sharon was simply to concentrate on taking the Chinese Farm.

The orders were less than an hour old when a disdainful Sharon and his forward headquarters crossed the Suez Canal. The Chinese Farm, he left to Amnon.

For Amnon, it came down to this: He would not quit. Last night his brigade had slipped right up into the heart of the Egyptian army. It had been so precise, a thing of beauty. And then it had turned ruinous. He refused to let it end that way. He gathered his exhausted, bleary-eyed officers. The battle would be won by the side that refused to quit, he said. If our men were spent, so were the enemy's. "Force Shmulik," he intoned, the words a revitalizing call to arms, "will not fail."

Determined, he put together a company of tanks and charged the Tirtur Road intersection. They went forward in a V formation with Amnon in the lead. A battle line of enemy tanks stood between them and the Chinese Farm. Amnon drove closer and closer, waiting to give the order to fire. But as he approached, the tanks retreated and the infantry raised a white flag. Jubilant, he charged ahead into the Chinese Farm.

But once again it was impossible. Hundreds of soldiers rose up from the irrigation ditches and enveloped the lumbering machines. The sky flashed with RPGs. Saggers passed overhead. "Withdraw! Withdraw!" he bellowed.

Still, he did not give up. He sent a new battalion to attack Tirtur from the east. These men, too, charged into a firestorm of missiles. Commanders stood in their turrets and raked machine gun fire into the swarm of gray uniforms. They hurled grenades into the tangle of men. The tanks tried to speed ahead, to burst through the fortified defenses. But the Egyptians would not yield. Amnon, beaten, turned the tanks and retreated to the Israeli lines.

But the bridges had to get through. And that meant the Chinese Farm had to be taken. He would do it, and neither pain, nor terror, nor all the fire and smoke and death, would stop him.

The plan Shazly outlined in the Operations Room that evening had a crude yet unforgiving symmetry. Box the Jews in on all sides at the crossing point and destroy them.

There would be two concerted thrusts. The Third Army would drive northeast, as simultaneously the Twenty-first Armored Division moved south along the Sinai bank. The Jews arrayed around Matsmed would be caught in the middle.

It was also crucial, he stressed as President Sadat and Minister of War Ismail listened in stony silence, to crush the enemy troops behind their lines immediately. They were a small force and could be stopped easily. Units from the Third Army, including the Twenty-fifth Armored Brigade with their fierce killing machines, the new T-62s tanks, should be sent back to the west bank to wipe out the raiding parties.

The enemy's presence on the west bank was only a minor annoyance, Ismail argued. Transferring forces back across the Suez Canal was unnecessary, and would only dishearten the men. The T-62s should move north along the water and lead the counterattack against the Jews.

Shazly knew this would never work. The Twenty-fifth Armored Brigade would need to advance twenty-five grueling desert miles, with its left flank trapped against the water and its right flank exposed. The enemy gunners would massacre them. He tried to control his rising sense of desperation as he explained this to Sadat.

Sadat exploded. Shazly had seen the president's anger before, but never had it been directed toward him. "Why do you always propose withdrawing our troops from the east bank," Sadat raged. "If you persist in these proposals, I will court-martial you. I do not want to hear another word."

It was a dangerous moment. If Shazly pressed on, he knew he would be relieved. Better to tell the president and Ismail that he had no faith in their plan, in their leadership, and could no longer serve. He saw only defeat ahead.

Only, he could not walk away. He had shared his men's triumphs, he had reveled in their cheers. It would be dishonorable to abandon them now.

Shazly held a steady, level gaze. And with a soldier's stoic discipline, he kept his silence. He listened as Ismail ordered the counterattack for tomorrow. The T-62s would lead the way.

La hawla wala quwata illa billah, Shazly thought. Man has strength for nothing without the strength of God. It was the Muslim prayer of resignation.

As the attack column of ninety-six T-62s moved north the next morning, the Israeli High Command was already locked in a fierce battle. Dado, Dayan, Bar-Lev, Sharon, and Bren knelt in the sand on a hill in Kishuf, south of the Akavish Road. Spread out in front of them was a map of the Sinai, and they referred to it as they argued about what should be done. And, no less important, who should do it.

Again Sharon insisted that men and tanks should be sent on rafts across into Africa. Forget about the fight on the east bank. Don't wait to lay the bridges across the Suez Canal. If armored brigades advance with speed through the Egyptian lines on the west shore, the enemy will collapse.

Bren, all cool logic to Arik's bluster, argued that the Matsmed bridgehead must be secured, and the bridges put in place across the

Canal. Until that was accomplished, it would be a tactical error to send a large force into Africa. And when the time came for the invasion, Bren made it clear he wanted his division to go across first.

Sharon erupted, but Bar-Lev cut him off. His frustration over the failure to get the troops across the Canal, to seize the opportunity to bring the war to an end, brought out a flood of hot indignation. "There is no resemblance between our aims and what has actually happened," he snarled at Sharon.

The accusation stung. Sharon wanted to slap Bar-Lev across the face. But he found control. He snapped, "I don't accept the judgment that expectations have not been fulfilled."

"What can I say," Bar-Lev answered, his words acid. "Nothing has worked out. The bridgehead hasn't been consolidated and there was no Egyptian collapse."

Sharon rose to his feet. "Any minute now you'll tell me I didn't take part in this war at all."

There was a sudden quiet. Something irrevocable was about to happen.

Dado intervened. "I have decided," said the chief of staff, "Sharon will continue with the task of consolidating the bridgehead, and Bren will cross westward according to plan."

"Arik," he added like a teacher admonishing a recalcitrant pupil, "complete the task assigned to you and then you can cross, too."

Sharon's anger was beyond words. He struggled to find the calm that would let him speak. But before he managed a word, an aide interrupted the meeting with an urgent message from Amnon. His four tanks were stationed on the south shore of the Great Bitter Lake and an Egyptian armored brigade of T-62s was coming toward them at full speed.

"I'll deal with that," said Bren, and raced to his command vehicle.

"They're coming! They're coming," Amnon shouted into the radio.

The Twenty-fifth Brigade's scout company was advancing toward him. But where was Bren?

"God bless them, let them come in—we're waiting for them!" one of Bren's commanders radioed back. They were hidden in the hills, hulls down. And below them, exposed on the flat desert, was the heart of the Egyptian counterattack.

Amnon fired. From long-range, he killed two of the lead tanks. On that signal, Bren opened up.

The Egyptians were caught in a perfect killing ground. In front of them were Amnon's tanks. On one flank, in good position on high ground, were Bren's forces. On the other flank, was the lake, and adjacent to it a vast minefield. Another of Bren's tank battalions had swooped down to block the rear. In desperation, the T-62s charged up the hill into the Israeli positions. Most were set on fire as they struggled up the slope. A few panicked and raced into the minefield. Escape was impossible.

Two hours of fighting later a battalion commander radioed Bren, "I think we can cross off this brigade."

In Center Ten, Shazly followed the battle. It had gone exactly as he had predicted.

Man has strength for nothing without the strength of God.

It would all be over soon. There was nothing more he could do.

That night, after midnight, Amnon again attacked the Chinese Farm. He came in with a squad of paratroopers and they moved across flat, exposed terrain. The Egyptians used night sights, and cut down the first charging wave. But now the two armies were on top of each other, and they fought hand to hand in the darkness. It was a night of private battles, vicious and intense. Yet the Egyptians would not yield. Finally, the outnumbered paratroopers were forced to retreat behind the tanks.

Amnon had been beaten back again.

* * *

But the battle had opened up Akavish Road and the convoy dragging the heavy pontoons moved forward toward the Suez Canal. At 7:15 A.M., the first pontoon splashed into the water.

And with the new day, Amnon returned to the Chinese Farm. This time he attacked from the rear. He was exhausted, but so much—the experiences of an entire war—urged him forward. He seethed with a corrosive hatred for this enemy who had tried to destroy his homeland. And he thought of the men he served with, their enormous capacity for sacrifice, their steady honor. "Force Shmulik," he once again repeated, as he rallied himself and his men for one more assault. His mind was set. He would not retreat.

He drove his tank forward into the farm, and today he was prepared. When the infantry rose up, his machine gun was ready. He mowed them down as they charged. By now his men knew the enemy's hiding places and they hurled grenades into the ravines. This time the Egyptians could not stop the tanks. The Centurions raced toward the farm buildings, and when their cannons fired, the Egyptians ran.

Later that afternoon, Amnon walked across the battlefield accompanied by a stunned Dayan. In all the days of fighting, Amnon had no perspective on what he had been caught up in. But now as he moved on foot through the destruction, the galloping chaos of war still and inert, he was overwhelmed. How had he lived through this? "Look at this valley of death," he whispered to Dayan.

"What you people have done," Dayan agreed, awed and woeful.

The two soldiers walked on in silence, the terrible smell of war all around them.

That evening, October 18, thirteen days after the war had begun, Bren rode at the head of his division to the Suez Canal. The moon was nearly full and the water sparkled in the light. "The bridge is a magnificent sight," he radioed his men. "The moment has arrived, and we are crossing into Africa." The invasion of Egypt had begun.

* * *

In Tel Aviv, Dado rejoiced. Then he left for home for the first time since a fateful call had awoken him before dawn on Yom Kippur morning. The war, he knew, would soon be over.

Shazly spent the day at the front with his men. He had led them this far, and he would stand with them in defeat. He looked across the Suez Canal and recalled the day when he had dared to wonder if a crossing were possible. They had lost, but they had not been broken. What might have been? he sighed. Victory had been in their grasp. But Sadat and Ismail had let it slip away. He felt an immense sadness. But he also felt no shame.

The next day Shazly met with Sadat and told him, "The war is over." Sadat fixed him with a cold anger. Then he relieved Shazly of his command.

The war sputtered on for three days. There were more battles, and more deaths. The Arabs would lose a total of 11,200 men, with at least 15,000 wounded. Israel counted 2,838 dead, and 8,800 wounded. More tears were shed by both sides. Then politics prevailed. On the morning of October 22 at dawn the UN Security Council passed Resolution No. 338. A cease-fire would go into effect by 6:52 that evening.

At sunset, the Yom Kippur War was over.

Two days later, Shmuli awoke from his coma. He looked warily about his room in Rambam Medical Center, and stared with incomprehension at his sister asleep in a chair across from his bed. He was charged with a very powerful feeling, but he could not make the words come. He managed to make a guttural noise, and that woke her, and she ran to him.

Speech was impossible. But he concentrated very hard, and he discovered he could move his right hand. He made a small gesture, as if he were writing.

His sister hurried out of the room, and then returned with a pad and a pencil. She gave it to Shmuli.

Slowly, with great effort, he began to write. When he was done, she took the pad.

"Why? Why? Why?" he had written.

She looked at her brother, and from the depths of her heart she tried to find an answer. But now she was the one who could not speak. Her lower lip began to tremble and hot tears fell down on him. She put her head on Shmuli's chest and sobbed.

Epilogue

THE WATCHMEN

Jerusalem / Cairo
Spring 2003

. . . and who shall be uplifted.

For months, Shabtai Brill had been forced to confront the fact that he was frightened. Once again, he needed to make a choice. And once again, his decision, the resolution of his own deep troubles, would reach out and shake the lives of others. Exiled to his custodian's office above the parking garage, he had believed his life had been settled. The days of crisis, of moral urgency, of responsibility—all belonged to his past. But now he knew: He had not escaped.

Thirty years ago, just days after the cease-fire had been announced, when Ben Porat had coolly informed him that he was being transferred, Brill had seethed with anger. It was a demotion, and a punishment. The end of his career in Intelligence and, with that stain on his service record, the beginning of the end of his life as a soldier.

And what was his crime? That he had put loyalty to the nation above a mindless obedience to the chain of command. That he had dared to make his case to General Lidor when Ben Porat, time after bad-tempered time, had rebuffed him.

Or was he simply the scapegoat for their guilt? His presence was a reminder that the surprise did not need to have happened. An incriminating mountain of evidence had been gathered and culled. But the minds in the High Command were firmly set. And as a consequence of their intransigence, their carelessness, Israel had been caught unprepared. It had been a bloody, wrenching fight, and for four anxious days the very survival of the nation hung in the balance. How many lives might have been saved if the reserves had been called up, the armored brigades deployed in fighting strength on the Golan and along the Suez Canal, the jets launched in a preemptive attack? Any answer, of course, would always be conjecture. But there was one certainty: It had not been inevitable. The nation had been warned. Brill understood that he had been chosen to pay for their sins. When he was gone, out of Military Intelligence and out of uniform, it would be easier to maintain the illusion of blamelessness.

"This transfer is being done out of jealousy and anger," he had railed at Ben Porat. "You have to undermine me. I could tell the world you did nothing."

But over the years, as Brill's life spiraled downward, the anger seeped out of him. He settled into a resigned understanding of the world. The high-minded principles that had led to the creation of the Jewish state had given way in the aftermath of the scandal and shock of the Yom Kippur War to a generation of moral complacency, to a politics of maneuvering simply for advantage, and to an era of escalating cycles of violence. He felt betrayed; and, no less, he realized the nation had been betrayed, too. It became harder to carry on.

He took no satisfaction when the Agranat Commission formed to investigate the Yom Kippur War and announced its findings. Zeira, "in view of his grave failure . . . cannot continue in his post as chief of Military Intelligence." Gonen was suspended from active duty. And Dado's career and reputation were ruined: "The chief of staff bears direct responsibility for what happened on the eve of the war, both with regard to the assessment of the situation and the preparedness of the IDF." Dayan and Golda Meir—all the politicians, for that convenient matter—escaped censure. Nevertheless, another lingering consequence of the war, in April 1974, Prime Minister Meir announced her resignation to the Knesset. That ended her government.

In his disillusionment, Brill retreated and his world narrowed. As a retired officer, he continued to receive *Maarakhot*, the IDF's periodical, yet he glanced at its pages more out of habit than out of any genuine interest. The war, he noted with a complacent shrug, had created a new generation of military heroes to replace those whose reputations had been tarnished. Avigdor Kahalani, for his stand at the Valley of Tears, had won the Medal of Valor, the country's highest decoration. Yanosh Ben Gal and Amnon Reshef, the men whose tenacity had cemented the frontline defenses, were promoted to generals. Yossi Ben Hanan, two years after being wounded, returned to command the Seventh Armored Brigade. And Shmuli Askarov became a celebrity; the very fact that, despite partial paralysis, he could walk, talk, and even drive a car, was reported in the press and on television as a miracle. Yet no less miraculous, Brill decided, was Sharon's rise to power. Only Arik could overcome his spotty and contentious leadership in the Sinai and reinvent himself, nearly three decades later, as prime minister. So many had been raised. While for his daring service, he had been lowered. It was difficult not to feel sorry for himself.

So with each passing year, Brill stepped further back. These public events were of no real importance to him. He put them in the category of things that no longer concerned him, and excluded them from his new life. He had his building to look after.

Then the intifada erupted, and that changed everything.

At first, as terror haunted the streets and cafés of his beloved city of Jerusalem, only sadness and anxiety dogged him. Brill clung to his helplessness and victimization; for all he knew, the next exploding bomb might claim him or, his larger fear, his family.

But this threat to his city gnawed at him. He had a sense of a national breakdown, that the entire country was besieged and at a loss: a mirror of his own floundering life. For the first time in years, he felt, though still in a vague, unarticulated way, he had to do something.

Slowly, without trying, Brill began to rediscover his past. All the training of his previous life had made him a slave to information. Without even planning to do it, he found himself sitting in his custodian's office and compiling a list of the bombings across the city. He began to mark the locations on a map. And as the grim symbols multiplied across his sheet, as this circle of evil was delineated, he began to see something.

It was not anything as startling as a pattern. Yet, he was convinced it was not as random as the authorities insisted. The bombers were moving through Jerusalem's neighborhoods and boulevards exploiting all the opportunities in one sector—a bus, a café, a restaurant—before heading on to a new, unprotected part of the city.

But no sooner had Brill worked this out, than he poured scorn on it. What foolishness, he told himself. It was a banished man's last gasp at self-aggrandizement. Besides, who would listen to him? He returned to the duties and routines of his dull job.

Then the bakery across Hakhayal Street was bombed. He passed it every day as he went to work; and each day the warm, fresh wafting aromas had been a small pleasure. Now the large plate-glass window lay shattered on the street, and he knew: His building would be next.

He could alert the building's owners in Tel Aviv. But what would they do? Look at him suspiciously? Tell him he was being irrational? Question his motivation? In the end, regardless of whether his prediction proved right or wrong, they would make him the scapegoat.

Just as Ben Porat had done. He could not endure another humiliation. They had left him with so little, but if they stripped him of this, too, he doubted he could go on.

Still, he could not walk away. He no longer was the nation's eyes and ears. He no longer had an ingenious array of electronic wizardry to assist him. But just like thirty years ago, he had his duty and he must obey it. He was still one of Zion's Watchmen. Only this time, he would not repeat his past mistake. He would not inform anyone of what he had discovered. Instead, he set a trap.

Weeks passed and nothing happened. Yet, his determination did not waver. He remained on guard, and began to look at the direction his life had taken with a new clarity.

The Yom Kippur War had not been his ruination. Rather, it had prepared him for this important moment: the opportunity to save his building and his tenants.

And with this personal realization, he found that he looked at the entire war differently. From his new perspective, the defining legacy of the war was no longer the surprise, or even Military Intelligence's failure to alert the nation to the attacks. Now he saw the war, in its tragic, painful way, as a historical necessity. It created the possibility of transcendence.

His new feelings focused on one event. On November 19, 1977, Egyptian President Sadat had arrived in Jerusalem and addressed the Knesset. He had come to Israel to make peace. It had been an intense moment, full of a faith in a promising future that would not have been possible without the events of October 1973. The Six Day War had broken the Arabs so completely that the subsequent conflict was a festering inevitability. But the Yom Kippur War—the epic crossing of the Suez Canal, the valor of the soldiers—had restored Arab honor. Their combat had revitalized the Arab's self-respect; and at the same time the Jews were forced to acknowledge the enemy's accomplishments. In the aftermath of war, they all could move on. They could work together, or at least begin to make an attempt.

With his newfound hopefulness, Brill worked all this out. And he waited. Then one winter afternoon, they came.

He purposefully kept the front door of the building locked. Residents had keys; guests had to be buzzed in. So the only way in would be through the garage. He expected they would try a car bomb. Drive in. Walk out. *Boom!*

When they came, he was ready. He saw the two Arabs drive in and start to head down the ramp. And as they did, he emerged from behind the pillar that had been his hiding place for so many weeks. He had his military Colt in his hand, a big gun, and he waved it at the car.

The driver looked at him, and Brill saw the panicked recognition on the boy's face. Without a word of warning, Brill fired a shot. The bullet missed.

The driver threw the car into reverse. The vehicle sped backward out of the dark garage. Gun in his hand, Brill ran up the ramp in pursuit. He could see the car retreating. He could hear its wheels racing. He wanted to get off another shot, but the angles made it difficult. By the time he was at the entrance, the car was gone.

Yet Brill felt only triumph. He had done his duty. He had averted tragedy. He had been given another chance, and this time he had not failed. After thirty years, his war was finally over. He walked back into the shadows of the garage, and disappeared into a different world.

In Cairo that winter, the Yom Kippur War was finally over for Dr. Ashraf Marwan, too. For so long he had believed he had escaped untouched into his prosperous, busy cosmopolitan life. In Egypt, he had a distinguished career in government service. He had been a confidant of both Nasser and Sadat, a roving ambassador, and the president's coordinator with the intelligence services. In England, he ran a London financial corporation that held a 3 percent ownership of the Chelsea soccer team and had publicly struggled with Mohamed Al Fayed over control of Harrods. Approaching his sixtieth birthday, he had achieved recognition and respect. And he was convinced, his secrets would be buried with him.

But Marwan had underestimated his enemies, and their bitterness. For thirty years, Eli Zeira had lived uncomfortably with his own brooding suspicions. "The national myth," as Zeira dubbed it, had blamed Military Intelligence, and Zeira specifically, for the failure to alert Israel to the surprise attacks that began the Yom Kippur War. But as Zeira sifted through history, the events leading up to the war took on a different significance. They became incriminating clues. And when he followed them, they led to a startling conclusion: Israel had been purposefully misled. The In-Law was a double agent. He was doing Sadat's bidding.

At Zeira's urging, the Mossad formed a special committee to examine the In-Law's role. Had he invented a false Concept? Had he deliberately "cried wolf" in May 1973 when he convinced Israel to call up its reserves? Had he artfully lied to Zamir at their midnight meeting the night before the war broke out? The Mossad committee, which included the In-Law's case agent and other Intelligence officials involved in running the operation, concluded that he was not a double.

But Zeira was unpersuaded. "What do you expect?" he complained. "They were asked to pass judgment on themselves as much as their agent. This was a whitewash."

As he grew older and saw in his mind's eye the condemning lines in his obituary, Zeira moved to salvage what he had lost in the Yom Kippur War. First, he began to talk openly about his theory. Then, as the debate went public, he started giving clues to writers and journalists. He never revealed the In-Law's identity. With a calculated caginess, he simply pointed them in a direction. But after a conversation with Zeira, it required only a few deductions to conclude that the man who had married Gamal Nasser's third daughter, Nuna, had led a very complicated life.

But in the end it was not the Jews who ambushed the In-Law. In January 2003, as the thirtieth anniversary of what was known in the

Arab world as the Ramadan War neared, the Egyptian press revealed that Dr. Ashraf Marwan was the spy who had met with the head of the Mossad.

Marwan said the charge sounded like something from a spy novel. Which was true. And, therefore, while not an admission, it was also not quite a denial.

Yet as the summer approached, it was tempting to believe that he had been forgotten, lost in the shuffle of history. After all, these were turbulent and momentous times in the Middle East. A new war in Iraq. A new Palestinian leadership. A new "road map" for peace. And new terror. The uncertainties of the future demanded full attention.

But Marwan knew that in the Middle East the past was never remote. It was too often the reason for tomorrow's unhappiness. And from this sad perspective, the defining legacy of the Yom Kippur War was not the hopefulness of Sadat's journey to Jerusalem. Rather, it was the event that occurred four years later on October 6, 1981. Four Muslim fundamentalists burst out of a military parade celebrating the eighth anniversary of the day the war began and rushed the reviewing stand firing automatic weapons. Sadat was killed, and with him the prospects for peace.

Would Marwan's time come, too? His secret now revealed, all the spy could do was wait, and hope. Such fearful, tenuous emotions, he realized. Yet they offered some consolation. After all, it was this shared humanity, this common fragility, that in the end still held out the only genuine possibility of uniting Arabs and Jews. All the wars, all the history, and this was all they had; and all there ever was.

Day after day, he sat alone on his terrace overlooking the ancient river. He lived uncomfortably with his past, and he wondered about his future.

A NOTE ON SOURCES

Nearly two years before my arriving for the appointment in the Haifa shopping mall, I had decided to write a book about the Yom Kippur War. I was driven by a few simple curiosities: How did Israel, with its vaunted intelligence network, get caught by surprise in October 1973? Why was Israel so unprepared that after three days of fighting many of its leaders believed the survival of the state was in jeopardy? And not least, how were Egypt and Syria able to execute both their deception plans and their invasions so successfully?

As I started my inquiries nearly thirty years after the war, I found my timing was fortunate. Israel, with a remarkable candor, had declassified transcripts of general staff and cabinet meetings leading up to and during the war. Many of the crucial Arab and Israeli participants had published memoirs. Key government and intelligence officials were at last willing to be interviewed (and, more often then not, take issue with what others had written). And the U.S. Air Force Air University Library at Maxwell Air Force Base had collected, I discovered, a treasure trove of unclassified research papers written by veteran Arab officers.

Yet by the time I arrived for the meeting in the mall, accompanied by my indefatigable research assistant and translator, Rachel Zetland, I was beginning to suspect that the answer to the original questions I had posed were not to be found simply in documents, conversations with officials, or the analysis, however penetrating, offered in research papers. Also, I had started to sense that my scope of inquiry was too narrow: there was a much larger, more humanly affecting and politically resonating, tale that needed to be told if one were to capture what the war was truly about.

Part of my concern was that the men I had interviewed and the documents I had read, while providing a fascinating and revealing insider's look at how military and intelligence decisions were made at crucial times, only detailed what was taking place within the corridors of power. No less compelling, I was learning, was the story of the people who had been caught up in the war, the view, if not from the trenches, from the wadis and tank cupolas. This was a true-life tale full of a human drama that would have inspired Macaulay: men "facing fearful odds for the ashes of their fathers and the temples of their gods." It was, to use an unfashionable term, the story of heroes, of Arabs and Jews who fought with great personal courage for their national honor.

I had also discovered something hiding in the "shadows" of the official histories of the war. This important, yet previously unreported factor in the war was a spy story. For three decades, this tale of intrigue had remained a secret drama, one only hinted at in the official reports or the memoirs. But as I probed, I found that the role of the In-Law was not simply a clandestine episode but a crucial element if one were to understand the psychology of national leaders who, despite an abundance of facts, refused to believe war was imminent. This, too, would need to be part of the story I would tell.

Further, by the time I entered the mall in April 2002, my curiosities—and my narrative ambitions—had also been tempered by events I had never anticipated when I had commenced my research.

Even in my leafy corner of suburban Connecticut, there was no escape from the tragedy of September 11. A father of a boy in my middle child's class had left his home at dawn for an early game of two-on-two basketball, only to arrive at his desk in the World Trade Center in time for Fate to catch up with him. At his memorial service, watching his red-eyed widow clutching their youngest of four sons in her arms, sitting surrounded by a grieving community of acquaintances from our previously insulated world of school pick-ups, Little League games, and children's birthday parties, I began to grasp that it would be a mistake to write a simple history. The Islamic fundamentalism that reached across the globe to catch this country by surprise, devastate New York City, and bring such sorrow to my well-tended suburb, had its roots in a past that had not vanished, but was still dangerously relevant. Similarly, if I told a story set in the Middle East that only looked backward, it would be incomplete. The Yom Kippur War was fought in 1973, yet it is an episode in a continuum of conflict between Arab and Jews. It cannot be understood simply as an isolated event, as something belonging to and affecting another generation. It needed to be seen as part of the region's ongoing history, as a factor in the present struggles, and of future ones, too. And as part of a swirl of politics, religion, and history that inevitably will have consequences for America.

These convictions hardened as I traveled that spring throughout Israel conducting interviews. It was a journey filled with a constant anxiety. The intifada was raging, and danger was a looming presence. I did not ride on buses, but there was no avoiding restaurants or cafés, or my suspicions about what could be lurking around the next corner. I began to appreciate that living with fear—a mind-set that in Israel embodied a sense of national duty as much as an existential dread—was an element in the story, too. And that the desperation that led people to the point where they were willing to blow themselves up—a volatile mix of disenfranchised rage as well as a quest for national and personal honor—had its antecedents in a past that still was not past. It, too, had to play a part in the history I would write.

All these elements, then, were weighing on me as I struggled to find a strategy to tell the story of the Yom Kippur War. I envisioned an account that would be personal as well as national in scope, a tale of men, women, and governments caught up both in the times in which they lived, as well as in ancient histories. And no less a challenge, for the consequences of the war to be accurately depicted, my book had to reach across the decades into the present disorders.

As luck would have it, these diverse strands began to coalesce into a literary whole—a narrative—in the aftermath of my going to the Haifa mall to meet Nati Ben Hanan. Wandering about the crowded shops as I waited for her to finish with a client at the travel agency where she worked was an uneasy excursion. As I searched every face looking for the commitment of a suicide bomber, as I considered every shopping bag as a potential hiding place for a bomb, the interview I had the previous day in Jerusalem with Shabtai Brill kept playing in my head. I realized that I, too, had become a Watchman. It was then that I made up my mind that both Brill's victimization and his sense of duty had to figure prominently in the book I would write.

But I still needed an approach that would allow me to weave all these complex strands—ancient history, contemporary politics, the intelligence drama, the decisions made in the Pit and in Center Ten, and the valor of the soldiers on the battlefields—into a sustained narrative. Nati gave it to me.

After our conversation in the mall, Nati escorted us to the house where her wedding took place. It was an emotional tour; the home had been sold after her father's death and this was her first visit in years. Afterward, we went to her apartment. Sitting on her small terrace around a table filled with bowls of humus and olives, she told the story of her marriage, the honeymoon journey, and the frantic trip back to Israel. Later in the evening, Nati spread her wedding pictures out on her living room coffee table, and as I looked at them, the book I would write seemed to leap up into my mind. The young soldiers, the generals, the celebrated politicians were all united on one joyous afternoon, and all were unsuspecting of the danger that loomed. Here was a way, I decided, to tell an epic story. It was the starting point from which I could carve a narrative path through a sprawling, complex history where the perspective needed to shift frequently from the battlefields to the cabinet room.

And any lingering doubts I had about using Nati and Yossi's wedding as the (symbolic) opening of this history were erased after I interviewed Zvi Zamir, the man who headed the Mossad during the Yom Kippur War. Toward the end of our conversation, I made a wild guess and asked him if he had attended the wedding. He answered with typical obliqueness. "I knew Yossi's family well. My wife studied math with his father." "But were you there?" I pressed. Finally, he conceded that he could not attend because of last-minute agency business in Europe. There was another spirited round of questions followed by more infuriatingly vague answers before the old spy conceded, "If you wanted to write I was meeting our agent that weekend in London, I would not disagree." And with that unexpected response, I knew I had a way of uniting the many animating elements in the book I was setting out to write.

The Eve of Destruction is a book that aspires to tell the story of the Yom Kippur War and its aftermath by juxtaposing personal and national dilemmas and conflicts. It is a narrative about people and governments.

It is also a true story, a reporter's history. Therefore, it is important for the reader to know how I researched this book. A summary of my sources follows.

Selected Interviews

I conducted more than 217 interviews for this book. Most were conducted in Israel, but there were also crucial conversations with intelligence sources and Arab officials and veterans in England, the

United States, and by phone from Egypt and elsewhere in the Arab world. Many of those interviewed—particularly my Arab sources—spoke on the condition that their names would not be used. It should also be noted with gratitude that Prof. Uri Bar Josef, author of an insightful and groundbreaking book published in Hebrew about the Yom Kippur War, *The Watchman Fell Asleep*, helped to arrange and accompanied me on many crucial discussions with members of the Israeli intelligence community.

A list of those interviewed who played a prominent role in shaping this book and who were willing to be cited for attribution follows:

Bren Adan
Omer Adan
Eliezer Agasi
Amos Amir
Meir Amit
Menahem Ansbacher
Shlomo Ardinest
Gideon Arenhalt
Motti Ashkenazi
Baruch Askarov
Shmuel Askarov
Shlomo Avital
Uri Bar Josef
Itamar Barnea
Yona Bendman
Yanosh Ben Gal
Nati Ben Hanan
Yossi Ben Hanan
Ahron Bregman
Shabtai Brill
Itzik Cnaan
Yehuda Duvdevani
Haim Erez
Yaakov Even
Yeshayahu Gavish
Gil Gazit
Uri Gazit
David Gdalia
Champa Gendler
Amir Gidron
Musik Gidron
Rani Hefetz
Yaakov Hefetz
Avigdor Kahalani
Zusia Kaniezer
Shlomo Levi
Rami Lontz
Danny Matt
Zeev Nesher
Shaul Nimri
Benjamin Peled
Yoel Ben Porat

Amnon Reshef
Yehoshoua Sagi
Eyal Sarig
Ran Sarig
Arieh Shalev
Eliyshiv Shimishi
Yiftach Spektor
Beni Telem
Ben Siman Tov
Nimrod Tzach
Mosher Tzurich
Refael Vardi
Avi Weiss
Aviezer Yaari
Zvi Zamir
Eli Zeira

Selected Bibliography

A bibliography for this book would be as thick as another book. I would suggest that anyone wishing to do further reading on this topic would be wise to get the twenty-seven page bibliography compiled by Janet L. Seymour of the Air University Library at Maxwell Air Force Base in Montgomery, Alabama. It is the most exhaustive one I found, and was an invaluable resource as I prepared this book. Also, Jehuda L. Wallach's *Israeli Military History: A Guide to the Sources* (Garland Publishing) has a very comprehensive list of books and articles on the Yom Kippur War, and I also frequently consulted these sources, too.

I relied on some books more than others as I wrote this account. Specifically, I am grateful for the following: Hanoch Bartov's *Dado* (published by the Ma'ariv Book Guild in Israel) is a masterly blend of biography, personal diaries, and government transcripts. I could not have portrayed with such accuracy and immediacy what was happening in the Pit and in GHQ meetings during the war without Bartov's skillful and resourceful account. Avigdor Kahalani's two autobiographical books—*The Heights of Courage* (Greenwood Press) and *A Warrior's Way* (published in Israel by Steimatzky)—were important supplements to the interviews I conducted with him. In the chapters where I quote conversations between Kahalani and other soldiers both in the field and over the battalion radio, his books served as the final arbiter for my re-creating the scenes and the dialogue he had shared with me.

My understanding of the Arab perspective on the war was greatly enhanced by several memoirs: Saad el Shazly's *The Crossing of the Suez* (American Mideast Research), Mohammed el-Gamasy's *The October War* (American University in Cairo), Mohammed Heikal's *Road to Ramadan* (Quadrangle), and Anwar Sadat's *In Search of Identity* (Doubleday). Moshe Dayan's autobiography, *Story of My Life* (William Morrow), provides a fascinating counterpoint to many of the incidents in the Egyptian accounts, and to Bartov's *Dado* as well. Uri Bar Josef's *The Watchman Fell Asleep* (translated from the Hebrew edition for me by Rachel Zetland and Dr. Bar Josef) is the definitive guide in detailing how Israel was caught by surprise. It is an impressively well documented response to the flawed, defensive books published in Israel (and which I had privately translated) on the intelligence failure, including Zeira's *Myth Against Reality,* as well works by Ben Porat and Ariyeh Braun. Many of the government transcripts and intelligence reports I cite in my book first appeared in Bar Josef's work and were graciously shared with me from his private collections. Additionaly, much of the ground-breaking revelations about the role of the Egyptian double agent were first mentioned in Ahron Bregman's *A History of Israel* (Palgrave Macmillian). And important original reporting on Israel's willingness to use nuclear weapons was documented in Seymour Hersh's *The Samson Option* (Random House), Dan Raviv and Yossi Melman's *Every Spy a Prince* (Houghton Mifflin), and Samuel Katz's *Soldier Spies* (Presidio). To my mind, the two most readable and informative books about combat during the war are Chaim Herzog's elegantly written and exhaustive *The War of Atonement* (Greenhill Books) and the Insight Team of the London *Sunday Times' The Yom Kippur War* (Doubleday), which, although compiled in the immediate aftermath of the fighting, remains a resourcefully reported and well-written account. And, of course, the official government inquiry into the war, *Report of the Agranat Commission* (Tel Aviv), was essiential reading.

I also consulted a tall pile of periodicals as I put this book together. Again, the list would make in itself another book. However, I would be remiss if I did not point out the debts I owe to Abraham Rabinovitch's "Killing Fields in Sinai," which appeared in the *Jerusalem Post Magazine* (September 13, 2002) and his two-part series, "Shattered Heights," which also had appeared in that magazine (September 25, 1998; October 2, 1998). Yossi Melman's article in *Haaretz*, "Double Trouble" (January 20, 2003), is a skillful journalistic analysis of the Marwan affair.

Special Collections

As previously mentioned, Professor Bar Josef's voluminous files of intelligence documents and government transcripts were an extraordinary resource. Anyone interested in obtaining an overview of his original research (and who does not read Hebrew) might want to obtain a copy of the paper he presented in English at the Handel International Strategy Conference held at the U.S. Naval War College in November 2001, "Intelligence Failure and the Need for Cognitive Closure: The Case of Yom Kippur."

Also, among the many documents I found at Maxwell Air Force Base Air University's collection, the following were the most helpful:

Abouseada, Hamdy, "The Crossing of the Suez Canal."
Awad, Tarek A., "The Ramadan War 1973."
Chorey, Moni., "Surprise Attack: The Case of the Yom Kippur War.
Cochran, Edwin S., "The Egyptian Staff Solution: Operational Art and Planning for the 1973 Arab–Israeli War."
Cooper, Gregory, "An Egyptian Perspective: 1973 Arab–Israeli War."
Faul, Karen W., "Intelligence and the Analytical Perspective."
Riedel, Bruce, "Intelligence Failures in the October War."
Sawah, Ossama, "Deception in Ramadan War"

Another special collection that offers revelatory as well as unexpectedly poignant reading is the volume of letters written by Egyptian soldiers in the Sinai that were "gathered" by Israeli intelligence and are now housed in the semi-official Center for Special Studies Intelligence and Terrorism Information Center outside Tel Aviv. Also, in the Tel Aviv University library is a master's thesis by Zeevi Ahron, "The 'Deception' in the Egyptian Plan of the Yom Kippur War." What makes this paper particularly valuable is that its author is the present head of the Mossad.

Specific Primary Sources for Each Chapter

Prologue

Interviews: Shabtai Brill (SB); Ahron Bregman (AB); Uri Bar Josef (UBJ); Zvi Zamir (ZZ); Eli Zeira; (EZ); Israeli Intelligence sources (II).

Books and Documents: *A History of Israel,* Bregman (HOI); *The Watchman Fell Asleep* (WFA); Sigma Securities company reports; "Double Trouble," Melman (DT).

Chapter One

Interviews: Nati Ben Hanan (NBH); Yossi Ben Hanan (YBH); Yanosh Ben Gal (YBG).

Books and Documents: *The War of Atonement,* Herzog (WA); *A History of the Israeli Army,* Zeev Schiff; *Life* (6/27/67).

Chapter Two

Interviews: NBH; YBH.

Chapter Three

Interviews: NBH; YBH; YBG; Shmuel Askarov (SA); ZZ.

Books: *Story of My Life,* Dayan (Dayan); *Dado,* Bartov (Dado); HOI; WA.

Chapter Four

Interviews: NBH; YBH; SA; YBG; Avigdor Kahalani (AK), Bren Adan (BA); Amnon Reshef (AR); EZ.

Books: WA; *Heights of Courage,* Kahalani (HC) and *A Warrior's Way,* Kalahani (WW); *The Yom Kippur War,* London *Sunday Times* Insight Team (YK); Dayan.

Chapter Five

Interviews: ZZ; EZ; UBJ; AB; II.

Books: *Soldier Spies,* Katz (SS); *Every Spy a Prince,* Raviv and Melman (ESP); WFA; HOI; YK; Dayan.

Chapter Six

Interviews: II; Egyptian sources (ES).

Books and Documents: *The Crossing of the Suez,* Shazly (CS); *The October War,* Gamasy (OW); HOI; WFA; WA.

Chapter Seven

Books and Documents: *Road to Ramadan,* Heikel (RR); *In Search of Identity,* Sadat (ISI); CS; OW; HOI; WFA; WA; "The Ramadan War 1973," Awad (Awad); "The Egyptian Staff Solution," Cochran (Cochran); "Deception in Ramadan War," Sawah (Sawah).

Chapter Eight

Books and Documents: CS; OW; RR; ISI; WFA; WA; *October Earthquake,* Zeev Schiff (OE); YK; Sawah; Awad.

Chapter Nine

Interviews: Syrian Intelligence sources (SI).

Books and Documents: CS; OW; RR; ISI; YK; Sawah; Awad.

Chapter Ten

Interviews: UBJ; ES; SI; NBH; YBH; YBG.

Books and Documents: SC; OW; RR; ISI; YK; WA; Sawah; Awad; Alexandria tourist information.

Chapter Eleven

Interviews: SB; EZ; Yoel Ben Porat (YBP); Aviezer Yaari (AY).

Books and Documents: SS; WFA; ESP; Dado; Bar Josef Collection (BJC).

Chapter Twelve

Interviews: Yiftach Spektor (YS); Amos Amir (AA); Tamar Zeevi (TZ); SB; NBH; YBH.

Books: Spektor memoir, private translation (SM); *Fire in the Sky,* Amir (Fire), WA; WFA; CS; Dado; BJC.

Chapter Thirteen

Books and Documents: CS; OW; RR, ISI; YK; WA; Sawah; Awad; "The Deception," Zeevi Ahron (ZA); BJC; Dado; Dayan.

Chapter Fourteen

Interviews: AY; UBJ; AK; YBG.

Books and Documents: HOI; WFA; BJC; Dado; CS; WW; HC.

Chapter Fifteen

Interviews: NBH; YBH; SB; YBP; EZ.

Books and Documents: WFA; BJC; Dado.

Chapter Sixteen

Interviews: SB; EZ; Arieh Shalev (AS)

Books and Documents: WFA; CS; RR; OW; YK; Dado; BJC.

Chapter Seventeen

Interviews: AK; YBG; YBH; II; EZ.

Books and Documents: *Duel for the Golan*, Asher (DG); *No Victor,*

No Vanquished, O'Ballance (NV); WW; HC; YK; WA; BJC; Dado; SS; Dayan; CS; OW; RR.

Chapter Eighteen

Interviews: AR; BA; SB; EZ; ZZ.

Books and Documents: Dado; BJC; WA; YK; *On the Banks of the Suez,* Adan (OTB); CS; OW.

Chapter Nineteen

Interviews: EZ; YBH; NBH; ZZ; II.

Books and Documents: CS; OW; RR; Dado; BJC; WFA.

Chapter Twenty

Interviews: EZ; ZZ; YS; AK; YBG; YBH; NBH; AB; SA; AR.

Books and Documents: BJC; WFA; Dado; WA; Dayan; HC; WW; WA; YK; OTB; CS; OW; DG; ISI.

Chapter Twenty-one

Interviews: AR; BA; YS; AA.

Books and Documents: WA; YK; CS; OW; Dado.

Chapter Twenty-two

Interviews: SB; AK; YBG, SA.

Books and Documents: SS; ESP; DG; WA; YK; WW; HC; "Shatterd Heights," Rabinowitz (SH); Dado.

Chapter Twenty-three

Interviews: AK; YBG; SA; AR; BA

Books and Documents: WW; HC; DG; SH; CS; OW; ISI; WA.

Chapter Twenty-four

Interviews: SB; AK; YBG; YS; AA.

Books and Documents: BJC; Dado; WFA; Dayan; WA; CS; OW; Fire; SM; YK.

Chapter Twenty-five

Interviews: NBH; YBH; AR; BA.

Books and Documents: Dayan; WFA; Dado; DG; OTB; YK; BJC.

Chapter Twenty-six

Interviews: SA; Baruch Askarov; AR; BA; Jackie Even (JE).

Books and Documents: SH; DG; WW; HC; WA; CS; OW; WFA; BJC; Dado; OTB; Dayan; YK.

Chapter Twenty-seven

Interviews: AR; BA; JE; SA; AK; YBH; NBH.

Books and Documents: Dado; WA; YK; OTB; CS; DG; SH; WW; HC.

Chapter Twenty-eight

Interviews: EZ; II; YS; YBH; SA

Books and Documents: Dado; Dayan; WA; YK; *Sampson Option*, Hersh; ESP; SS.

Chapter Twenty-nine

Interviews: SB; YBP; EZ; YS.

Books and Documents: Dayan; WA; YK; *Myth Against Reality*, Zeira (MAR); Dado.

Chapter Thirty

Interviews: YBG; AK; YBH; SA.

Books and Documents: SH; DG; WA; YK; HC; WW; CS.

Chapter Thirty-one

Interviews: YBG; YBH; AK; SA.

Books and Documents: HC; WW; DG; SH; WA; Dado.

Chapter Thirty-two

Interviews: AR; BA; JE.

Books and Documents: Dado; WA; OTB; YK; CS; OW; CS; "Killing Fields In Sinai," Rabinovitch (KFS); Dayan.

Chapter Thirty-three

Interviews: SA; NBH; YBH; YBG; AK

Books and Documents: SH; Dado; *Secret Soldier,* Muki Betser (MB); WA; DG; HC; WW.

Chapter Thirty-four

Interviews: YBH; YBG; AK

Books and Documents: SH; DG; WA; HC; WW; MB.

Chapter Thirty-five

Interviews: BA; AR; JE; SB.

Books and Documents: CS; OW; INS; WA; YK; OTB; Dado; Dayan.

Chapter Thirty-six

Interviews: YBH; YBG.

Books and Documents: SH; MB; Dayan.

Chapter Thirty-seven

Interviews: EZ; UBJ; AR; BA; JE.

Books and Documents: Dado; CS; OW; ISI; WA; YK; OS; OTB.

Chapter Thirty-eight

Interviews: YBG; AK; NBH; YBH; SA

Books and Documents: WW; HC; SH

Chapter Thirty-nine

Interviews: AB; AR; JE
Books and Documents: OTB; WA; YK; Dado; KFS; CS.

Chapter Forty

Interviews: BA; AR; JE; SA.
Books and Documents: CS; OW; ISI; WA; YK; OTB; KFS; Dado.

Epilogue

Interviews: SB; AB; II; ES
Books and Documents: HOI; DT; WFA.

ACKNOWLEDGMENTS

In my life as an author I have learned that each book is its own unique battle. But this one was fought under truly sorrowful and complicated conditions. Therefore, I am particularly indebted and grateful to those who helped me out along the way.

At HarperCollins, it was a blessing to have so many people in my corner. Cathy Hemming's support, kindness, and friendship were always appreciated. David Hirshey was the sort of editor who said what he meant, and meant what he said—and that's a rare quality in any business. Plus, he's a smart guy to boot. Jeff Kellogg brought his insightful and incisive pen to my prose and improved everything he touched. And Nick Trautwein came in at the tail end of the process and graciously put up with all my ill humor.

I was also lucky to have Lynn Nesbit and Cullen Stanley at Janklow-Nesbit on my side. We've been together forever, or so it seems, and I value them both as agents and friends.

In Los Angeles, Bob Bookman and Jill Cutler not only read early drafts and offered encouragement, but also were friends I counted on. And Alan Hergott continues to be the wisest man I know.

In Israel, Uri Bar Josef's assistance was invaluable. He is a scholar and a gentleman and I owe him plenty. Rachel Zetland helped me out on this book as she had on *The Brigade,* and once again I could not have gotten this done without her hard work and intelligence.

My sister, Marcy, was a generous and hovering presence. And every day my children, Tony, Anna, and Dani, were a source of joy and pride.

Books by Howard Blum:

THE EVE OF DESTRUCTION
The Untold Story of the Yom Kippur War
ISBN 0-06-001400-8 (paperback)

Howard Blum delivers a riveting account of the Yom Kippur War of October 1973—a war that took Israel by surprise and might have destroyed the Jewish state, but for the courage and sacrifice of the Israeli people. At once a war drama, a political history, and an espionage story.

"A lively and informative account of a pivotal conflict." —*New York Times*

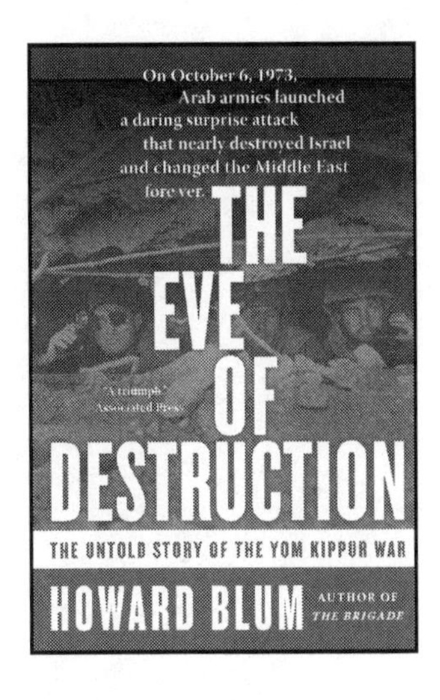

THE BRIGADE
An Epic Story of Vengeance, Salvation, and WWII
ISBN 0-06-093283-X (paperback)
ISBN 0-694-52658-4 (audio)

A gripping historical adventure tracing the formation and wartime activities of a Jewish Palestinian brigade that overcame great odds to fight the Nazis in World War II. These soldiers, with yellow Stars of David emblazoned on their uniform sleeves, show the world that a Jewish army can fight back—and win.

"Remarkable. . . . An illuminating addition to the annals of World War II."
—*New York Times Book Review*

26479224R00235

Made in the USA
Middletown, DE
30 November 2015